KU-490-367

EDUCATION POLICIES: CONTROVERSIES AND CRITIQUES

Education Policy Perspectives

General Editor: **Professor Ivor Goodson**, Faculty of Education, University of Western Ontario, London, Canada N6G 1G7

School Organization and Improvement Series

Editor: David Reynolds, University College, Cardiff, United Kingdom

Education in general and schools in particular are at the forefront of public debate in most industrialised societies. Only a decade ago, there was a pervasive belief that education 'didn't matter' and that educational reform and expansion as attempted worldwide in the 1960s and 1970s would inevitably produce failure and disillusionment.

Now, however, the work of academics, practitioners and policymakers in the effective schools movement shows that schools can generate excellence *and* equity if they are run in certain ways. School improvement researchers and practitioners also are showing how schools can be made more effective and efficient.

This series aims to bring to the attention of teachers, administrators, policymakers and academics the latest research, practice and thinking in these fields. It aims to stimulate academic debate about school effectiveness and improvement, and to provide practitioners with the detailed analysis and description of effective school strategies that they need as societal and legislative pressures on schools grow even stronger. Now more than ever before, educationists need to know about 'good schools' and about 'how to make schools good'. This series aims to provide just that information.

THE COMPREHENSIVE EXPERIMENT
David Reynolds and Michael Sullivan with Stephen Murgatroyd

IMPROVING THE QUALITY OF SCHOOLING
Edited by David Hopkins

THE SELF-MANAGING SCHOOL
Brian J. Caldwell and Jim M. Spinks

SUCCESSFUL SECONDARY SCHOOLS
Bruce L. Wilson and Thomas B. Corcoran

WHOLE SCHOOL APPROACHES TO SPECIAL NEEDS
Edited by Arlene Ramasut

Education Policy Perspectives

EDUCATION POLICIES: CONTROVERSIES AND CRITIQUES

Edited by
Andy Hargreaves
and
David Reynolds

The Falmer Press
(A member of the Taylor & Francis Group)
New York • Philadelphia • London

UK The Falmer Press, Falmer House, Barcombe, Lewes, East Sussex, BN8 5DL

USA The Falmer Press, Taylor & Francis Inc., 242 Cherry Street, Philiadelphia, PA 19106-1906

First published 1989

Library of Congress in Publication Data available on request

Printed and bound in Great Britain by
Redwood Burn Limited, Trowbridge, Wiltshire.

Contents

Preface

This volume is based on a series of papers given at the British Educational Research Association annual conference in Autumn 1986, with the addition of two later papers on the General Certificate of Secondary Education by Roger Murphy and on Teacher Education by Jean Rudduck. All papers have been revised and up-dated to take into account any policy changes since that time.

Our original motivation in organising the seminar was a simple one. At the time we felt — and still feel — that educational research in general and the sociology of education in particular had not been sufficiently concerned with the dramatic changes in educational and social policy that had taken place since the 1979 General Election. The absence of policy related research and discussion had, we felt, numerous damaging consequences — within sociology of education it meant that elaborate flights of theoretical fancy could take place that had no empirical reference. The discipline was also unable to participate at a professional level in the contemporary public discourse on educational policy and, most damaging of all, the absence of knowledge about the nature of current policies hindered any creative thinking about the sorts of alternatives that might be envisaged. It also seemed disappointing to us that the perfect experimental situation whereby education was being substantially changed in its forms of organisation would have enabled — if it had been studied that is — the complex relationships between policy and outcomes, and between the educational system and the wider society, to be better understood.

The papers in this volume are an attempt — we think the first on offer — to describe, explain and understand the nature of contemporary educational policy in Britain, although of course many of the trends described in this volume are not peculiar to only one culture. Our own contribution and Brian Simon's chapter are both overviews of policies, attempting to relate these policy changes to wider political, economic and social changes, an attempt which Andy Hargreaves' own chapter attempts to take further with its analysis of assessment policies and their relationship to the perceived 'crisis' in education.

The next four chapters describe policy initiatives that are targetted at different portions of the pupil ability range — James Murphy looks at GCSE,

Roger Dale and colleagues examine TVEI, Hilary Radnor and colleagues look at the Certificate of Prevocational Education, and Penny Weston/James Harland assess the value of initiatives for low attainers.

The subsequent three chapters move discussion away from the secondary school sector and look at the increased State sponsorship of the independent sector (Geoff Whitty and colleagues), differentiation and specialisation in the primary sector (Jim Campbell) and changes in the control of teacher education (Jean Rudduck).

Three sets of conclusions and reflections are offered lastly. David Reynolds attempts an overview of governmental initiatives and considers the possible responses to them from the educational 'left' that may be appropriate. David Hargreaves and Maureen O'Connor offer their reflections on the collection of papers from the perspective of a local education authority administrator and a journalist/parental consumer of education respectively.

We are grateful to Maureen O'Connor of *The Guardian* for chairing the seminar and to the large number of colleagues who gave helpful advice to all of us at the seminar and subsequently as we prepared material.

ANDY HARGREAVES
DAVID REYNOLDS

Introduction

Decomprehensivization

Andy Hargreaves and David Reynolds

There is never a moment in state education when policies are not changing in one respect or another. Stability and consolidation are infuriatingly elusive as policy goals. But in our view, the chapters in this collection and the evidence they lay out before us, do not just represent yet one more set of policy changes, no different in character from the innumerable policy changes which preceded them. They are not concerned merely with isolated, disconnected initiatives, targetted at quite discrete and unrelated aspects of educational practice. Rather, taken together, the initiatives seem to us to have a remarkable coherence and logic signalling a fundamental shift in the orientation and goals of educational policy in late twentieth century Britain.

As we shall see, the coherence is not absolutely uniform, the logic not impeccable. There are contradictions and inconsistencies in the policies themselves and in their interrelationships too. But looking across the policies as a whole, the impetus behind late twentieth century educational change in general is of a very different order than that which directed educational reform from the immediate post-war years to the 1970s.

As each of us points out more extensively in our own later chapters, the two decades leading up to the late 1970s were ones in which educational reform, at least at secondary level, addressed an agenda of comprehensive reorganization and development. Widening educational opportunities, improved identification of talent, postponement and reduction of educational selection and differentiation, broadened curriculum entitlement — these were the issues, principles and goals that dominated the educational reform agenda during that period. The establishment of comprehensive schools themselves; the replacement of streaming first by broader systems of banding and setting, then increasingly by arrangements for mixed ability grouping too; and the eventual efforts to redefine the comprehensive curriculum in ways different from the watered down academic one which the comprehensives had first inherited from the grammar schools — these things marked a continuous attempt in educational policy and practice to define and develop a distinctive identity and rationale for comprehensive education. As this book goes to press, the evidence is that after a long period of struggle and uncertainty, this identity of what Reynolds, in his chapter, calls 'authentic comprehensive education' has finally begun to take a definite shape. Moreover, some of the most recent educational research findings from Scotland suggest that this is being achieved alongside improvements in conventional academic standards too (McPherson and Willms, 1987).

Yet, just as the era of comprehensivization is reaching maturity, the signs are that in the late 1980s, it is about to be cut off in its prime. Comprehensivization characterized the two decades from the 1950s to the 1970s. In the late 1980s, we are, in effect, entering an era of decomprehensivization. We are entering a period of reduced state support for education overall together with increasing state control over what remains; a period where quality not equality is the *motif* of educational debate; where earlier, more systematic and more finely tuned differentiation is taking the place of egalitarian and opportunity-conscious programmes of postponed selection; and where the restoration of the subject-based academic curriculum is undermining earlier attempts at a broadening of curricular entitlement. Severed by the axe of state stringency, drained of its most able and privileged pupils, and depressed by powerful ideological forces which run counter to the hopes and aspirations of those countless teachers who have matured professionally with the comprehensive system, the vitality and sheer existence of state comprehensive education as we have come to know it is now in serious jeopardy.

The process of decomprehensivization is a complex phenomenon. It contains several interconnected strands, each with their realization in specific educational policies and initiatives. That interrelationship is becoming increasingly clear with the maturation of Conservative government policies in education. Indeed, the Education Act of 1988, crystallized exceptionally well the extent to which modern educational policy is increasingly being organized around the principle of decomprehensivization. We will pick out seven strands of this emerging policy orientation: privatization and market competitiveness, centralization, differentiation, specialization, vocationalization, dispositional adjustment and surveillance.

Privatization and Market Competitiveness

There are two broad aspects to the policy of privatization in modern British education. First, there is the privatization of the financial means for purchasing or gaining access to good quality education. More education for more of the people is made dependent on private financial support and investment (Pring, 1986). Second there is the privatization of decision-making in relation to the supply and demand of educational services. Here, the kind and quality of education offered is made more dependent on consumer (parent) choice within a market place of competitive provision. With deregulation of direct state involvement in education, advocates of this sort of privatization claim that the character and standards of educational provision will increasingly come to reflect the public will (Holmes, 1987).

Privatization is in part an economic response on the part of the state to an intensifying crisis of capital accumulation; an attempt by the state to unburden itself of economic responsibility for education at a time of mounting financial stringency (Offe, 1984). The privatization of things like school cleaning services, for instance, is part of this response. In addition, privatization is also a response to an escalating crisis of legitimation in education and in state institutions more generally (see Andy Hargreaves' chapter in this volume). In education, privatization has come to be regarded an as alternative to the failed vision of comprehensive education: the comprehensive system's apparent incapacity to deliver economic productivity, social consensus and equality of opportunity. If the state cannot efficiently regulate the educational system, it is believed, then the market place will. In this respect, responsibility for any educational crisis is 'exported' into the domain of private, individual choice (Apple, 1986). Measures to accommodate more parental choice in education fall very much within this interpretation of privatization.

Within educational policy and practice, privatization manifests itself in three major ways: in development of, and support for, private provision outside the state system, in shifting of responsibility for certain kinds of provision within the state system to private sources, and in reorientation of the style and pattern of state operation and provision in education towards market economy principles.

In the first case — support for and promotion of take up of private education outside the state — recent years have seen the development and expansion of the Assisted Places Scheme, and a general drift towards growing parental take-up of independent education. Whitty, Fitz and Edwards in their chapter describe their extensive evaluation of the early years of the Assisted Places Scheme. They find that while the scheme does indeed offer a state financed independent education for children who come from low income families, these are not, in the main, working-class families. The families of Assisted Places pupils are predominantly middle-class ones who have, for some reason — for instance, because of single parenthood — fallen into less favourable financial circumstances. The scheme therefore does not really cater for bright working-class children, but for children coming from middle-class families of modest means, many of whose parents are very much within the 'independent frame of reference' and who would strongly support the retention and restoration of grammar schools.

The Assisted Places Scheme, as an element of privatization, therefore appears to offer disproportionate advantages to middle-class children compared with their working class counterparts. Because of its experimental nature, the scheme's immediate impact may not be great, although, at the time of writing, the returning Conservative government has committed itself to extending it. The scheme is likely to have a more substantial indirect impact, however. First, as Whitty, Fitz and Edwards suggest, the Assisted

Places scheme is, in many respects, a 'precursor of a radical new policy of privatization' in educational policy. The establishment of separately funded city technical colleges (CTCs) can be read as a further move within the development and extension of just such a policy. Reynolds, in his chapter, predicts that these CTCs will tend to draw predominantly on middle and high ability pupils. If that is the case, they would create what Reynolds calls a 'creaming of the state comprehensives'.

Just as important as any such direct creaming of able, middle-class pupils and their articulate parents from the state system by specific initiatives like the CTCs and the Assisted Places Scheme, is the symbolic value such initiatives have as publicly visible indicators of declining confidence in state education. Initiatives of this sort, coupled with poor governmental financial support for and powerful governmental ideological critiques of the state education system and its teachers, are likely only to increase the recent yet growing emigration of pupils, particularly able pupils, from the state to the private sector (Salter and Tapper, 1986; Walford, 1985).

Privatization in the form of state supported creaming of able middle-class pupils from the comprehensive system is being accompanied by privatization of a second sort within the state system itself. This involves making more of what would hitherto have been provided by the State now dependent on private investment. In some cases, this is made mandatory upon schools, as when some local education authorities contract out school meals and school cleaning services to private enterprise (Pring, 1986). Provisions in the new Education Reform Act to hand over more budgetary control of school finances to headteachers will almost certainly increase these trends. At the same time, the transfer of budgetary control to heads will, if anything, strengthen existing tendencies towards parents having to take increasing financial responsibility for their children's education. This will take place through the private individual purchase of what are increasingly regarded as non-essential areas of the curriculum like swimming and music tuition, through the combined parental purchase of computer equipment increasingly viewed as essential to children's education in the microchip era, and through the combined purchase even of basic texts, library books and the like. A survey published in 1985 by the National Confederation of Parent-Teacher Associations revealed that parents were by that point supporting the state system to the extent of 30 per cent of capitation in primary schools. Inevitably, of course, as schools draw on different catchment areas with different economic capacities to provide private aid, the resource differentials between schools in favoured and less-favoured areas will be magnified. Class differentiation in educational provision and opportunity will be increased.

Third, as privatization is creaming off many of the able and class-advantaged pupils from the state sector, what remains is itself being subjected more and more to the principles of market competitiveness. Legislation in the 1980 Education Act to widen parental choice in schools is being strengthened through further measures, in the 1988 Education Reform Act, to remove from local education authorities the power to place entry ceilings or planned admission limits on particular schools. Schools, and secondary schools in particular, it seems, will be allowed to flourish or founder according to the market dictates of parental choice. Schools are being and will increasingly be placed in the position of competitive enterprises bidding for parental custom.

Within the competitive market economy model of educational provision, headteachers, with their increased budgetary power, will be placed in the position of corporate managers of educational enterprises. From being primarily and directly responsible for the development and improvement of teaching and learning in their schools, their role will shift to interpreting and manipulating local parental markets and to making entrepreneurial bids for those forms of state investment which are increasingly being supplied to schools on a competitive basis in terms of money 'earmarked' for particular initiatives. And should the local state in the form of the LEA impose regulations on schools which would curtail the opportunities of some to establish a particularly advantageous market position for themselves, then these schools will be allowed to opt out of LEA control altogether and receive their funds direct from central government instead.

Supporters of privatization (for example, Holmes, 1987) claim that it

- widens educational choice;
- fares no worse in terms of alleviating educational inequalities than previous patterns of educational provision which were underpinned with stronger egalitarian purposes;
- increases the responsiveness of the educational system to the public will;
- thereby moves the system towards providing a more traditional form of education which in turn raises academic standards.

In response to such claims, the privatization of education can be criticized on the grounds that:

- While privatization does indeed create an overall increase in individual choice of school, for many people this ability to choose is nominal. The exercise of such choice depends on the prior possession of appropriate financial or cultural capital — to purchase an independent education, to pay for music tuition, to cover transportation costs, to build an informed understanding of the system, its differences and the choices that can be made within it etc. Privatization thereby brings with it powers to choose and to acquire a socially advantageous education which are distributed unequally on class and ethnic lines. This, in turn, almost certainly has adverse consequences for those pupils whose parents have not 'chosen' or not been able to exercise their choice and who must remain in the underresourced and undervalued schools that serve their own locality and from which many of the most able pupils and their articulate parents will have been creamed.

- In recognizing the limited power of educational systems to reduce social inequalities in Western capitalist societies, educational privatization turns a social vice into a legislative virtue by introducing a set of rules and procedures which will, if anything, exacerbate these inequalities.
- Educational privatization may assist responsiveness to particular public wills, to the wishes of particular communities of interests. What it does not satisfactorily resolve, however, are conflicts of interest between particular public wills and the will or interests of the public as a whole. Some white Anglo-Saxon Protestant communities, for instance, may have no wish to see their local school diverting its energies and attention towards preparing its pupils to live in a multicultural society. If schools were to preserve their individual market position by responding to such local public wills among particular communities of interest, would this not in turn sometimes offend the wider public will and threaten the moral order of society in general?
- Can the public will be regarded as objective, neutral and rational? Can it indeed be neatly encapsulated within the private domain of civil society? Is it itself altogether protected from that influence and intervention of the state from which advocates of privatization claim detachment? What matters here, of course, is how far the terms according to which choice is exercised, the criteria of choosing, emerge spontaneously from the private, familial domain of civil society, and how far those terms and criteria are themselves defined by the state! What limits to choice does the state set? How far does the state's ideological steering of educational discourse, for instance, and its more direct legislative intervention in educational provision set the terms of market competition and influence patterns of parental choice? In other words, once we inspect it carefully, just how private *is* privatization?

Centralization

An apparent paradox of educational policy in contemporary Britain is that while the state is apparently shedding many of its responsibilities for educational provision through policies of privatization, it is also, at the very same time, tightening its own centralized grip on the educational policy-making process. Privatization and centralization are therefore operating side by side. They are the unlikely bedfellows of modern British educational policy.

Some analysts of educational policy see these processes as contradictory, representing different and conflicting stands of Conservative thinking, along with the constituent interests from which those strands have arisen (Ball, 1987; and Simon in this volume). Others argue that in the long run, 'the frontiers of the welfare state cannot easily be "rolled back" in the face of the self-crippling tendencies of the capitalist economic system' (Offe, 1984: p. 27). For them, the push for privatization will eventually be overtaken by the need for centralization to contain and control the crises of modern capitalist society.

We agree that privatization and centralization do indeed have different ideological roots. We recognize also that privatization has its limits. To open up the entire process by which the next generation will be socialized to the free run of market forces, runs social and political risks that no government will seriously contemplate, especially at times of severe economic crisis and social uncertainty. But we want to argue that a limited commitment to privatization is in many respects not at all in conflict with the spread of centralized control of educational policy. As coordinated arms of educational policy, the two processes can, in fact, hold the course of educational change firmly within a powerful grip.

At times of mobility scarcity, privatization encourages the materially and culturally advantaged to take some independent responsibility for purchasing educational and social opportunities for their children. Where rewards are scarce, opportunities are few and mobility is squeezed at the margins, where success cannot easily be taken for granted by class advantaged parents, then privatization, contrary to the policy rhetoric, does not so much facilitate the purchase of cultural and religious choice in education, as encourage the purchase of additional opportunities and advancement which particular institutions seem able to provide. For many parents, privatization means booking passages for their children on ships of opportunity sailing under flags of religious and cultural convenience.

In times of mobility scarcity, therefore, to control the criteria of success and opportunity is in many respects to control the criteria of choice. Once control is exercised over the criteria of choice, then the state maintains significant steering capacity over the privatization process as a whole. The requirements, under conditions of widened parental choice and intensified competition between schools, that schools publish their examination results, closely circumscribes the terms of parental choice and market competition. The state thereby exerts ideological control over the privatization process. Moreover, by focusing institutional competitiveness around its own examination-based, academic criteria of success and effectiveness, the privatization process reciprocally reinforces the centralized power of the state. The processes of privatization and centralization therefore hold a recursive, reciprocal relationship to one another. Through the combined use of privatization and centralization, the state in fact enhances its control over education, while at the same time divesting itself of some of the financial responsibility for achieving this.

The fulcrum of the state's operation of a pincer movement on schools, gripping them between the recursive forces of privatization and centralization, is therefore its ideological control over the criteria of educational success and failure, over the means of mobility. The growth of centralized control over the curriculum, the examination system and over teachers themselves is pivotal here. All three of these areas have seen very substantial shifts in the locus of control towards the centre since the mid-1970s.

Central government, and particularly the Department of Education and Science, has significantly tightened its grip upon the curriculum (Lawton, 1984). Hargreaves, in his chapter, traces the growth of central interest in control over the curriculum to a major crisis of legitimation running through the institutions of the state in the mid-1970s as recession bit particularly hard into the British economy. Worries about education's capacity to deliver the economic goods, concern about its apparent dislocation from the needs of working life, and anxiety about the system's apparent unresponsiveness and lack of accountability to shifting social expectations and demands, provided the occasion for DES intervention. James Callaghan's Prime Ministerial pronouncement on the curriculum, a proliferation of DES and HMI documents designed to shift the agenda of curricular debate, requirements placed upon LEAs to undergo a process of curricular review and to inform the centre about the outcomes of that review, regulations imposed on teacher training institutions to devote more attention in recruitment and programme design to subject specialist expertise of a conventional kind (see Rudduck's chapter in this volume) — these things turned out to be but preludes to the main orchestral theme. This is the legislative imposition of a national curriculum: an academic curriculum of a conventional, subject based, grammar-school kind. This curriculum is not a broad and balanced curriculum. It is a comprehensive curriculum only in the sense of being common. It is not comprehensive in the sense of being wide-ranging. We shall return to the implications of this shortly. For now, we need only note the importance of this nationally-determined and redefined curriculum as the centrally-minted currency of choice and success within the educational system.

In addition to its control over the curriculum, the centre has also strengthened both the place of public examinations and testing within the educational system, and its own hold over those important mechanisms of educational assessment. As Broadfoot, (1984) argues, in addition to recognizing individual *competence*, public examinations also strongly influence curriculum *content*, they regulate the terms of educational *competition* and they exert a powerful measure of *control* over educational change. Examinations, in important respects, determine the curriculum; a point which Her Majesty's Inspectorate (1979 and 1983), the professional conscience of government bureaucracy, has itself acknowledged. Control of the examination system carries within it extensive control of the curriculum itself. Government, and the DES in particular, has firmly seized that control through reform of examinations at 16+ in the shape of the new GCSE. Murphy, in his chapter, notes how, through the creation of national criteria to which all GCSE syllabuses must conform, the power of the DES has been strengthened at the expense of different examination boards (also Salter and Tapper, 1987). Through laying down national criteria, the DES has been able to determine the inclusion or exclusion of particular subject contents— for instance, exclusion of the social uses of science from physics courses. It has placed serious bureaucratic constraints on the development of new curriculum titles, and in doing so has tended to cluster curriculum provision around an academic and subject-norm rather than a topic or theme-based one (Torrance, 1987). The proposed development of benchmark testing of pupil performance in a limited range of academic subjects at ages 7, 11 and 14, represents still further moves, on the part of government, to control the process of curriculum by controlling the patterns of assessment. It is not hard to predict that coupled with the earlier discussed procedures for publishing examinations and test scores as a basis for school-by-school comparisons in a competitive market economy of parental choice, both of the new assessment initiatives — GCSE and benchmark testing — will lead to clustering of curriculum provision around the subject-based, academic mean.

Should teachers prove unsympathetic towards or unable to implement the centrally generated initiatives in curriculum and assessment, control of their preparation and professional development has been moved into central hands also. The governmentally-established and appointed Council for the Accreditation of Teacher Education (CATE) has laid down criteria which teacher education courses must meet if their students are to be awarded Qualified Teacher Status (QTS), or, quite simply, the right to teach, at the end of them. Indicators of strong commitment to subject specialist learning and qualification rank high amongst those criteria. Rudduck probes some of the serious areas of difficulty with this policy in her chapter. The establishment of Grant Related In-Service Training (GRIST) in 1986 has provided the DES with a mechanism to steer LEA in-service provision towards its own preferred priorities, through allocating a high proportion of its funding only to patterns of INSET which fall within those priorities (Harland, 1987). Finally, the introduction of compulsory teacher appraisal on a continuous basis will help ensure that teachers comply with government policy initiatives and objectives.

Curriculum, assessment and the teaching force itself: these are some of the most significant areas in which central influence has been exercised and strengthened. But exactly how has this been achieved? By what channels and mechanisms has the power of the centre been significantly enhanced in these different areas?

Firstly and most obviously, the centre has made extensive use of the power of *legislation and regulation*. Centrally imposed dictat! The end of local-central partnership on which educational reform of the post-war period has been built! A national curriculum, examination reform, control of initial teacher education, compulsory teacher appraisal: these are just some of the changes that have been bulldozed through by legislative and regulatory means.

Second, alongside legislative compulsion, the centre — in the form of the DES and the Manpower Services Commission (MSC) — has used financial persuasion. It has used *categorical funding* — not additional to existing budgets but earmarked within them — to promote particular initiatives and developments. Schools and LEAs, short on more general funding allocations, have found it hard not to bid competitively for these separately allocated resources. The Technical and Vocational Education Initiative (TVEI), LAPP, GRIST, and a range of initiatives funded by Educational Support Grants (ESGs), have been promoted in this way. Here again we see centralization and privatization operating in concert.

Third, through an overwhelming proliferation of discussion documents and policy statements across an astonishing range of educational initiatives, the centre, and increasingly the DES in particular, has come to exert a profound *ideological influence* on the basic agenda of educational debate, on the very terms in which educational development and change are discussed. The replacement of a discourse of equality and opportunity by one of quality and standards is one example of this process. Campbell, in his chapter on primary education policy, discusses how subject specialization and differentiation have emerged as central items of educational policy discourse in recent years, not least, perhaps, because of HMIs' growing responsiveness to preferred DES agendas. We will say more about differentiation and specialization shortly.

Fourth, the centre has reduced the power and efficacy of intermediate administrative levels of the policy making system that might hinder the committed and efficient take-up of its developments and initiatives. The erosion of the power of the LEAs is the most startling example of this process (Ranson and Tomlinson, 1986). Beginning with general though increasingly complicated restrictions on educational financing through capping of the Rate Support Grant (RSG), then moving on to restraint and redirection of LEA priorities through categorical funding (ESGs and GRIST), the centre, under legislation in the 1988 Education Reform Act, has subjected LEAs to the particular indignity of allowing schools to opt out of LEA control altogether if they wish, and receive their financing direct from central government instead. At a stroke, the centre thereby eliminates the controlling interest of LEAs in large numbers of state schools. What we are supplied with instead is an educational franchising model of policy implementation. The DES decides the policies, the shape and texture of the educational products that are to be made and even the style and standard of service by which those products are to be delivered. Headteachers, paid directly by central government and placed in independent control of their school budgets, then manage their individual educational enterprises on competitive market principles. The rhetoric is consumer choice and diversity. The reality is product standardization. Kentucky Fried Schooling!

Fifth, the centre has eliminated or displaced potential sources of questioning, critique and opposition to its policies. In winding up the Schools Council, it eliminated the main, indeed the only, significant body of curriculum development and policy formation to enjoy substantial independence from direct government control. Decimation of the research budget of the major 'independent' research council — the ESRC— has seriously curtailed opportunities to fund a wide range of substantial projects that might prove critical of government policies (Hargreaves, 1986a). The research on the Assisted Places Scheme reported by Whitty and his colleagues in this book is a rare exception to that trend. The other major government initiatives in education have been evaluated through direct funding by the DES and MSC themselves. Yet for all the myriad local evaluations of TVEI, for instance, scarcely any findings have surfaced into the public and published domain. It is arguable that the politics of educational evaluation, as opposed to educational research in 1980s Britain, may be more to do with suppressing independent public scrutiny of government educational initiatives than promoting it. The passing of control of the educational research process from the independent research councils to the DES and the MSC may yet prove to be a highly significant strategy in depressing and displacing sound, empirically-based critiques of government policy. To control and co-opt the means of systematic enquiry is to control the credibility of dissent. Without substantial research-based foundations, the legitimacy of academic criticism of government policies can easily be denied.

Differentiation

Centralization can be explained in part as an attempt to exert more direct and tightly managed state power over the education and socialization of future generations. At times of severe economic crisis, privatization is in some measure a strategy for offloading some of the state's financial burden for this task. Strengthened ideological control, state setting of the terms of market competition, to a large extent prevents the privatization process from running counter to the interests of the state. But the development and construction of these new modes of state control are also explicable as strategies to recapture and redefine the social purposes and outcomes of education in modern British society, in a way that is different from those purposes and outcomes that had been associated with the development of comprehensive school reform until the mid-1970s. Such processes are designed to secure not greater social equality or even equality of opportunity, but earlier and more explicit forms of educational and social differentiation. In other words, centralization and privatization have become the state guardians of increased differentiation in education.

The resurrection and reconstruction of explicit differentiation and selection in education has been most publicly visible in debates surrounding the reintroduction of grammar schools in some local education authorities. Solihull was the first and most controversial of the critical LEA cases here, closely followed by Berkshire, Wiltshire and Redbridge. In all cases the proposals were defeated, for which the Left claimed victory (for example, Simon, 1984). In many ways, though, that victory was hollow and premature. Certainly in Solihull, much of the pressure against the reintroduction of selection came from middle-class pressure groups who had, through investing financial capital in expensive homes in desirable catchment areas, effectively purchased cultural capital for their children by giving them access to prestigious comprehensive schools with an academic bias and an intake heavily skewed towards the middle-classes. The reintroduction of grammar schools threatened to undermine this heavy investment that such parents had already made to secure educational advantages for their children (Walford and Jones, 1986).

There was also another sense in which the defeat of grammar schools was a hollow victory for the left. Reports compiled by Colin Humphrey, Director of Education for Solihull, on the selection question were heavily criticized by pressure groups and indeed by the editors of this book at the time (see *Birmingham Evening Post*, 27 February 1984), for misuse of evidence, selective use of existing research and misinterpretation of statistics. Such criticisms certainly helped undermine the office's educational justification for reintroducing selective schools. Throughout this critical process, however, a second and, in retrospect, possibly more significant section of the Director's second report was overlooked entirely (Humphrey, 1984). This was concerned not with selective schools in particular, but with a more general review of the education service in Solihull.

This part of the report opened with a discussion of school organization, and in particular of mixed ability teaching. In a paragraph displaying remarkable insensitivity to the accumulating body of research evidence on mixed ability grouping, Humphrey advanced a number of strident assertions about mixed ability.

> 'Some theorists argue that mixed ability teaching is a logical consequence of comprehensive education and a necessary concomitant to equality of opportunity . . . Personally, I would not agree with any of this, and my view is that mixed ability teaching all too often leads to inequality of opportunity. (*ibid*, p. 19)

Still writing in apparent blissful or wilful ignorance of the large body of relevant research, Humphrey went on,

> Whatever social gains are claimed under a mixed ability organization, they are at the expense of academic achievement . . . I have the feeling that the disappearance of mixed ability teaching would generally be welcomed, certainly by parents . . . I would not regret its disappearance. (*ibid, p. 20)*

The research evidence on pupil grouping in fact shows inconsistent findings in relation to attainment, although the most recent study in the US indicates that streaming or 'tracking' has negative consequences for academic attainment (Oakes, 1986). What *has* been consistently found is that streaming and banding have adverse personal and social consequences for large numbers of children in terms of behaviour and self-esteem (Hargreaves, 1967; Lacey, 1970; Ball, 1981). Moreover, there is also evidence in primary mathematics teaching that teachers of setted groups are more likely to use 'safer' whole class teaching methods than those teaching mixed ability groups (Barker-Lunn, 1984). The evidence of Her Majesty's Inspectorate on setting in 8–12 schools also tends to run counter to assertions such as Humphrey's, as Campbell notes in his chapter.

The matter at issue, though, would appear to be not one of evidence but of ideological preference. In this sense, it is somewhat disturbing that a group hitherto as impartial as HMI, should increasingly be seen to be adopting a language of differentiation in their reports on various parts of the education service. Moreover, these reports make no effort at all to distance themselves from possible interpretation of HMI's advocacy of differentiation as being support for grouping by ability in terms of streaming, banding or setting (Hargreaves, 1986; and Campbell in this volume). HMI, under some pressure, one suspects from the DES, have helped insert and establish differentiation in the newly defined hegemonic discourse of current educational policy. They have helped make differentiation an acceptable, discussable, legitimate, agenda-setting element of normal educational debate, inside the school and out.

'If . . . selection between schools is largely out, then I emphasize that there must be differentiation within schools.' So remarked Sir Keith Joseph, former Conservative Secretary of State for Education and Science (quoted in Simon, 1984, p. 21). In this respect, the defeat of proposals to reintroduce grammar schools on a system-wide basis looks, in retrospect, to be a minor one. There is more than one way to skin the egalitarian cat. Honing the technology of differentiation within schools is arguably the most efficient of these, not least because it is less visible, less open to public objection.

Privatization fosters increased differentiation between the state and independent sectors. Differentiation between schools that will have class and ethnic associations will also be enhanced by policies boosting principles of market competitiveness and parental choice, along with deregulation of local state control over individual schools. Opting out of LEA control may well prove to be a more effective back-door route to the reintroduction of selective schooling on a gradualist basis.

Within schools, the reintroduction of streaming, banding and setting in an ideological context of growing endorsement for ability grouping policies; the separation of academic from vocational routes at age 14 through LAPP, TVEI and the remaining subject-specialist curriculum; the retention of a differentiated examination structure within the GCSE and between the GCSE and the prevocational assessment system: all these are indicators of the increasing commitment to earlier, more finely graded, more carefully monitored yet also more covert processes of differentiation within the secondary and primary educational systems. Differentiation is at the heart of decomprehensivization. Its presence and influence on modern educational policy run throughout most chapters in this book.

One of the key strategies of differentiation is the establishment of more distinct and separate academic and non-academic routes within the secondary system. Underpinning this division are processes of subject specialization and vocationalization within the educational system, with which we shall now deal in turn.

Specialization

The 1960s and 70s in British education was a period which accommodated a wide range of innovations in the school curriculum. Topic work, thematic approaches to the curriculum and learning through play gained more time and attention at the primary level. The secondary system witnessed the emergence of a wide range of new subjects: social studies, integrated studies, European studies, computer studies, technology, health education and the like. These innovations promised new classifications of the curriculum which cut across and potentially challenged existing and long-standing subject-based decisions. For many years though, this challenge was a muted one. The new subjects and curriculum categories, and the kinds of knowledge and learning they privileged, were very much confined to lower attaining, 'non-academic' pupils. Newsom studies (Burgess, 1984) and European studies (Goodson, 1988) for instance, certainly fitted this mould.

The hegemony of the academic, subject-based curriculum — abstract intellectual, and unrelated to practical issues and concerns — remained intact for more able pupils (Connell, 1985). The curriculum which led to high status examinations, which provided the route to social and educational opportunity, and which drew on and legitimized the academic inheritance of cultural capital in which the advantaged middle classes were already steeped, continued to be protected. There was no serious threat to redefine the cultural capital, the forms of knowledge and learning, that constituted the currency of educational and social success (Hargreaves, 1988b). Middle-class advantage was not in jeopardy.

The mid-1970s marked the beginning of a period of challenge to this hegemony of the academic curriculum. As Hargreaves records in his chapter, a crisis of curriculum emerged during this time, a crisis for which a decisive settlement is only now beginning to emerge. Blame placed upon schooling for economic underperformance and mounting unemployment, coupled with a crisis of confidence in state and welfare institutions as a whole, created an economic and ideological pretext for the government to pursue increased control over the curriculum and to redefine its fundamental purposes.

The government was not however 'united' in its views regarding how that curriculum was to be redefined and reconstructed. Varying, indeed conflicting, interpretations and preferences between the DES and HMI were particularly visible in the early stages of curricular debate (Lawton, 1980 and 1984). Nor was the argument about curriculum confined to different arms of central government either, as other groups, most notably the LEAs, and especially the ILEA, also contributed to the debate.

One of the arguments for curricular reconstruction was clearly counter-hegemonic in its implications. The view of the curriculum promoted here was one which challenged existing subject boundaries and promised learning experiences which cross-cut and extended beyond them. For those holding to this position, the dominance of the subject-based academic curriculum and its imposition on virtually all secondary school pupils was broadly responsible for the disaffection and disillusionment that many low attaining, working-class pupils felt with regard to their school experience. Her Majesty's Inspectorate (1979 and 1983) therefore advocated and indeed actively sought to implement a policy of providing all young people, as a matter of entitlement, with a broad and balanced range of educational experiences.In the ILEA, an influential committee reviewing and making recommendations concerning secondary education in the Authority, argued that the school system currently recognized and rewarded only a very narrow range of educational achievements: ones residing in the academic, intellectual-cognitive domain (ILEA, 1984). A wider definition of achievement, the Committee argued, which embraced social and personal and practical achievements as well as the usual intellectual-cognitive ones, would maximize opportunities for success among all young people, but especially among many working-class ones who had traditionally not fared well in the narrowly interpreted academic domain.

Challenges to the subject-based, academic hegemony of the school curriculum were taking place at school level also. This was perhaps most apparent in the rapid development and spread at local level of programmes of 'active' tutorial work (Bolam and Medlock, 1985) and personal and social education (David, 1983; Pring, 1984; Hargreaves *et al.*, 1988). These courses addressed the affect as well as the intellect: feeling as well as thinking. And increasingly, after originally being provided for low attainers only, they offered personal and social education to *all* pupils, whatever their ability. Such programmes shifted the principle of relevance from the insulated low status confines of the less able, into the cloistered enclaves of the academic elite. Boundaries were becoming blurred; categories confused. Able and less able, rigour and relevance, affect and intellect — the things which the secondary school and its curriculum had assiduously kept apart, were now being mixed together. Lepers were tolling their bells amongst the clean.And in the ears of the powerful and the privileged, the chimes were not at all sweet. The New Right in particular voiced especially strong objections to the emergence of peace studies, world studies, and development education in the curriculum, on the grounds that they raised issues that were too difficult conceptually for children under 16 to handle, that they were often taught in an emotionally loaded and politically biased way, that they were not 'real subjects', and that they took precious learning time away from the fundamental subjects of the school curriculum (Scruton, Ellis-Jones and O'Keefe, 1985; Scruton, 1985; Cox and Scruton, 1984; Marks, 1985; O'Keefe 1986; for a critique see Hargreaves *et al.*, 1988).

Against this counter-hegemonic thrust, a second version of curricular reconstruction was simultaneously being promoted. This was designed to strengthen, not weaken, the existing academic, subject-base of the school curriculum. Its central rationale was a proposed improvement of the quality of subject teaching, given supposed evidence, collected by HMI, that the quality of teaching suffered where there was a poor match between the subject taught and the subject expertise and qualification of the person teaching it. As Hargreaves argues in his chapter, HMI's evidence and their interpretation of it is open to serious criticism (also Hargreaves, 1988b). Nevertheless, that evidence was used to justify various measures, introduced by the DES and the Secretary of State, to improve the quality and provision of subject specialist teaching.

Teaching Quality (DES, 1983) and *Better Schools* (DES, 1985) urged schools and LEAs to pay more attention to the quality of subject specialist provision in primary, middle and secondary schools, especially in the making of new staff appointments (see Campbell's chapter). Circular 3/84 (DES, 1984), and the deliberations of CATE (see Rudduck's chapter), imposed new regulations on courses of teacher education, requiring institutions to allocate at least 50 per cent of their time for students to study a subject of the school curriculum. This was no policy of tepid encouragement. It was backed by the force of legislation and statutory requirement. Within this approach to curriculum renewal, the quality of teaching was to be improved by strengthening rather than weakening the grip of school subjects upon the curriculum.

For a while, these two different interpretations of curriculum change competed for supremacy as the crisis of curriculum brought with it processes of conflict and contestation in the struggle to create a new curriculum consensus. The hegemony of the academic curriculum was being contested. Those seeking to deconstruct school subjects, and to widen definitions of achievement were, in effect, bidding for a new, widened curricular hegemony, in which cultural capital, the criteria of success and achievement, would be redefined and extended beyond the academic domain. By contrast, the advocates of subject match and increased specialization, were reconstructing and refurbishing the traditional, subject-based academic curriculum; stripping down and renovating the traditional, 'quality' stock of school subjects. They were reinforcing cultural capital, not redefining it; reasserting the hegemony of the academic curriculum, not questioning and challenging it.

The terms of the newly-proposed National Curriculum suggest very powerfully that reconstruction, not deconstruction, has now virtually won this particular struggle (see our own chapters for extended commentary on the National Curriculum). The foundation and the core subjects which are to occupy up to 90 per cent of the school timetable, are predominantly academic in character. They are defined in traditional, very traditional subject terms. There is history and geography, but not humanities or social studies. Health education and computer studies are to be taught through existing subjects, not aside from them. 'Clutter such as peace studies', as one DES official has estimated, may well be squeezed out altogether. Development education, environmental education, political education, if they are to be catered for at all, must be offered within the remaining 15 per cent or so of curriculum time. The New Right, it seems, is having its way.

In this way, existing forms of cultural capital and the hegemony of the academic curriculum are being reasserted (Hargreaves, 1988a). What is currently contentious, will quickly become normal, natural, reasonable, taken-for-granted. New subjects will be eclipsed, forgotten, or consigned to older, less able groups. 'Real' subjects will be distinguished from and thereby presented as self-evidently superior to mere 'clutter'. Integration will be inhibited. Questioning and controversiality will be muted; relevance pushed back; definitions of achievement narrowed. The decisive hegemonic resolution which the National Curriculum is delivering will, in this way, restore and reinforce processes of educational and social differentiation which recognize and reward the cultural inheritance of the middle classes. The curriculum will be narrowed. Differentiation will be increased. In both these senses, specialization will hasten the development of decomprehensivization.

Beyond age 14, when the hegemonic curriculum and the cultural capital it rewards and recognizes has done its work, more choice and experimentation will then be permitted — indeed, encouraged. The able will likely pursue yet more traditional academic subjects — more science, a second foreign language, and the like. The less able, having already been selected out by the strict application of narrowly interpreted academic criteria, will then be allowed to follow what might facetiously be called the 'MFI curriculum'. Modules for Idiots!! Having been safely selected out, the 'less able' will be permitted to furnish themselves with a low-cost, self-assembled set of technical, social and life skills to help them adjust to and cope with the many changes that rapid shifts in societal circumstances and the occupational environment will demand of them as less academic, less qualified, less skilled. A modular way to a modular life! (Hargreaves, 1987).

To designate the modular curriculum as the 'MFI Curriculum' is, of course, less than generous. Modular initiatives, particularly within TVEI, have often shown considerable imagination and experimentation. They have sometimes opened up less conventional, less subject based areas of inquiry to the more able. And advocates of the modular curriculum claim significant success in its raising the motivation and achievement of the less able (Moon, 1987; Warwick, 1987). In principle, there is nothing in itself wrong, and a good deal that is praiseworthy about the modular curriculum. But, like much curricular innovation, the context of small-scale experimentation is very different from the context of wholesale implementation. Experimentation has been possible with supportive and committed schools and heads, often working with imaginative and challenging understandings of curriculum change. Experimentation has also been possible in a context which has still allowed curriculum change to be implemented according to an agenda of common and broad comprehensive entitlement. The context of wholesale implementation, however, looks as if it will be rather different. As well as encountering the familiar problem of having to deal with a large number of unconvinced and less-than enthusiastic schools and heads, the widely implemented modular curriculum will also be developed in the imposed and unavoidable context of a National Curriculum. This, it will be recalled, is an academic, subject-based curriculum, a curriculum which divides able from less able according to narrowly interpreted academic criteria, a curriculum which builds up subject allegiances and option choice preferences of a subject-based nature at an early age, and a curriculum which strongly discourages or prohibits curricular experimentation before 14, since that would lead to redefinitions of cultural capital and threats to middle-class interest and inheritance. Within this inescapable context of National Curriculum reform, widespread implementation of modular structures is likely to lead only to thinly disguised and selective systems of subject option choice. Under such circumstances, it seems to us that despite its radical origins, widespread modularization will in fact reinforce the principles and processes of differentiation and decomprehensivization, not challenge them.

Vocationalization

Vocationalization is, in many respects, the antithesis of specialization. Against an academic and bookish learning, it counterposes principles of practicality and relevance. It concentrates less on the acquisition of knowledge, than the development of attitudes and skills. And instead of didactic modes of exposition, it tends to promote active and experiential learning.

Vocationalization is not new to the school system. The relationship between education and economic performance has long been a preoccupation of educational policy makers (Gleeson, 1985). And there have been continuing and repeated attempts to put technical education on a firm footing in British education (McCulloch, 1986). But the relationship between education and employment, and in particular between schools and industry, gained a greater prominence and sense of urgency within educational policy, as unemployment rose, especially amongst the young. Prime Minister Callaghan, in his Ruskin College speech in 1976, voiced anxieties about pupils who may become 'unemployed because they do not have the skills', and the whole relationship between schools and working life subsequently formed a major item in the Great Debate of 1976. These anxieties about industrial competitiveness and economic performance were in turn compounded by a mounting moral panic about the threats to social order and stability that might be caused by jobless youth (Mungham, 1982). And so a magnificent irony was visited upon the education system: just when there were fewer and fewer jobs for young people to go to, so was there more and more of a vocational emphasis within the secondary school curriculum. As Finn (1982, p. 49) crisply puts it 'Schooling for unemployment involves, paradoxically, more efficient education for employment: it is as if teachers now have to instil the work ethic deeply enough for it to survive lengthy periods out of work.'

The early initiatives in vocational education, though numerous, were somewhat disparate and disconnected, however. Project Trident, Understanding British Industry, the Schools Council Industry Project, Young Enterprise and other schemes like them — such innovations were launched to make industrial and vocational inroads into the experience and curriculum of secondary schooling. Although there was evidence that these schemes had some impact on the development of work experience programmes,and the study of industry and work within the context of personal and social education courses, the impact was not systematic (Holmes and Jamieson, 1986). Pressure was piecemeal. Take-up was uneven. At the end of the day, adoption by schools was optional and dependent upon the persuasive power of HMI, the DES and the industry lobby (Jamieson, 1985). Against a deep-rooted historical tradition of suspicion and antipathy towards vocational values and enterprise culture in many parts of the educational community, the responsiveness of schools in industrial initiatives was consequently localized and less than whole-hearted. Old humanist values preserving classical liberal education were still holding out against the enterprising ambitions of the industrial trainers (Whitty, 1985; Ball, 1987).

The apparent inability of the localized educational system to respond to economic change, and the administrative incapacity of the DES to force the hand of schools in adopting new vocational initiatives, occasioned the intervention of the Department of Employment through the Manpower Services Commission, and with it, a massive shift towards centralization of government control in the curriculum. As Dale and his colleagues argue in their chapter, the intervention of the MSC in the curriculum through the establishment of the TVEI, created a hybridization of the spheres of education and employment, a bringing together of different social values and different managerial principles of operation and innovation.

TVEI itself has tended to be confined to the middle and lower ability ranges, and in that sense, the contradiction alleged by some (for example Ball, 1987) between the old humanist academic curriculum and the industrial trainer vocational one, has been less great than might be imagined. The two traditions have remained relatively well insulated from one another. But if an explicitly 'vocational' curriculum still tends to exclude the most able, TVEI has nonetheless brought about more indirect changes in other parts of the school system. In particular, its modular course structures have helped stimulate modularization elsewhere in the secondary school curriculum (the implication of which, we have already alluded to, and which we will examine further in the next section). Moreover, the style of innovation — which Dale (1986, p. 43) identifies as following a business and commercial model — with its swift time schedules, rapid movement of resources into priority areas, sponsorship of competitive bidding, and procedures of regular evaluation and auditing — has been quickly emulated by the DES, keen to retrieve its own control over the secondary school curriculum.

The Further Education Unit (FEU), attached to the DES, has, in fact, itself made a significant contribution to the content and style of courses for the young unemployed. Having relied in the past on teaching of traditional crafts and skills on a day-release basis for apprentices in manufacturing and service industries, and on catering for an expanding academic intake of students taking GCEs, qualifications in business studies and the like, further education in the late 1970s was beginning to cater for a third, and rapidly expanding sector. This was unemployed youth; the tertiary modern intake, as Gleeson (1986) calls them. Through documents on such areas as Active Learning (FEU, 1974), Pupil Profiles (FEU, 1982 and 1984) and their influential *A Basis for Choice* (FEU, 1979), the FEU mapped out basic principles of curriculum and pedagogy for what euphemistically came to be labelled as the new 'prevocational' courses.

In *A Basis for Choice*, the prevocational curriculum was divided into three fundamental components; core, vocational and job specific studies. This structure was later broadly incorporated into the Certificate of Prevocational Education (CPVE) which Radnor, Ball and Burrell describe in their chapter. A pattern of provision originally designed for the post-school unemployed was therefore now making substantial inroads into the school system itself. Taken together, two related aspects of the MSC's and FEU's influence on the secondary school curriculum are particularly important; more important, indeed, than the emergence of specific, identifiable components of vocational training. One is the spread of what Dale (1986) calls 'the new FE pedagogy' throughout the secondary school curriculum. We shall deal with this shortly. The other is the increasing emphasis being attached to 'generic' or 'transferable' as opposed to job-specific skills.

As the legitimacy of work-orientated programmes in a work-scarce world became increasingly tenuous, the 'discovery' was made that there were, in fact, basic generic skills that would equip young people with the ability to adapt to changing technological requirements rather than to any particular job, and that these generic skills relevant to work were, in fact, also skills that were relevant to life in general. Such claims were based on an influential document identifying eleven 'occupational training families' of skill areas (IMS, 1983) which, critics have argued, had no identifiable philosophical or empirical basis (Reid and Holt, 1986; Gleeson, 1986). The newly defined vocational-cum-life skills are therefore empirically suspect. They are often labelled skills, when closer inspection reveals they really refer to attitudes (much more socially contentious!). And the programmes that arise from them tend to emphasize individual responses of coping and adaptation to life difficulties such as unemployment, rather than to developing capacities for critique, or strategies to secure change. Such possibilities of a more radical nature have indeed been explicitly excised on the grounds of their being 'political'. That their excision is also political, has not been a matter for policy discussion, however.

A mandatory requirement of both the CPVE and the TVEI, is that they provide compulsory programmes of personal and social development (within core studies, for instance). These initiatives have, indeed, had considerable influence on the spread of personal and social education throughout secondary schools more generally (Hargreaves *et al.*, 1988). Yet we have seen how the skills and attitudes fostered in such programmes may well be constructed from an agenda of vocational values and skills which have magically been reinterpreted as having wider relevance to life in general. It is here, where its influence is most covert and pervasive, where it is less open to direct challenge by subscribers to alternative value systems, that vocationalization is ethically and politically at its most questionable.

In some cases, the spread and importance of vocational values has become so taken for granted and pervasive that employers are involved in, and consulted about, educational initiatives in which it could be argued they should have no legitimate stake at all. It has been a matter of virtually universal acceptance, for instance, that employers be actively involved in the design and development of pupil profiles and records of achievement — an initiative designed for pupils of *all* abilities, across the entire secondary age-range span. Yet, given continuing youth unemployment, the extent to which employers will be direct users of young people's records of achievement at 16 is extremely small. Employers' role as users therefore gives them little warrant for involvement in this important development. And yet their influence both direct and indirect, has been substantial — blurring the distinction between universally worthwhile personal qualities and those particular qualities required by commerce and industry: or more worryingly, allowing the second to pass as the first (*ibid*).

Vocationalization is therefore influencing the redefinition of secondary school experience in two ways. First, it is a policy which is being applied to particular ability groups after age 14, to maintain differentiation, to perpetuate the work ethic, and to eliminate more 'academic', cognitively rigorous and rational appraisals of the social world in general and the world of work in particular (which more 'liberal' forms of education might well provide). Second, vocationalization is contributing to a more general, less visible, yet perhaps more potent process of socialization of the young as a whole, where personal qualities are being aligned with vocational values, and where the existing organization and relationships of business and commerce are being placed above appraisal and beyond reproach. Vocationalization therefore fosters differentiation and it suppresses dissent. In the form it has adopted within British secondary schools, it has become a major facilitator of decomprehensivization.

Dispositional Adjustment

Social differentiation requires individual adjustment. It requires individual adjustment of many pupils to institutional and social positions of lesser advantage than their more academic peers. And it requires individual adjustment of teachers to a system which in practice denies those principles of comprehensiveness to which many of them have become committed. In a penetrating analysis of changes in modern secondary education Hartley, (1986) argues that newly developed classroom pedagogies and strategies of staff training bear a striking similarity to one another. There is, he argues,

> an emerging isomorphism in the forms of collaborative control in education . . . a non-directive and collaborative pedagogy in the classroom; and a similar collaborative strategy on the part of officialdom . . . when trying to persuade teachers to implement the new progressivist pedagogy for low achieving and possibly disruptive pupils in the (later) years of secondary education. (p. 229).

Such points are amplified by Hargreaves in his chapter on the 'Crisis of Motivation and Assessment' which finds, in current emphases on pupil motivation, a policy interest in manufacturing and manipulating diffuse dispositions among the less able to secure their loyalty to institutions and purposes which may be working to their objective disadvantage. The new pedagogy, with powerful roots in the 'new FE' pedagogy described by Dale (1986), emphasizes pupil collaboration, negotiated curricula, 'active' or experiential' learning, pupil self-assessment and so forth. And the new pedagogical agenda for lower attaining pupils, also described in the chapter by Weston and her colleagues, has, in echoing many of the sentiments of 1960s progressivism, secured the support of many radical teachers keen to subvert the grip of the traditional academic curriculum and its associated didactic modes of pedagogy, on secondary school experience. Yet close inspection of the new progressivist pedagogies raises serious questions about their appropriateness within the context of a secondary system increasingly committed to earlier and stricter principles of differentiation.

First, the pedagogies are mainly applied to the less able, not the more able. Second, they tend to emphasize affect more than intellect, emotion more than reason, coping more than critique. They are pedagogies of individual adaptation rather than pedagogies of social change. Third, negotiation is often exceedingly one-sided and conducted within strict limits of an agenda externally decided elsewhere — political examination of the causes of unemployment or the nature of work lies outside the remit of most personal and social education programmes, for instance (Hargreaves *et al.*, 1988). Fourth, the technological apparatus of subject-based graded assessments often substitutes the motivational trickery of extrinsic grades and certificates, for the instrinsic motivational values of 'really useful' knowledge.

Progressivism is not always radical or subversive (Hartley, 1987). In a highly stratified society where the ruling government has a powerful ideological grip on the means of mobilizing mass loyalty, experiential, affective, emotional learning can shape dispositions and loyalties and inhibit the emergence of rational and rigorous critique. No less a figure of political authoritarianism than Italy's Mussolini grasped this principle with great perceptiveness. His first Minister of Education, Gentile, was very much an educational 'progressive' who favoured state schooling giving high importance to spiritual development. Expressing his confidence in Gentile's reforms, Mussolini himself proclaimed that 'from the future fascist schools and universities, the nation's new and ruling class would issue' (quoted in Entwistle, 1979, p. 185). Such are the possible consequences for political indoctrination of too strong an emphasis on the affective, emotional, spiritual aspects of children's education! As Entwistle (*ibid*, p. 82) puts it in summarizing this historical evidence 'an innovative, democratic society requires not merely "spontaneity" but also citizens who are well informed'. The new pedagogy, it would seem, set as it is within a wider context of differentiation, has very little to do with developing a socially and politically well-informed citizenry among the less able.

As Hartley (1986) notes, very similar principles are at work in the new approaches to in-service training among teachers and management. Not only have extensive programmes of in-service *education* been replaced by brief, intensive programmes of in-service *training*, compressing the time available for studied reflection about educational innovation. But the training, as training, has become more emotional and experiential, and less rigorous and rational than the in-service provision it replaced.

Courses of training in the widely adopted programmes of Active Tutorial Work (Baldwin and Wells, 1981), have in many ways provided the exemplar for further training models within the GCSE, TRIST (TVEI Related In-service Training) and GRIST. Practical, experiential, short, intensive — this is now the style of in-service provisions. Yet, an evaluation of Active Tutorial Work training has revealed that while some space is allocated to open discussion within training programmes, the time for this is usually compressed and (in ironic contrast to the rest of the training), the discussion itself is often rather unstructured in nature. In their evaluation, Bolam and Medlock (1985, p. 21) found that in an introductory school course, 'the least successful activity was the question session at the very end of the course . . . owing to lack of time, the questions were limited in number and several course members did not get the opportunity to raise matters of significance to them'. Similarly, after observing an LEA course, they concluded that 'some teachers would welcome a clear and coherent statement of the ATW approach, including its theoretical and curriculum underpinning, both for themselves and to explain to colleagues' (p. 25). The fact that Bolam and Medlock nonetheless found the ATW training method to be impressively 'effective', compounds rather than mitigates the anxieties and ethical doubts we have already raised.

In ATW training, as in patterns of in-service training that have succeeded it, the overwhelming emphasis appears to have been on transmission of information about, and practical experience in, using a particular approach. The structure of such in-service experiences denies teachers the opportunity to engage in sustained critical questioning and to make autonomous judgments about the programmes to which they are being exposed. This pattern of training should itself be understood within a wider context of escalating pressures and constraints on teachers' work where teachers are being required to respond to a growing range of multiple and simultaneously mounted initiatives, but under conditions where little extra time or resources are allocated for coping with, still less reflecting on such initiatives. The implementation of such innovations in simultaneous, multiple fashion is part of what Apple (1986) calls the *intensification* of teachers' work; a qualitative change in the labour process leading not just to greater pressure towards productivity (more work), but reduced opportunity to reflect on the worth and rationality of what is being produced too. It would seem, then, that in the new pedagogies of classroom learning and in-service training, teachers and pupils alike are being disenfranchized of their entitlement to intellectual independence and of the means which would allow them to express rigorous and rational criticisms, where appropriate, of the systems in which they work.

To sum up: the structural isomorphism between pedagogies for the less able and in-service training for their teachers is, we believe not merely coincidental. Experiential, affectively based pedagogies are, in effect, being deployed in such a way as to secure the dispositional adjustment of pupils and teachers to a centrally controlled system embodying increased educational differentiation. They are pedagogies which repress reflection and depress dissent.

Surveillance

Dispositional adjustment is one strategy by which the socially destabilizing effects of heightened differentiation are averted. Intensified state surveillance is another. In his classic study of changing attitudes to punishment and discipline over the centuries, Michael Foucault (1977) points to discipline and surveillance as the most modern and sophisticated microphysics of power and control. Discipline and surveillance are not, in his terms, punitive. They do not extract forms of public retribution as in older, more traditional forms of punishment. Nor are they simply preventative, in the sense of actively and openly discouraging crime and deviance. Discipline and surveillance are not particular kinds of act or intervention, stopping and starting, visible at the moment of their imposition. They do not intervene to sustain or restore social order. They are a fundamental, integral part of that order itself and the principles by which it operates.

Discipline and surveillance are systems of minute, state-regulated anticipations and restructurings in the mundane, day-to-day business of everyday life. They are especially appropriate for, and increasingly common in, the exertion of centralized state power over social systems of great complexity. They comprise systems and processes of information and intelligence gathering, and of increasingly intensive and all-encompassing observation, where it is the knowledge that one is being watched or may be watched that inhibits infraction and discourages deviance even before it occurs. Foucault himself summarized it thus:

> Discipline had to solve a number of problems for which the old economy of power was not sufficiently equipped. It could reduce the inefficiency of mass phenomena: reduce what, in a multiplicity, makes it much less manageable than a unity; reduce what is opposed to each of its elements and of their sum . . . That is why discipline fixes; it arrests or regulates movements; it clears up confusion; it dissipates compact groupings of individuals wandering about the country in unpredictable ways . . . It must also master all the forces that are formed from the very constitution of an organized multiplicity; it must neutralize the effects of counter-power that springs from them and which form a resistance to the power that wished to dominate it. (Foucault, 1977, p 219).

The formidable functions and requirements of modern social discipline, call for processes of immense sophistication:

> The disciplines have to bring into play the power relations, not above but inside the very texture of the multiplicity, as discretely as possible: to this correspond anonymous instruments of power, co-extensive with the multiplicity that they regiment, such as hierarchical surveillance, continuous registration, perpetual assessment and classification (*ibid*, p. 220).

The department store camera and the soccer match 'hoolivan' with their high profile technology whose visibility announces that private behaviour is potentially ever-open to public observation; these things, along with the ubiquitous computer data bank are the more obvious parts of the state's apparatus of social surveillance. But the record card, the pupil profile, the staff appraisal document and the community involvement programme — these things too are part of the school's, and with it the state's growing network of inclusionary control. Such things are part of that widening network of state practices where more of the person is open to continuous assessment, intervention and control in more of their life for more of the time. In the name of personal welfare and social improvement, the state delves deeper into the hitherto private realm of personal space, and spreads wider into more dimensions of social living, into neighbourhood and community, in order to fulfil its task of social integration. Two examples will illustrate the point: pupil profiles and community education.

One of us has previously written about the possible use of newly-developed pupil profiles, processes of self-assessment, negotiated assessment, and recording of personal experiences, as instruments of social surveillance (Hargreaves, 1986b). Pupil profiles, it was argued, were in danger of opening up pupils' emotions for hierarchical inspection, assessing personality as well as performance. They were designed to do this not just as a matter of entitlement, but of inescapable, enforced entitlement. And it appeared they would apply the process on a regular, routine basis where the pupil's knowledge of future inescapable 'negotiated' reviews would suppress deviance or non-conformity even before it arose. Profiles, it was suggested, might well lead to the build-up of sinister written or mental dossiers on pupils, which could be retrieved for possible future use at later points in the child's educational career. They would subject emotion, feelings and intentions to mandatory scrutiny. And despite rhetorics of negotiation, this process of compulsory 'review' would in most cases probably be predominantly one-sided, the teacher observing and judging the child, rather than vice versa.

Since that point, while arguments about the advantages and disadvantages of pupil profiles and records of achievement have continued, three interesting points have come to light. First, in one local education authority (Warwickshire), parents have been asked to fill in questions on their children's behaviour at home in terms of such things as how often they do the vacuuming, how well they manage their pocket money and how good they are at getting up in a morning (Hargreaves *et al.*, 1988). Here we have the parent co-opted into the apparatus of state surveillance; community living being brought under state regulation and subjected to state normalization. Second, a remark was leaked from the DES that information collected from pupil profiles about behaviour and demeanour might be used to compile public data on the effectiveness or otherwise of schools in terms of their social outcomes. (*Times Educational Supplement*, 28 August 1987). And third, if such events and initiatives have not offered sufficiently clear pointers to likely future social uses of pupil profiles, recent research on pupils' responses to profiling clearly suggests that very many pupils believe that what they reveal about themselves of a personal nature, may well be used in evidence against them at some future point of their education (Phillips and Hargreaves, 1987).

Like pupil profiles, community education has also been founded on a rhetoric, by no means empty, of welfare and improvement. Yet the social consequences of its development too, are in many ways running contrary to those desired by many of the movement's most ardent supporters. Baran (1987) has analyzed how community education first emerged in the context of rural Cambridgeshire in the 1920s, as part of a programme of rural reform and restoration, promoted by Henry Morris. According to Baran, the context of community education in the 1970s and 80s, however, is rather different. Community education now provides an occasion for the insertion of modern surveillance practices into the inner city. Socially at-risk groups are drawn into a structure of care and opportunity which is also one of regulation and control, by being brought within the ambit of the school in the form of play groups, coffee mornings and the like. Similarly, through home visiting schemes, community profiles and now pupil profiles too, the school is moving into the community, gathering and collecting information on an intensive and extensive scale, as a possible basis for intervention, referral and official interpretation at any future point. As Cohen (1985) puts it in his discussion of the emergence of 'soft', inclusionary patterns of control of crime and deviance in the modern state, the external environment is manipulated to prevent the initial infraction (p. 214). 'Urban environments and situations', he argues, 'will become sites for behaviour control' (p. 232). Schools, families, neighbourhoods, youth organizations will increasingly fall within the state's embrace. 'The aim is to discourage anything from being casual — leisure, family, child rearing, sexuality' (p. 232). The conflicts of class and ethnicity within the community will be played down, anticipated, reinterpreted. Spontaneous cultures of class and race will be restructured, reorganized. Through community festivals, displays and theatre, the state, through the school, re-presents the community to itself as a diverse but integrated unity — steeped in harmonious tradition (*ibid*).

Through modern developments in British schools, we can, therefore, see ways in which the state through the school penetrates the private, polices the personal, and coordinates the community in its disciplinary monitoring and organization of everyday social life. Pupil self-assessment and personal recording, processes of compulsory staff appraisal and institutional forms of self-evaluation — all these things are part of a coordinated, integrated state strategy of management by hierarchical assessment, of surveillance by the intensive but unobtrusive means of judgemental observation. The school, in this sense, is increasingly becoming a powerful instrument of state surveillance.

Summary and Conclusions

The educational era we are now entering is one of growing fiscal scarcity and resource contraction within the schooling system and within society at large. As the availability of social rewards and opportunities contracts, dominant social groups along with those who politically and administratively represent them, are working hard to preserve their cultural and economic advantage. This is, in many respects, what explains the movement from comprehensivization to decomprehensivization; from the pursuit of equal opportunity to the institution of earlier and more finely graded processes of educational and social differentiation. That differentiation is itself in part secured by a reassertion of traditional forms of academic cultural capital as the criteria for curricular achievement and recognition. The subject specialist, academic, national curriculum with its benchmark testing and early separation of success from failure therefore converts educational differentiation into a process of social class differentiation; recognizing and rewarding particular versions of scholastic ability in which the advantaged middle classes already have a rich cultural inheritance and investment.

Following something of a hegemonic crisis in the curriculum in the late 1970s and early 1980s, vocationalization no longer appears to present a major threat to these existing forms of cultural capital and the social privileges they protect. Through principles of practicality and relevance, vocationalization works more to contain and motivate those who have already categorically failed. Only now are those without the required cultural capital permitted the alternative curriculum and the alternative forms of achievement that go with it. It would take much earlier applications of extensive vocationalization to challenge seriously the hegemony of the academic curriculum, the forms of cultural capital on which it rests, and the processes of differentiation which advantage those classes and groups who already possess such capital.

Earlier and more extensive processes of differentiation bring with them more intensive and extensive procedures of state control, to offset their potentially destabilizing effects. State control undergoes centralization to monitor and manage the distribution of disadvantage, and to establish and legitimate the criteria of curricular worth and educational success according to which that distribution is secured. Because of the state's powerful ideological role in this respect, the apparently contradictory process of educational privatization, in fact creates not choice and diversity, but enforcement of traditional academic homogeneity through the state-regulated market of parental choice. Privatization facilitates the state in divesting itself of financial responsibility for educational and social reproduction under conditions of economic scarcity.

But in other respects we have seen that privatization also supports the state's ideological reconstruction of the academic, hegemonic curriculum. It successfully converts political wishes into private wants.

In the coalescence of privatization and centralization, the boundaries between public and private become increasingly blurred, and under rhetorics of pupil welfare, parental partnership and community involvement the state increasingly extends its activities of surveillance and dispositional adjustment into the hitherto private domain. Privatization and personalization become integrated with and indistinguishable from centralization and control. Surveillance and control therefore underwrite the processes of differentiation and decomprehensivization.

The process of decomprehensivization is of course, by no means complete. In many ways, it has indeed only just begun. The evidence is that resistance is persisting in many forms. Teachers are not always implementing the GCSE as intended (Radnor, 1987). Pupils are highly perceptive about the surveillance potential of pupil profiles and edit what they are prepared to disclose accordingly (Phillips and Hargreaves, 1987). Work experience sometimes does not so much instil vocational values as perpetuate scepticism and criticism about the nature of work in modern British society (Shilling, 1987). The new hegemony is therefore not being reasserted entirely unproblematically, without contradiction or resistance. But all the same, we have, it seems, now entered a decisively different phase in British education, in which the broad parameters of differentiation and decomprehensivization have been set down. A new hegemonic settlement is beginning to emerge. In this introduction we have described its central and interconnected principles. The chapters in the book amplify some of those principles more fully. For those who would want to defend an educational system according to values of fairness, entitlement and opportunity, these are the principles we believe should be widely and actively contested. Gentle compromise, polite persuasion, and muted deference to governmental authority in attempts to claw back minor concessions; these things are no longer tenable as a strategy for the defence and reconstruction of comprehensive education. A vigorous and coordinated campaign in support of very different educational and ethical values is now required. The evidence so far, however, is as Reynolds suggests later, that the Labour Party, still landlocked in its late 60s social democratic policies of access and resources, is not even remotely in a position to supply this. Distinctive educational policies which speak to the central issues of curriculum and assessment are also conspicuously wanting in the programmes of the liberals and the social democrats. We would now urge those parties, along with other bodies of political and professional opposition (such as the teacher associations), to begin to regain or even seize for the first time their intellectual initiative on state education and the curriculum. The first move in such a strategy might be for opposition groups to reestablish or build again their links with an active base of rigorous and properly critical educational research. We hope this book and the chapters in it begin to lay out the kind of intellectual critique of current educational policy, that politicians and administrators who subscribe to the sorts of ethical and educational principles we have outlined, may find valuable.

References

APPLE, M. (1986) *Teachers and Texts*, London, Routledge & Kegan Paul

BALDWIN, J. and WELLS, H. (1981) *Active Tutorial Work: Books 1–5*, Oxford, Basil Blackwell.

BALL, S. (1981) *Beachside Comprehensive*, Cambridge, Cambridge University Press.

BALL, S. (1987) 'Comprehensive schooling, effectiveness and control: An analysis of educational discourses', unpublished mimeograph, London, Kings College.

BARKER-LUNN, J. (1984) 'Junior school teachers: Their methods and practices', *Educational Research*, 26, 3, November.

BOLAM, R. and MEDLOCK, P. (1985) *Active Tutorial Work: Training and Dissemination – An Evaluation*, Oxford, Basil Blackwell.

BROADFOOT, P. (1984) 'From public examinations to profile assessment: The French experience' in BROADFOOT, P. (Ed) *Selection, Certification and Control*, Lewes, Falmer Press.

BURGESS, R. (1984) 'It's not a proper subject: It's just Newsom' in BALL, S. and GOODSON I. (Eds) *Defining the Curriculum: Histories and Ethnographies*, Lewes, Falmer Press.

COHEN, S. (1985) *Visions of Social Control*, Cambridge, Polity Press.

CONNELL, R. W. (1985) *Teacher's Work*, London, Allen and Unwin.

COX, C. and Scruton, R. (1984) *Peace Studies: A Critical Survey*, Occasional Paper No. 7, Institute for European Defence and Strategic Studies, London, Alliance Publishers.

DALE, R. (1986) 'Examining the gift-horse's teeth; A tentative analysis of TVEI' in WALKER, S. and BARTON, L. (Eds) *Youth Unemployment and Schooling*, Milton Keynes, Open University Press.

DAVID, K. (1983) *Personal and Social Education in Secondary Schools*, Schools Council Programme 3, London, Longman.

DEPARTMENT OF EDUCATION AND SCIENCE (1983) *Teaching Quality* (Cmnd 8836), London, HMSO.

DEPARTMENT OF EDUCATION AND SCIENCE (1984) *Initial Teacher Training: Approval of Courses* (Circular 3/84), London, HMSO.

DEPARTMENT OF EDUCATION AND SCIENCE (1985) *Better Schools* (Cmnd 9469) London, HMSO.

ENTWISTLE, H. (1979) *Antonio Gramsci – Conservative Schooling for Radical Politics*, London, Routledge & Kegan Paul.

FINN, D. (1982) 'Whose needs? Schooling and the "needs" of industry' in REES T. L. and ATKINSON, P. (Eds) *Youth Unemployment and State Intervention*, London, Routledge & Kegan Paul.

FOUCAULT, M. (1977) *Discipline and Punish*, Harmondsworth, Penguin.

FURTHER EDUCATION UNIT (1974) *Active Learning* London, FEU.

FURTHER EDUCATION UNIT (1979) *A Basis for Choice*, London, FEU.

FURTHER EDUCATION UNIT (1982) *Profiles: A Review of Issues and Practice in the Use and Development of Student Profiles*, London, HMSO.

FURTHER EDUCATION UNIT (1984) *Profiles in Action*, London, HMSO.

GLEESON, D. (1985) 'Privatization of industry and the nationalization of youth' in DALE R. (Ed) *Education Training and Employment*, Oxford, Pergamon Press.

GLEESON, D. (1986) 'Further education, free enterprise and the curriculum' in WALKER, S. and BARTON L. (Eds) *Youth Unemployment and Schooling*, Milton Keynes, Open University Press.

GOODSON, I. (1988) 'The micropolitics of curriculum change; The case of European studies' in GOODSON, I. (Ed) *The Making of Curriculum*, Lewes, Falmer Press.

HARGREAVES, A. (1986a) 'Research and policy: Some observations on ESRC educational research projects', *Journal of Education Policy*, 1, 2.

HARGREAVES, A. (1986b) 'Record breakers?' in BROADFOOT, P. (Ed) *Profiles and Records of Achievement*, Eastbourne, Holt-Saunders.

HARGREAVES, A. (1987) 'A modular way to a modular life'. *Times Educational Supplement*, 21 August.

HARGREAVES, A. (1988a) 'HMI perceptions of pastoral care and personal and social education in middle schools: A critique' in LANG P. (Ed).

HARGREAVES, A. (1988b) 'Teaching quality: A sociological analysis,' *Journal of Curriculum Studies*, 20, 3, pp. 211–31.

HARGREAVES, A. (1989) 'Curriculum policy and the culture of teaching' in GOODSON, I. and MILBURN, G. (Eds) *Reconstructing Educational Research*, Lewes, Falmer Press.

HARGREAVES, A., BAGLIN, E. HENDERSON, P., LEESON, P. and TOSSELI, T. (1988) *Personal and Social Education: Choices and Challenges*, Oxford, Basil Blackwell.

HARGREAVES, D. (1967) *Social Relations in a Secondary School*, London, Routledge & Kegan Paul.

HARLAND, J. (1987) 'The new INSET: A transformation scene', *Journal of Education Policy*, 2, 3, pp 233–44.

HARTLEY, D. (1986) 'Structural isomorphism and the management of consent in education', *Journal of Education Policy*, 1, 3.

HARTLEY, D. (1987) 'The convergence of learner-centred pedagogy in primary and further education in Scotland: 1965–1985', *British Journal of Educational Studies*, 35, 2, June.

HER MAJESTY'S INSPECTORATE (1979) *Aspects of Secondary Education*, London, HMSO

HER MAJESTY'S INSPECTORATE (1983) *Curriculum of Secondary Education*, London, HMSO.

HOLMES, M. (1987) 'The funding of private and independent schools', unpublished mimeograph, Ontario Institute for Studies in Education.

HOLMES, S. and JAMIESON, I. (1986) 'Jobs and careers: Class, schools and the new vocationalism' in ROGERS, R. (Ed) *Education and Social Class*, Lewes, Falmer Press.

HUMPHREY, C. (1984) *Structure of Secondary Education: Selection and Standards*, report of the Director of Education, Solihull, Metropolitan Borough of Solihull.

INNER LONDON EDUCATION AUTHORITY (1984) *Improving Secondary Schools*, report of the Committee on the Curriculum and Organization of Secondary Schools, London, ILEA.

INSTITUTE OF MANPOWER STUDIES (1983) *Training for Skill Ownership*, Falmer, University of Sussex.

JAMIESON, I. (1985) 'Corporate hegemony or pedagogic liberation: The school-industry movement in England and Wales' in DALE, R. (Ed) *Education Training and Employment*, Oxford, Pergamon Press.

LACEY, C. (1970) *Hightown Grammar*, Manchester, Manchester University Press.

LAWTON, D. (1980) *The Politics of the School Curriculum*, London, Routledge & Kegan Paul.

LAWTON, D. (1984) *The Tightening Grip*, Bedford Way Papers, London, Institute of Education.

McCULLOCH, G. (1986) 'Policy politics and education: The Technical and Vocational Education Initiative', *Journal of Education Policy* 1, 1.

McPHERSON, A. and WILLMS, D. (1987) 'Equalization and improvement: Some effects of comprehensive reorganisation in Scotland', *Sociology*, 21, 4 pp. 509–40.

MARKS, J. (1985) *'Peace Studies' in Our Schools: Propaganda for Defencelessness*, London, Women and Families for Defence.

MOON, R. (1987) 'Module myths and innovation', *Education*, 170, 11.

MUNGHAM, G. (1982) 'Workless youth as a "moral panic" ' in REES, T. L. and ATKINSON, P. (Eds) *Youth Unemployment and State Intervention*, London, Routledge & Kegan Paul.

NATIONAL CONFEDERATION OF PARENT-TEACHER ASSOCIATIONS (1985) *The State of Schools in England and Wales*, Gravesend, National Confederation of Parent-Teacher Associations.

OAKES, J. (1986) *Keeping Track: How Schools Structure Inequality*, New Haven, CT, Yale University Press.

OFFE, C. (1984) *Contradictions of the Welfare State*, London, Hutchinson.

O'KEEFE, D. (Ed) (1986) *The Wayward Curriculum*, Exeter, Short Run Press.

PHILLIPS, P. and HARGREAVES, A. (1987) 'Closed encounters', *Times Educational Supplement*, 11 September.

PRING, R. (1984) *Personal and Social Education in the Curriculum*, London, Hodder & Stoughton.

PRING, R. (1986) 'Privatization and education' in ROGERS, R. (Ed) *Education and Social Class*, Lewes, Falmer Press.

RADNOR, H. (1987) *GCSE – The Impact of the Introduction of GCSE at LEA and School Level*, final research report, Windsor, NFER.

RANSON, S. and TOMLINSON J. (Eds) (1986) *The Changing Government of Education*, London, Allen & Unwin.

REID, W. and HOLT, M. (1986) 'Structure and ideology in upper secondary education' in HARTNETT, A. and NAISH, M. (Eds) *Education and Society Today*, Lewes, Falmer Press.

SALTER, B. and TAPPER, T. (1986) *Power and Policy in Education: The Case of Independent Schooling*, Lewes, Falmer Press.

SALTER, B. and TAPPER, T. (1987) 'Department of Education and Science – Steering a new course' in HORTON, T. (Ed) *GCSE: Examining the New System*, London, Harper & Row,

SCRUTON, R. (1985) *World Studies: Education or Indoctrination?* Occasional Paper no. 15, Institute for European Defence and Strategic Studies, London, Alliance Publishers.

SCRUTON, R. Ellis-Jones, A. and O'KEEFE, D. (1985) *Education and Indoctrination*, London, Sherwood Press.

SHILLING, C. (1987) 'Work experience and schools: Factors affecting the participation of industry', *Journal of Education Policy*, 2, 2.

SIMON, B. (1984) 'Breaking school rules', *Marxism Today*, September.

TORRANCE, H. (1987) 'GCSE and school-based curriculum development' in HORTON, T. (Ed) *GCSE: Examining the New System*, London, Harper & Row.

WALFORD, G. (1985) *Life in Public Schools*, London, Methuen.

WALFORD, G. and JONES, S. (1986) 'The Solihull adventure: An attempt to reintroduce selective schooling'. *Journal of Education Policy*, 1, 3.

WARWICK, D. (1987) *The Modular Curriculum*, Oxford, Basil Blackwell.

WHITTY, G. (1985) *Sociology and School Knowledge: Curriculum Theory, Research and Policy*, London, Methuen.

Chapter 1

Education and the Social Order: The Contemporary Scene

Brian Simon

My specific concern is to relate educational policies, especially those discussed in this book, to 'the national political dimension'. This, in my view, raises questions about their relation to the social order. Looked at historically, it seems clear that mass, organized education, through schooling, has always been perceived as a major means of social control; that is to say, of ensuring both the stability and the perpetuation of the existing social order. This was probably the leading motivation for bringing universal education into being. For many thinkers, politicians, clergymen and others in the past, revolution seemed just round the corner. Are things so very different today — or can we find here a clue which would help to unravel the complexity of contemporary educational initiatives?

Here is the title of a book published in 1806 by Robert Colquhoun — in the days when titles really meant something. It reads:

> *A new and Appropriate System of Education for the Labouring People as practised at the free school at 19, Orchard Street, Westminster . . . with details explanatory of the particular economy of the institution and the methods prescribed for the purpose of securing and preserving A Greater Degree of Moral Rectitude as a means of preventing criminal offences by habits of Temperance, Industry, Subordination and Loyalty among that useful class of the community comprising the Labouring People of England*

This, says Geoffrey Best (1964, p. 156), the historian, writing in the early 1960s was perfectly representative of the dominant attitude among the upper orders towards the education of the lower. It was, he points out, both ideological and vocational. Some would fasten on the one, some on the other branch of it. Quite so, I thought, reading this recently. Surely the terrible twins to a tee. Keith Joseph — ideology, the importance of teaching 'national myths in history', 'the moral virtues of free enterprise and the pursuit of profit', and entrepreneurial values in particular. David Young — and the 'new vocationalism'. Skills for all, banausic and high grade (but mostly the former), social and life skills, CPVE in the schools, TVEI. The two prongs of the contemporary attack.

Here is a modern statement of the role of education within this syndrome as enunciated by an anonymous, but leading, DES official (with acknowledgement to Stewart Ranson, who recorded it):

> We are in a period of considerable social change. There may be social unrest, but we can cope with the Toxteths. But if we have a highly educated and idle population we may possibly anticipate more serious social conflict. *People must be educated once more to know their place.* (Ranson, 1984, p. 241, my emphasis)

Of course, the rhetoric has changed with the times. Since universal education was successfully imposed a century or so ago, it has been no longer politic to speak so frankly about plans for what Colquhoun called 'the useful class of the community' — that is 'The Labouring People of England'. The anonymous DES official is unusual in this respect. Normally, everything is now shrouded in an uplifting rhetoric which sometimes conceals the very opposite of the overt meaning. *Better Schools*, 'raising standards', concern with 'the quality of education' — and so on. One of the means of achieving these objectives (taken almost at random) is 'teacher appraisal'. But what is the social significance of teacher appraisal in the present context? It means teacher control. And by whom? By those in authority. As contradictions sharpen, direct control from the centre appears the more imperative.

The contributions in this book cover most of the main contemporary policy initiatives within the state (or maintained) sector. One aspect of them — the private, or so-called 'independent' sector — is, however, perhaps even more important than the collective emphasis of this book suggests. Is there a Low Achieving Pupils Project at Eton? or CPVE at Winchester? The private sector, since it reacts on the public sector in all sorts of ways, provides an essential dimension in any overall assessment. Rehabilitated and reconstructed after a period of near crisis just before and during the war, through such measures as the Assisted Places Scheme (see Whitty, Fitz and Andrews in this book), this sector has been successfully shored up and officially encouraged (indeed as a model) vis-a-vis the maintained sector. It continues to play a crucial, if changing role within the social context. To ignore it is to distort reality — a failure to effect an overall analysis. But here we are concerned with the maintained sector, and so, confining ourselves to schools only, what can be said?

If education is to fulfil its function of ensuring, or reinforcing, social stability, then, as circumstances change, education itself must change. In particular it must adapt to new social trends — particularly those resulting from deep-seated economic and technological change. The massive decline in the manufacturing and extractive industries, the substitution of high-tech processes, and other such changes, have led, and are leading, to rapid changes in the social structure, and, more generally, to substantial change in the relative position of this country compared to others — as all are aware.

The tensions that result (deriving, for instance, from mass unemploym... especially among young people) require quite new measures and initiatives.

There is now a clearly perceived danger of over-education (in spite of the supposed alienation of a proportion of school students). 'There has to be selection', Ranson (1984, p. 241) reported another high DES official as saying,

> Because we are beginning to create aspirations which society cannot match. In some ways [he continued] this points to the success of education in contrast to the public mythology that has been created . . . [so] we have to select; to ration the educational opportunities so that society can cope with the output of education.

Quite so. And this is the key.

So we have the Technical and Vocational Initiative (TVEI), Certificate in Prevocational Education (CPVE), General Certificate of Secondary Education (GCSE) and the Lower Achieving Pupils Project. So we have also the drive to central control and direction — the end of the 'partnership' in any meaningful sense. So we have in addition the enhancement of so-called 'parental choice'; deliberate resource starvation of the schools — and official encouragement for parental funding so building in new differentiation processes between schools budgetary measures to assist this and to assist the 'independent' schools, the Assisted Places Scheme. So, in a recent shiftaround, a woman from the Manpower Services Commission (MSC) is put in charge of curriculum at the DES; the Schools Council closed down; the Central Advisory Council simply abolished — an action which required Parliamentary sanction and connivance. No independent advice of any kind is either welcomed or sought. The centre takes control. The situation is clearly perceived as critical; hence the continuing series of critical actions — adaptations — the search for new solutions to the problems posed by the social order.

We may take these phenomena in turn.

First, the inner school restructuring, as imposed through both the DES and MSC. What is the emerging pattern?

It is arguable that, in place of the evolution of a common curriculum, or core, offering a broad, general education for all and including science and CDT (craft, design, technology), what is being aimed at is the imposition, of course on a new level, of the old tripartite division of schools which, of course, comprehensive education was designed precisely to overcome. Andy Hargreaves analyzes this whole development in his chapter in this book. Is it significant that it is just at the point in time when comprehensive education is becoming universal that these initiatives are undertaken?

TVEI, as we know, is to be generalized — though according to the critics (who, oddly enough, include the MSC itself) with totally inadequate funding. A condition of the pilot experiments was that TVEI courses should be available to *named* students only in each school. If this is also to be generalized, we have here the creation of a specific technically and vocationally-oriented 'track' within the comprehensive school for students aged 14 and upwards.

It may well be that some extremely good work (in terms of educational criteria) is being, and will be done, within TVEI (though overall evaluation is incomplete). But this is not the issue in terms of our analysis. The issue is the imposition of divisive procedures (and curricula) within the very heart of the comprehensive school (see also chapter 10).

The recent White Paper, *Working Together — Education and Training*, in spite of assurances to the contrary, gives full control of the ten-year TVEI extension programme in the schools directly to the MSC, which is answerable to the Employment Secretary, and which proposes to monitor its development very closely indeed. This is a clear defeat for the DES, and education generally. Kenneth Baker said, after this announcement, that the aim was to give a new dimension to what was taught in schools. 'Learning has to become practical', he said — putting a brave face on things (*Times Education Supplement*, 4 July 1986).

Then there is the much less publicized LAPP initiative, which Penelope Weston discusses in her chapter. The object here is to develop 'appropriate' curricula for Keith Joseph's 'bottom 40 per cent' — that is, for four-tenths of the three-and-a-half million students in secondary schools — a total of 1.4 m students; or, in modern terms, Colquhoun's 'useful class' — the 'Labouring People of England'. Of course, in the present circumstances, this is all about motivation (or, if you like, assimilation) — in any case the active countering of alienation is clearly important both in terms of social cohesion, and in terms of the objective that people should learn once again 'to know their place'. Here again, much good work is certainly being done, but again this is not the issue for us now. The objective significance of this initiative — in terms of new forms of differentiation and subordination — is clear enough. The more effectively the projects are carried through in terms of the project's own, pre-determined criteria — and then, presumably, generalized as is the intention — the more effectively its wider social objectives will be achieved.

And how does GCSE fit into the picture? The fusion of the two existing exams might surely be regarded as an advance. It was certainly a priority demand on the part of comprehensive school teachers and heads for very many years. But, as Desmond Nuttall (1985) put it at the 1985 conference of the British Educational Research Association (BERA), the new examination has created a precedent in that, for the first time, it includes differentiating procedures within its very structure. The new examination is, in fact, both seven graded and bifurcated (which is quite an achievement). It may be that schools will find their way round the difficulties this structure will pose; and I have no doubt that the criteria do embody some much-needed reform in terms of content and pedagogy. But again, viewed objectively, differentiation is its chief characteristic — as indeed was very strongly emphasized by Sir Keith Joseph when he made his first announcement in the House of Commons in June 1984. The GCSE, he said, '*will be a system of examinations, not a single examination*'. There will be 'differentiated papers and questions in every subject (*The Times*, 21 June 1984). Only four months earlier, after the defeat of the Solihull attempt to reintroduce selective schools, Joseph had emphasized that, since selection between schools 'was largely out', then 'I emphasize that *there must be differentiation within schools*' (*Times Educational Supplement*, 17 February 1984). This he was ensuring through the design of the new GCSE.

What has happened to all the talk, official pamphlets from DES and HMI, and so on, about the common curriculum? This issue has been dropped like a hot brick, as the new, differentiating curricula initiatives take over. In place of cohesion and unity — as so effectively proposed in the ILEA report *Improving Secondary Schools* that David Hargreaves discusses in his chapter in this book — the perspective is one of enhanced differentiation; if not quite of the character of the conveyor belt system of streaming and selection which was the dominant model up to twenty years ago, then of a more complex and perhaps diffuse character in keeping with contemporary requirements. But the outcome, generally speaking, may be very similar.

I have not mentioned the CPVE nor the extraordinary rhetoric being developed around this initiative — and that of the 'new vocationalism' in general (Pavett, 1986); nor have I analyzed its specific social role at this particular conjuncture. As Geoffrey Best said, vocationalism has always been one of the prongs of the attack — the inculcation of 'temperance, industry, subordination and loyalty', as Colquhoun put it. But today there is a difficulty — there are very few jobs for young people. The contradiction between the evangelizing surge of the new vocationalism and the actual sharp erosion of job opportunities cries out for explanation. The one the MSC used for years — that it will mean that, when the 'economic up-turn' comes, young people will be ready and equipped with skills — no longer carries the least conviction. The 'new vocationalism', then, appears as a strategy for social control. The Emperor really has no clothes.

Added strength is given to this interpretation by the recent report of the Working Party on Pre-vocational Courses for students aged 14 to 16. Work experience and work skills are to be 'demoted'; instead the report 'emphasizes the goals of personal development, learning skills, and what used to be called life and social skills' (*Times Educational Supplement*, 18 July 1986). Members of the Committee are reported as holding 'that the main function of the courses' will be to provide 'an alternative general education for pupils who do not respond to traditional teaching'. In other words, what the *Times Educational Supplement* has recently described as 'a fork in the road' is being designed — one route to GCSE, the other through CPVE. sixty per cent to the first, Keith Joseph's 'bottom 40 per cent' to the other. This, the *Times Educational Supplement* claims, is 'the brute reality' of the situation.

The imposition of a clearly delineated, differentiated, functional structure on a school system that has its own, inner logic or thrust of development is no easy task. Educational institutions, and indeed whole systems, are essentially conservative — in the sense that, having a degree of autonomy, they develop (through their historical experience as institutions) procedures and practices, an ethos or outlook, that is exceptionally tenacious and highly resistant to change. This, I think, is confirmed by the whole history of curriculum innovation, at least from the early 60s. Hence the bid for central control is now pressed with increasing energy — even desperation, and all kinds of new, centralized procedures, having the aim of thrusting through the new initiatives, are being resorted to. Returning to our DES official, we can clearly see the reason for his cri-de-coeur to Stewart Ranson (1984, p. 224).

> Our focus must be on the strategic questions of the content, shape and purpose of the whole educational system and absolutely central to that is the curriculum. *We would like legislative powers over the curriculum* and the powers to control the exam system by ending all those independent charters of the examining bodies. (my emphasis)

And again, on the same issue:

> I see a return to centralization of a different kind *with the centre seeking to determine what goes on in institutions*: this is a more fundamental centralization than we have seen before. (my emphasis)

It certainly is. 'To determine what goes on in institutions' — that is exactly the point, and the current necessity.

When, early in March 1986, the crisis in education, underlined by leaks about Thatcher's electoral strategy, hit the headlines in all the national newspapers, the running, it may be recalled, was at first made by the Radical Right within the Tory party. The quality press — and the others — were full of the outpourings of men like Oliver Letwin, Arthur Selden and others, arguing strongly for the introduction of voucher schemes, or variants there-of, as well as for wholesale privatization of the school system generally. But — and this is where the politics of the day-to-day variety enter into the picture — the Tory party appeared as split between two sections with different attitudes and policies. On the one hand there were what might be defined as the maverick privateers who for a time *seemed* to be making the running. On the other hand there were the mainline centralizers. Each group had its own candidates for the succession of Sir Keith Joseph as Secretary of State. It seemed at the time that the logic of events, in terms of this sort of analysis, would ensure victory for the centralizers (Simon, 1986). And so it was, aided probably, by the debacle of the May elections, both local and parliamentary. There was no way in which this accelerating, and, if you like, politically and socially necessary drive could or would be diverted — and certainly not into harebrained schemes which might put the thrust at risk, with the possible resulting loss of control. Hence the appointment of Kenneth Baker — the expert communicator. The thrust has to be sold. Baker was soon reported as pressing his Cabinet colleagues 'for open-ended powers to control educational spending direct from the DES'. (*Times Educational Supplement*, 27 June 1986). While said to have been opposed to specific grants when Environment Secretary, he has, the *Times Educational Supplemement* reports, 'quickly espoused the cause of greater central funding in his new role'. This, in the circumstances, is exactly what might be expected. The intention to establish twenty 'city technical colleges' is precisely in line with this thinking.

Nevertheless, the new Secretary protests (significantly to the Council of

Local Education Authorities (CLEA)) that he is not a centralist. His image of the 'partnership' as a wheel (when speaking to CLEA) was perhaps rather unfortunate — if the spokes do not radiate from the centre (or hub), and if they are not very precisely aligned and tightly welded, the wheel will disintegrate. Leading DES officials argue (and I have heard them) that the term 'partnership' implies 'senior' and 'junior' partners — as apparently in a firm of solicitors (as one of them put it). However that may be, the traditional partnership — between Ministry, local authorities, teachers, lies in tatters, as everyone knows. It will take a massive, determined effort to reconstruct it. Indeed it can be argued that the destruction of the partnership has been the necessary condition for the imposition of the new structures on the schools. For this, as in the case of other initiatives in other areas (for instance initial teacher training, in-service training, non-advanced further education), enhanced central control was seen as a necessity.

Now I hope eveything fits together, and that I've left my readers suitably depressed. But such was not, and is not, my intention. I have attempted to fit the pattern together as a contribution to understanding the strategy, and the tactics, of those in authority. It is not necessary, incidentally, to postulate a conspiracy theory. Rather to see these policies as a logical outcome of existing problems and tensions, given the structure of society, the particular economic pressures which form the context of present circumstances, and assuming, and I think it's a reasonable assumption, that education still plays a key role (or at least is perceived as playing a key role) in the perpetuation of the existing social order, just as it did in the past.

Two points may be made. First, that such strategies, or policies, even when apparently very precisely formulated, cannot always easily be put into practice in their pure form, owing to the complexity of circumstances and the in-built resistance of social institutions derived from their historical formation and so traditions. Second, that for a number of reasons policies may have unintended outcomes — even opposite ones. New developments may take place which may turn things on their heads. Take, for instance, the parents' movement now gathering force. We saw the establishment of ALPAG and PRICE (Put Resources into Children's Education). Now we have PARENTS, uniting parent/teacher associations through their federation with teachers' organizations (and now, possibly, also the main local authority organizations) in the defence of public education. Or again, the continuing pressure on the part of teachers to strengthen non-discriminatory and non-selective processes within the schools — anti-racism, anti-sexism, and the determination of many to preserve and extend the unity of the single comprehensive school (the GCSE may not be designated as a single exam, as Sir Keith Joseph insisted, but may it not be transformed as such?). Or again, and finally, local authorities, proud of their systems, and highly experienced in their administration, may not lightly concede control — or so at least it may be hoped. The ILEA is perhaps the leading example here, but of course there are others which wish to pursue their own, independent policies.

The British Educational Research Association itself is, of course, committed in its constitution to improving schools, and also has a part to play — the symposium, of which this publication is the outcome, rightly focussed on policy issues, and will certainly encourage further research evaluating new developments from the standpoint of educational criteria — and this, in my view, is a very important function. Therefore, although the outlook appears bleak, there are many points where a brighter future may be discerned, struggling to get through. The history of education does not record a straightforward, linear development. On the contary, there are advances and rebuffs; periods of crisis and periods of the resolution of such crises, often involving compromises, sometimes defeats or victories. We are living through just such a period now. Its outcome is not pre-determined. What actually happens depends on *human* action. This is the key issue that must be consistently borne in mind.

References

Best. G. F. A. (1964) *Temporal Pillars*, Cambridge, Cambridge University Press.

Nuttall. D. (1985) 'Evaluating progress towards the GCSE', unpublished paper delivered at the annual meeting of the British Educational Research Association, Sheffield, August.

Pavett, D. (1986) 'The joint boards and the CPVE', *Forum*, 29, 1, pp 9–11.

Ranson. S. (1984) 'Towards a tertiary tripartism: New codes of social control and the 17+' in Broadfoot. P. (Ed) *Selection, Certification and Control*, Lewes Falmer Press.

Simon. B. (1986) 'The battle of the blackboard', *Marxism Today*, June, pp 20–6.

Chapter 2

The Crisis of Motivation and Assessment

Andy Hargreaves

Introduction

The 1980s has been a period of intense, rapid and far-reaching change in educational policy and practice. One of the main areas in which reforms have been concentrated has been educational assessment. Assessment, more than curriculum or pedagogy, has been the prime focal point for educational change. Indeed it would be no exaggeration to say that the 1980s has been the era of assessment-led educational reform.

Interest among policy makers in educational assessment is not at all new, of course[1]. But no previous developments in this sphere match up to the breadth and intensity of activity on the assessment front that we have witnessed during the 1980s. The implementation of the General Certificate of Secondary Education (GCSE) with almost indecent haste; the rapid proliferation of schemes of subject-based graded assessments beyond their early confines in a small number of subjects only, like music and modern languages; the development of the new Certificate of Prevocational Education (CPVE) along with other attempts to rationalize the system of prevocational qualifications; and the widespread adoption of pupil profiles and records of achievement at a rate of almost geometric progression — these are just some of the major assessment initiatives that have been launched in recent years.[2]

In the case of pupil profiles and records of achievement alone, it is interesting that as recently as 1980, fewer than 1 per cent of all secondary schools offered anything more than a structured testimonial, and scarcely twenty-five schools had a profile that was non-confidential, available to *all* pupils, included some reference to cross-curricular skills and personal qualities, and was in a structured format (Balogh, 1982). Yet, by 1984, the DES had issued a clear policy statement on Records of Achievement; had earmarked some £10m of its budget to fund nine pilot schemes in the area; and has since declared its intention that every secondary school issue its pupils with a record of achievement by the 1990s.

This is expansion and innovation on a scale and at a pace of remarkable proportions. What explains it? What accounts for the intense political and professional interest in changing patterns of educational assessment? Explanations for these developments have not been wanting. Some have attributed the changes to growing impatience, especially among the Inspectorate, with the adverse effects of public examinations on teaching and learning processes, and on the secondary curriculum as a whole (HMI, 1979; Burgess and Adams, 1980; D. Hargreaves, 1982; Hitchcock, 1986). Others have pointed to a sense of growing disillusionment amongst employers with the value of examination results as an effective screening device and predictor of job performance (Goacher, 1984; Jones, 1983). A number of politicians and educationalists with views ranging right across the political spectrum, have voiced concern about the plight of low attaining pupils in circumstances of growing youth unemployment — and about the need, therefore, to recognize and reward alternative kinds of achievement among the young.[3] Some see new patterns of assessment as devices that can unlock curriculum innovation where other strategies of whole-school curriculum change have failed (Moon, 1984). And a few shrewd cynics have noted that the diversification of assessment activity and support for new initiatives by examination boards may have less to do with a new found liberal conscience on their part than with their entrepreneurial search for new sources of income as their existing ones are being eroded by falling rolls (Hargreaves *et al* 1988, chapter 6).

These factors, and others too, have undoubtedly been influential in the emergence of new patterns of assessment.[4] They have often been treated as if they were separate, though, as if they were only accidentally related to one another, just happening to coincide at the same point in time (for example, Hitchcock, 1986, p. 11). Picking off causes, influences and precedents individually in this way, however, does not allow us to get to grips with the interrelationship between them; to recognize the social patterns that bind them together. In this sense, I want to suggest, we would do well to heed the advice of the French sociologist, Emile Durkheim, that in educational changes of considerable scale, one can usually find reflections (and refractions) of much broader transformations within society as a whole.

What social transformations have led to recent changes in assessment policy and practice, then — to assessment being an issue at all, in fact? If we are to understand the emergence of assessment as a major educational issue, we clearly need to locate it in some more general *social* theory of educational change in post-war years. We need to understand why assessment, and not something else, has emerged as a dominant strategy of educational change. And we need to understand what strategies of educational change have preceded assessment-based ones and why they have now been put aside.

In order to explain the emergence of educational assessment, we must go beyond it, therefore. We must address ourselves to major shifts in strategies of educational reform as a whole in Britain over the past three decades or so. In analyzing such shifts, I want, in particular, to examine how well each of these strategies, assessment-led ones included, has addressed itself to two important social purposes: creating some measure of social consent amongst the young on the one hand, and meeting some definition of comprehensiveness, of equal access, common entitlement, or shared experience on the other. My purpose, that is, is to examine the relationship of assessment-led reform to patterns of reform that preceded it and to evaluate the contribution of these different reform strategies to the comprehensive experience. When assessment is itself assessed, our questions should not end with matters of mere technical efficiency, with whether the new patterns of assessment improve motivation or not, for instance. They should surely extend to the whole purpose and direction of comprehensive education and the contribution of changing patterns of assessment to it. This is my purpose in this chapter.

Explaining Educational Change

What kind of social theory might best explain the changes in educational policy focus and reform strategy in post-war years? There is no shortage of theories purporting to explain the relationship between education and society. Most of these theories, however, have difficulty explaining major shifts of direction in educational policy. They tend to be stated at such a high level of generality that reproduction, resistance, relative autonomy, bureaucratization and so forth, become general *qualities* of education under Western capitalism, not variables that might help us understand shifts in policy strategy from one period to another.

At the same time, research focused more directly on policy issues — whether as a pragmatic response to the current exigencies of research funding, or as a way of providing a more solid foundation of evidence for theoretical claims — has sometimes made it difficult to see the wood for the trees. In developing detailed understandings of the workings of TVEI, low attaining pupils projects and the like, they have often lost sight of the social trends and requirements that give these disparate initiatives a more general coherence and logic. Critical overviews of the social context of different educational policy initiatives have been rare. Indeed, the decline of 'basic', independently-funded educational research and the emergence, in its place, of more cursory and politically-tied evaluations of particular initiatives actively discourages such overarching critiques (which might reflect poorly on the sponsors).

What we require, then, is a social theory that can begin to explain how and in what ways the dominant focus of educational reform has shifted over the past three decades or so, since the commencement of comprehensive school reform. My starting point for such an explanation is loosely derived from two general theories of social change that have an evolutionary quality about them — a capacity to identify phases of social development and to explain why there are shifts from one phase to the next. One of the theories is Jurgen Habermas' (1976) explanation of crisis developments in the modern capitalist state. The other is Michel Foucault's (1977) interpretation of changing approaches to punishment, discipline and surveillance in Western societies.[5]

Both theories focus on social change in Western society. Both are developmental or evolutionary in character. Both identify three major phases of social development. Together, they have a significant capacity to illuminate the major patterns of social and educational change in recent times; to show them in a new light. But the theories also have their limitations. The periods to which they refer are very different — Foucault's model spans several centuries, Habermas' restricts itself to modern capitalism only. And neither of these periods coincides exactly with the period of educational change I am reviewing here. Nor are either of the theorists predominantly concerned with education — Habermas makes only passing reference to education in his writings on crisis development while Foucault confines most of his remarks on the subject to his final phase of development, where education and examinations in particular are said to play a major part in maintaining discipline and social surveillance.

I am not therefore claiming to offer a 'correct' or 'literal' interpretation of the theories. Neither am I suggesting that they are applicable or generalizable to educational policy developments in other societies. Nor do I want to claim that there is any evolutionary 'necessity' about the phases of educational reform that I identify — for as Habermas himself argued in the case of his own more general theory, such evolutionary claims have to be decided by empirical research, they cannot be theoretically assumed beforehand.

All I *am* suggesting is that the work of these two theorists has generated a set of ideas, concepts and interpretations, and a broad evolutionary model, which seem to me to resonate particularly well with what I take to be some of the most significant aspects of educational change in post-war times. They help bring together and give coherence to an otherwise disparate and disconnected range of educational initiatives and developments.

Social Crises and Educational Crises

In explaining the social context of educational change, it is important to recognize, with Habermas and Foucault, that most organized education is part of the state.[6] The fortunes of education are therefore closely bound up with the fortunes of the state as a whole. The state has the task, amongst other things, of managing, intervening in, creating appropriate conditions for and compensating for the unwanted effects of, economic activity. Its management of specific spheres like education is therefore powerfully affected by the fortunes of the economy, and by the strategies deemed appropriate for dealing with the problems the economy throws up.

Notwithstanding the partial 'boom' in the late 1950s and early 1960s, post-war Britain has witnessed an underlying trend of economic decline and therefore an experience of intensifying economic crisis — some would call this a capital accumulation crisis. As this overall crisis has intensified, the state has developed different strategies for dealing with it, so that, in many respects, the economic crisis has come to be displaced into the state. This in turn has generated different kinds of crisis and patterns of adaptation within the state as the state tries to manage the wider economic problem and all its destabilizing effects. These crises in the state reverberate throughout its different parts, not least within educational policy, which experiences its own particular crises. These take the form of a succession of critical points where a significant gap is perceived between educational policy and practice on the one hand and society's needs on the other; where existing solutions are seen to be exhausted or to have failed, or where new needs are felt to have emerged. It is under such conditions that support grows for new styles of state management, different patterns of initiatives; for a new overall strategy which promises to produce a closer match between schooling and society's needs.

Following the work of Habermas and to a lesser extent Foucault, I want to propose that British education has, in fact, passed through *three* such phases since the 1950s, that it has responded to *three* sets of perceived crises as attempts have been made to restructure education to society's purpose. These are phases of reorganization by *administrative, curricular* and *assessment-led means.* Each of these phases has been precipitated by a particular kind of social and educational crisis — a crisis of administration and reorganization, a crisis of curriculum and belief, and a crisis of motivation and assessment, respectively. I shall now review each of these critical phases in turn, paying particular attention to the contribution each has made to the development of the comprehensive experience. For the advent of the crisis of assessment and motivation and all the problems accompanying it, can only be fully grasped if we also understand why previous reform strategies have been rejected. As a point of early reference, a summary of my overall argument here is presented in diagrammatic form in table 1.

The Crisis of Administration and Reorganization[7]

In the 1950s and 1960s, the dominant strategies of educational policy reform were administrative ones. The educational system responded to the problems with which it was presented in administrative terms, through forms of institutional reorganization and expansion. Throughout this period, state intervention in education extended as a way of generating a technically equipped, socially productive workforce, and an expanding economy, during an era of post-war reconstruction. Investment in education increasingly came to be seen not as a burden on the social purse, as a claim on state expenditure, but as an investment in human capital, in Britain's economic future.

These public attitudes were reflected in and reinforced through some of the major education reports of the period. The thrust of these reports was that the existing selective arrangements and restricted range of opportunities in secondary and higher education were leading to a 'wastage of ability' among pupils of high measured intelligence, especially working-class ones, who left school early, did not proceed to higher education, gained modest qualifications and secured only low-grade jobs.[8] There was, allegedly, a

Table 1: CRISES IN EDUCATION

Period	Type of social crisis	Type of educational crisis	Point of application	Locus of change	Policy focus
Late 1950s–mid-1970s	Rationality	Administration and Reorganization	Body	Access and Opportunity	Comprehensive education
Mid 1970s – early 1980s	Legitimation	Curriculum	Mind	Consciousness and belief	Common curricular entitlement
Early 1980s – ?	Motivation	Assessment (and appraisal)	Mind	Disposition and discipline	Records of achievement

'hidden pool of talent' among the young people of Britain which the educational system needed to tap, not only to maximize individual opportunities but to secure economic regeneration also.[9] Even the Plowden Report on primary education which has often been read as a testament to the importance of individual creativity and personal development in children's education, nevertheless justified child-centred education in terms of its capacity to produce flexible, adaptable citizens, able to switch jobs many times in their lifetime, as technological change required.[10]

Such reports, together with a mounting body of educational research which showed that many able working-class children were not fulfilling their intellectual potential within the existing selective secondary system, furnished a case for institutional reorganization and expansion in education on *economic* grounds. But commitments to reorganisation and expansion also appealed to lingering post-war sentiments of fairness and social justice. In a sense, these policies 'bought' social loyalty by opening access, widening opportunities and meeting rising aspirations. They offered one way of responding to and accommodating the welfare demands of a socially aspirant post-war population. Policies like comprehensive reorganization were therefore designed to boost economic performance, enhance social consent, and respond to rising social aspirations, though processes of *administrative* change. The worth of the kind of education on offer (the traditional, academic, grammar school curriculum) was not in question. What mattered at this time of relative prosperity was increasing access to the demonstrably worthwhile social and educational opportunities that were available. Reform at this stage was therefore very much concerned with the movement of bodies into buildings; with investment, expansion and administrative reorganization in a broad context of optimism about expanding opportunity and social improvement. The new policies of comprehensive reorganization were therefore underpinned by a strong degree of social and political consensus and optimism. Existing education offered a demonstrably beneficial route to individual improvement and economic growth. All that was needed was more of it, for more of the people.

By the mid-1970s, however, this faith in the social and economic benefits of administrative expansion and reorganization had collapsed. There were two reasons for this. First, by that time, the bulk of comprehensive reorganization, the main administrative reform, was already under way. The strategy of educational reform through comprehensive reorganization had begun to exhaust itself (Simon, 1985). This exhaustion of existing policies provided one of the preconditions for new initiatives to flourish. As time ran out for the reorganization strategy, a second precondition for change, already rooted in the economic logic of state intervention and educational expansion itself, began to make itself felt more keenly. A fundamental paradox was built into the very heart of this pattern of reform. While the state, during this period, was expanding its involvement in, and expenditure on, social and economic life in order to provide support for economic development, the financing of this itself entailed deduction of expenditure from the very thing (profits and revenue) the intervention was designed to enhance. What this meant for educational policy was that while there was investment in comprehensive education for economic development and to secure social loyalty, the investment could not be too costly, the price not too high. Despite broad rhetorics of expansion, therefore, actual educational expenditure, even at a time of relative prosperity, was somewhat limited. This meant that comprehensive reorganization, like many other educational reforms, was carried out very much 'on the cheap', by principles of administrative convenience, using existing buildings, wherever possible. Indeed Ministry of Education and DES regulations insisted on this.[11]

Junior high schools, middle schools, split-site schools — all these major new developments in educational provision were the result of this basic paradox working its way through educational policy decisions (Hargreaves, 1986a). Such policies revealed a certain *irrationality* in the administrative pattern of educational intervention — that education was taking place in buildings ill-equipped for the purposes that were intended. Middle schools in inflexible, old secondary modern premises; large comprehensive schools of Kafkaesque proportions which subjected 11 and 12-year-olds to the experience of vast, impersonal bureaucracies for the sake of retaining a large sixth-form of academically able youngsters; split-site schools with their chaotic trudging of pupils, staff, or both between premises; open-plan schools, often established more to cut costs on use of space than to realize the principles of child-centred learning — these were some of the irrationalities that administrative convenience introduced into the comprehensive system.

However, as long as the economy remained relatively buoyant, as long as jobs were available, opportunities appeared to persist and aspirations had a chance of being met, these irrationalities scarcely surfaced as a public issue — or if they did, as among the Black Paper writers in the late 1960s, for instance, they were given little serious attention. But with the waning of growth and the deepening of recession of the early-to-mid 1970s, the 'irrationalities' became more noticeable and overt. Education, and comprehensive education in particular, like many other state institutions, became subject to what Kogan (1978) called the 'onset of doubt', and now found itself in the midst of a *crisis of rationality*, a crisis in which the adminstrative system was patently failing to fulfil the economic requirements demanded of it. From being a much needed investment, educational spending quickly came to be regarded as a non-productive luxury the nation could no longer afford.[12] Expansion and reorganization, it seemed, were not just too expensive in the new climate of severely curtailed public spending, but they had not worked either — and they quickly fell out of political fashion.

This period of educational reform therefore culminated in a crisis of rationality. Administrative reorganizations continued, of course — school amalgamations, tertiarty reorganizations and, most ironically, unscrambling of many middle school systems which expediency had brought into being as recently as the late 1960s and early 1970s. But these new administratively expedient changes were no longer part of a major strategy of intervention and unification, but simply an exercise in pragmatic cost-cutting with scarcely any educational justification added. It was in other strategies of educational change that the language of educational justification began to prosper.

The Crisis of Curriculum and Belief

With educational institutions no longer apparently meeting the ideals and aspirations of openness, opportunity and improvement that had come to be expected of them during the period of post-war reconstruction, doubts began to emerge and questions began to be asked about the value of what these institutions had to offer, about the character and quality of the processes that went on within them. The crisis of administrative rationality was therefore quickly compounded by a crisis of belief in the very legitimacy of society's basic institutions. In education, this crisis of legitimation led to a questioning of the quality of schooling itself and set in motion a reexamination of its basic purposes and processes.

There were accusations by the now more seriously regarded Black Paper writers of the 'New Right' that comprehensive education and educational progressivism more generally were undermining Britain's industrial competitiveness (Cox and Boyson, 1975). Events at the William Tyndale Junior School in London were given wide publicity which pointed to the dangers posed by extreme progressivism which prospered when the curriculum was not subject to public accountability and control (Gretton and Jackson, 1976). And there was media-hyped treatment of research findings claiming to show that 'informal' teaching methods produced lower standards of attainment in reading and mathematics than more formal ones (Bennett, 1976). All these things both reflected and reinforced a deepening moral panic about the failure of the educational system, in the absence of political and public control, to sustain economic growth and political stability.

The wider crisis of legitimation and belief therefore created, in schools, a crisis of curriculum. (Reid, 1978) This crisis of curriculum not only reflcted the diffuse dissatisfaction with education's capacity to deliver the economic goods, however. It was not just that the curriculum, cast adrift from public control was apparently failing to meet existing economic requirements. The curriculum was also invested with a positive social role. It was a basis for hope as well as a source of despair. As confidence in the institutions of state and government more generally came under threat, the school and its curriculum came to be identified as having a major ideological role in creating a new set of social beliefs, a new basis for social consent and cohesion.

The curriculum may have become the target for increased political control on the one hand — as Prime Minister James Callaghan's Ruskin College speech on education and the Great Debate that followed it indicated. The contents of the curriculum garden were no longer to be kept a professional secret — as became evident in a whole series of HMI and DES pronouncements on the curriculum in the late 1970s. But political incursions into the curriculum also opened up a new and important phase in the development of the comprehensive experience — where the essential nature of that experience came to be seen not as a matter of common institutional *access* (with curriculum decisions left to the professsionals), but of *common curricular entitlement*: entitlement by right of all pupils, whatever their abilities, to the same breadth and balance of educational experiences.

Potentially, this could have been a radical departure for the development of comprehensive education. The existing subject specialist basis of the secondary school system, geared towards public examinations and slanted towards the academic interests of 'grammar school' pupils, could have been overturned in favour of new curriculum categories, designed to foster useful and rigorous education for all in the furtherance of the common good. A new common entitlement curriculum might, for instance, have embraced Raymond Williams' (1961) recommendations that all young people up to 16 should learn the language *and culture* of at least one other country, that they should be familiar with the workings of national, local and community politics, and so on. It might have offered support for innovative categories like integrated studies or community studies as the basis for a common curriculum in the way that David Hargreaves (1982) suggested in the early 1980s. It might even, just as controversially, have followed the lead of the new educational right and, like Rhodes Boyson (1967), have proposed specific curriculum contents such as key book titles and named figures in political history as required elements of study.

But the new proposed common curriculum did none of these things. Instead, HMI avoided controversial value questions of this kind and the social and political choices and commitments that necessarily accompany them, by defining the curriculum in terms of eight (now nine) broad areas of educational experience to which all pupils had an entitlement (HMI, 1977). These categories and the way HMI suggested they be applied in the school did not challenge the continuing academic, specialist base of the secondary curriculum and the purposes of social selection and elite recruitment that it served. HMI advised that the 'areas of experience' be used as a kind of checklist, against which current curriculum coverage, including that taking place within existing subjects, could be monitored, to try and ensure balance and breadth. The categories were added to the curriculum. They did not imply or recommend that anything be taken away. They were a complement to, not a substitute for, existing coverage. The vague way in which the areas were defined, the fact that they were purely an advisory basis for curriculum planning and included no statutory requirements for minimum coverage on a cross-curriculum basis; along with their additive, complementary character — may all have helped secure a measure of professional consensus, but they did nothing to foster a radical and practical re-examination of existing curricular arrangements (Halpin, 1980).

As a result, at this broad level of policy formation, continous choices between subject contents were avoided, allocations of timetable priority not established, and implications for the status and importance of existing subjects not spelt out. It was left to teachers and schools to make their own decisions about these matters. And as HMI themselves discovered when they worked with teachers and schools in five LEAs using the areas of experience as a basis for whole school curricular appraisal, teachers did indeed make such practical curriculum judgments but in a way which served only to reinforce existing subject specialist interests. In a critical commentary on the fate of this exercise, HMI (1983b) candidly recorded that 'since the major commitments and loyalties of most teachers are within subject departments, it has often been more difficult for them to identify and explain those aspects of their specialisms which contribute to cross-curricular concerns' (pp. 14–15). Similarly, they noted that 'it has proved extremely difficult to avoid aligning (the areas of experience) with subjects when considering issues of balance within the curriculum. It has also been too easy to justify each subject in terms of the eight areas.'

Just as importantly, HMI drew attention to the problems posed by formal examinations, by 'society's requirement that young people should possess qualifications at the end of their formal education in the subjects of the conventional curriculum' (p. 13). This pressure, they noted, has if anything been heightened in recent years. They did not go on to say that, in part, this is actually a direct consequence of government policy, through the 1980 Education Act's requiring schools to make their examination results public. But they implied as much when they said that

> The schools see themselves increasingly at the mercy of the market force of parental choice in a time of falling rolls, and they judge their examination results to be among the major factors which determine the exercise of parental choice. This has led them to be understandably cautious in making decisions about the acceptablity of change in the current curriculum even where there has been considerable agreement about the desirability of such modification. (p. 14)

The GCSE, developed subsequently to these observations of HMI, offers little hope of modifying these pressures and patterns. Indeed, by fixing broad subject criteria at national level through cumbersome procedures of discussions and development, it looks likely to inhibit the creation of new and innovative curriculum titles (Torrance, 1987) And there is evidence to suggest that in the early phases of GCSE implementation at least, teachers have been 'teaching syllabuses as close as possible to ones with which they are familiar' (Radnor, 1987).

By the early 1980s, then, the curriculum as a whole was no longer seen as a dominant strategy for securing social consent, restoring common belief, re-establishing broad legitimation for society's purposes and institutions at a time when opportunities remained sparse, jobs scarce and rewards thin. The reluctance to decide upon competing political values, to attack high status subject specialist interests in the school system and the position of those who benefit from them, and to devote expenditure to the time, staffing and resources that effective whole-school curriculum change requires — these things have put paid to common curriculum reform as a dominant strategy of state managment, and as a widely held ambition for comprehensive education.

Lip service of a muted kind continues to be paid to common curricular entitlement within HMI documents — in *Curriculum 5–16*, for instance (HMI, 1985). But the recommendations are, if anything, made in an even more tepid and advisory form than in previous documents. They are given neither the force of statutory requirement, nor the stimulus of financial incentive. Such requirements and incentives can, however, be found in the new curricular policies of the 1980s — policies which emphasize and reinforce subject specialization, and support broad principles of educational differentiation. Here, it would seem that having been unable to break the academic subject-based hegemony of the secondary school curriculum, the DES and HMI have decided to strengthen it still further. 'If you can't beat them, join them' so to speak.

The interests of subject specialization have been promoted by measures, announced in the DES's influential document on *Teaching Quality*, to improve the match in schools between the subjects in which teachers are qualified and those which they are required to teach (DES, 1983, p. 9). Subject specialist interests were further aided by various HMI surveys which claimed that 'mismatch' of qualifications to task and low specialist emphasis overall was often associated with poor standards of work (HMI, 1982 and 1983c).[13] And as Rudduck describes in more detail elsewhere, specialist interests were given powerful support through the imposition of new regulations in initial teacher training which required teacher education institutions to allocate at least 50 per cent of their curriculum to 'subject studies', and to ensure that applicants selected for the PGCE possessed degree qualifications appropriate to teaching some part of the existing school curriculum.

This swing to specialization in curriculum policy has been further reinforced by the government's increasing commitment to educational differentiation. The details of its policy in this area are outlined more fully in other contributions to this collection. But within the 14–16 curriculum in particular, one can already detect the trial of prototypes for the reintroduction and refinement of selective, tripartite principles within the existing comprehensive structure. At the apex of this pyramid of provision is the existing and now strengthened academic, 'grammar school' curriculum, supported by the new policies on subject specialization, and reinforced by the introduction of a GCSE with a differentiated entry structure, and with a virtually complete absence of reference to vocational interests and criteria (McKay, 1987). In the centre is a broad vocational and technical band, the principles of which have been piloted through schemes which, as Dale and his colleagues show elsewhere, tend to exclude the most and least able groups of pupils (who 'choose' not to opt in to TVEI). And at the base of the pyramid are the types of programme currently being experimented with under Sir Keith Joseph's Low Attaining Pupils' Project, which, notwithstanding the detailed variations between particular schemes, tend to stress practicality, community links, residential experience, and social and lifeskills (see Weston *et al.* in this volume).

In the 1980s, then, the secondary curriculum is no longer a basis for social consensus or comprehensive entitlement, but a mechanism of social and educational differentiation. The pronouncements made by the Secretary of State, on a possible National Curriculum, show no positive signs that these trends will be reversed either. The National Curriculum seems geared to setting standards of attainment of a traditional kind within conventional high status subject specialisms — the 'basic' subjects as the Secretary of State calls them — such as English, mathematics, science, modern languages, history, geography and (the one innovatory concession) technology. This kind of National Curriculum will serve only to reinforce existing academic specialist interests within the secondary curriculum, and to perpetuate the process of educational differentiation which specialization fosters (indeed the age-based attainment targets make specific provision for such differentiation). Admittedly, it also proposes to give some coverage to areas like health education and education in personal and social qualities, attitudes and values too, but by not being tested, it is likely these will be given lower priority than the 'old', 'traditional' grammar school subjects dressed up as the 'new' basics. Moreover, some areas of the curriculum, vital to the forging of common purpose and the development of the social good — such as political education, development education, social studies, environmental education and integrated studies will be excluded from the National Curriculum and will therefore be consigned to lesser, optional status in the school curriculum or omitted altogether. Given such developments in National Curriculum policy towards increased specialization and differentiation, it is in assessment that the last vestiges of comprehensive ambition and the continuing attempts to secure some kind of common social cohesion are being invested.

The Crisis of Motivation and Assessment

As what the state has to offer looks increasingly ill-coordinated and ineffective; as belief in the value and legitimacy of society's basic institutions subsides; as aspirations are eroded and hopes are dashed; society then begins to experience what Habermas calls a crisis of motivation — a generalized reponse of 'Why should I conform?'. 'Why should I bother?', 'Why should I care?' There are, Habermas argues, two reasons for such deficits of motivation.

First, the reasons for conforming to established norms are taken away. In British secondary education, for instance, while public examinations have long been recognized as having a stultifying effect on the process of teaching and learning, many young people were prepared to endure this experience because of the qualifications they might attain at the end, and because of the social opportunities these qualifications could purchase. Like the CSE 'ear 'oles' interviewed by Paul Willis (1977), many young people were, until recently, prepared to trade their obedience for qualifications. But once there are very few or no jobs at all available for school leavers, and once a few qualifications can no longer guarantee employment, therefore, then the existence of these qualifications can no longer be relied upon to secure classroom consent or effort. As John Gray and his colleagues (1983) have remarked, 'pupils on a course in which success is either assured or virtually unattainable will . . . tend to lose motivation'.

A second cause of motivation deficits, Habermas (1976) argues, arises from the erosion of existing cultural supports as the state intrudes more and more into community and family life, and existing bonds of loyalty and association are weakened. Frustrated aspirations no longer have their compensations in the solidarity of working class community life, as in the 1930s. Unemployment, lack of opportunity, absence of hope increasingly becomes an individual, solitary experience. Without the support of friends and community, without an alternative basis for the development of a meaningful identity and sense of worth or purpose, the experience of unemployment or frustrated aspiration can become a lonely one and have serious consequences for motivation.

It seems likely that, together, the impact of economic recession on the wage economy, and the decline of traditional forms of emotional or cultural support, will have profound implications for the motivation of the young. This thesis still awaits firm scientific proof, of course, and indeed, it has been contested on the basis of Scottish truancy statistics which appear to show a *fall* in rates of truancy (as an indicator of motivation) at a time of rising youth unemployment (Raffe, 1986). In the end, however, the actual levels of decline in motivation among young people, even if they could be measured accurately, are not important from the point of view of educational policy. It is the political and public perception of the threat that matters. This public and political reading of trends in employment and pupil behaviour is the vital lever for policy change.

The importance of motivational factors in stimulating educational policy change can be seen very clearly in the development of pupil profiles and Records of Achievement. In HMI's review of ten secondary schools experimenting with early profile schemes, one of the two major reasons that schools put forward for their development was their capacity to increase motivation among the less able (HMI, 1983a). In her survey for the Schools Council of profile provision in nine secondary schools, Janet Balogh (1982) found that the 'desire to improve pupil motivation by involving students in their assessment process or by making it clear that their behaviour and attitude could affect their leaving statement' was a very important factor in their development. Goacher (1983), following up Balogh's research with a programme of action-research to develop records of achievement in other schools, found that many of the schools participated because the 'pupils would benefit from improved motivation due to a better indication of what was expected'. And Andrew Harrison (1982), in his review of over sixty Graded Objectives in Modern Languages (GOML) schemes, found that the advocates of these schemes pointed to their capacity to increase pupil motivation and, as evidence for this, cited increases in the proportions of third year pupils opting for modern languages since the introduction of GOML. By the time of the publication of the DES policy statement on records of achievement in 1984, the improvement of pupil motivation was listed as one of the four major justifications for their introduction into secondary education (DES, 1984, p. 3) And pupil motivation is persistently mentioned as a justification for records of achievement in the many documents and newsletters accompanying the numerous local and regional schemes currently being piloted around the country.

Improved motivation, it is claimed, is secured in several ways within records of achievement. First, the recording of personal and social experiences and achievements broadens the definition of achievement valued by the school beyond the academic domain, stimulates the school to give more emphasis to these other achievements, and thereby increases the amount of success experienced by pupils, particularly the non-academic ones most susceptible to motivation deficits. Second, where pupils record their own personal achievements on a regular basis, this gives them the opportunity to define and declare their own identity as a way of increasing their self-awareness and independence. Third, the negotiation of records of progress on a continuous periodic basis between teacher and pupil, involves pupils more in their own assessment and encourages them to take more responsiblity for their own learning once they can see they have some positive and influential stake in it. Fourth, the assessment of subject learning on a continuous step-by-step basis, through a series of graded, hierarchical levels with certificates to be gained at each level, provides pupils with a clear structure of rewards and incentives. Fifth, the breaking up of the curriculum into a series of separate levels, or discretely assessed modules of a few weeks each in length with a 'course credit' to be collected at the end of each module, replaces the dispiriting trudge for public examinations over two years between 14 and 16, with a set of more immediate, achievable targets.

Elsewhere, I have discussed some of the difficulties of achieving these motivational purposes in an educational context which, as we have seen, still values and promotes educational selection. (Hargreaves 1985 and 1986b). The use of new patterns of assessment for the purposes of personal development, for instance, are in tension with their use as a device to aid employee recruitment, and as a way of developing the qualities that employers value. Declarations of personal worth may, for many young people, not always mesh with the selective interests of employers or with the more narrow range of work-related characteristics like perseverance and enterprise that teachers, with an eye on job prospects, might want to emphasize. It is doubtful, then, whether the purposes of records of achievement in enhancing pupil motivation and in providing a 'document of record' to be used by employers, are altogether compatible.

While this argument that selection undermines motivation within reords of achievement is an important one, I believe that it has not yet been taken far enough. For existing critiques of records of achievement (including my own), in taking issue with the inequities of employee selection, have tended to adopt rather uncritically the dominant assumption within the records of achievement movement that motivation is a good thing, a thing of unquestioned educational value, worthy of positive support and encouragement. Is it the case, I want to ask, that motivation, as understood within the records of achievement initiatives, is indeed such a good thing?

Motivation or Manipulation

One of the major educational justifications for profiles and records of achievement is that they are not just a 'bolt-on' addition to the existing curriculum in the sense of a more extended leaving statement or a separate set of tutorial discussions, but that they are integral to the curriculum itself, central to the learning partnership and the process of curriculum review. In this sense, the new patterns of assessment are seen as being intimately tied up with curriculum change. This indeed is why people speak of assessment-led curriculum reform.

However, the association between assessment reform and curriculum change applies in only two respects, and not in an important third one. Assessment reform is certainly intended to serve as a device for changing the *process* of curriculum construction — involving pupils in self-assessment necessarily involves them in negotiating their teaching and curriculum too, which leads to a re-negotiation of the curriculum, where possible, to meet their individual needs (Burgess & Adams, 1985). Assessment reform is also intended to help change the *structure* of the curriculum, by encouraging the development of modular or accumulated credit schemes (Moon, 1984; ILEA, 1984). What is absent, however, is any discussion of the relationship between the new patterns of assessment and the *content or focus* of the curriculum. There is virtually no discussion within the new assessment initiatives of the social purposes of the curriculum; of the essential knowledge and experiences to which all pupils are entitled. The profound implication of this is that in records of achievement, we have a system designed to enhance pupil motivation but without any broadly-based political or professional discussion and agreement about what pupils are being motivated *towards*; about what sorts of things we are committing young people *to*, and whether these have any educational or social legitimacy. We run the risk, that is, of taking on the characteristics of objectives-based educational developments in the United States as described by Popkewitz (1986, p. 277) where 'learning, motivation or satisfaction become ends in themselves'; where 'what is to be learned, motivated, counselled or satisfied is left vague and unimportant'. Under circumstances such as these, the enhancement of pupil motivation shifts from being an *educational* process of positive disposition to learning worthwhile knowledge; to a *sociopolitical*, state-managed process of accommodation to the realities of economic crisis; of adjustment to diminishing prospects of employment and economic reward and to an educational experience that, for many pupils, can no longer promise social and economic benefits in adulthood. Motivation that is, becomes transformed from a process of educational encouragement, to a strategy of social crisis management.

Consequently, where assessment strategy is developed in isolation from discussions of curricular purpose and entitlement, the development of pupil motivation can even, with the best intentions, become equivalent to a manipulation of generalized dispositions, habits and inclinations — the adjustment of young people to whatever the social, economic and political system requires of them, especially, as even the relatively radical ILEA review of secondary education acknowledged, adjustment to the experience of failure (ILEA, 1984).

There are then, serious objections to assessment-led reform *unless* it is developed in conjunction with a clear sense of curricular purpose. Otherwise, motivation-inspired changes in assessment will be but vehicles to undermine the principle of comprehensivism. For people will no longer be given access to common and socially valuable experiences. They will only be furnished with a common and diffuse disposition to adjust them to any purpose within the social system in present or later life — however suspect or iniquitous it might be. In present government policy, then, assessment initiatives have been unhooked from important earlier discussions about common curricular purposes and entitlement. The development of common diffuse human dispositions has been divorced from any intention to forge common social and technological knowledge and belief.

More than this, if we reflect back on the fate of common curriculum reform, we can see that the new assessment-led system of dispositional adjustment, of generalized inclinations towards institutional and social loyalty through negotiation, discussion, establishment of contracts and the like, has been grafted on to an increasingly differentiated and divided curricular system. In this sense, the development of common motivational dispositions within a differentiated curriculum, works to adjust young people to their social fate and, through complicated systems of credit accumulation and modular study, denies them access to an overall grasp of the processes, structures and mechanisms by which such differentiated adjustment is achieved. (Hargreaves, 1988)

Through the use of graded assessments and stepped levels of achievement, horizons are not just shortened, but limited too (a modular step-by-step curriculum, for a modular scheme-by-scheme life, perhaps?) Through the use of pupil profiles, processes of negotiation and target setting, institutional loyalty and adjustment are secured. Through the development of elaborate, modular, credit-based structures, the system is bureaucratically mystified and made non-accountable to those who use it and whose opportunities are affected by it.

When we view assessment reform strategies in this light, it is clear that *common* motivation and disposition developed through profiling and related assessment strategies on the one hand, and the new forms of curricular *differentiation* on the other, are not at all unlikely bedfellows. Their interrelationship is exceedingly intimate. Indeed it is incestuous. They are both very much part of the same political family. Assessment-led strategies of curriculum reform, that is, look as if they might well be adjusting many pupils to their failure, underwriting this adjustment through the establishment of agreed contracts and other consent-gaining processes (Hartley, 1986), and through the development of modular structures, obscuring the means by which all this is achieved. To many, the patterns of common assessment in the form of records of achievement for all appear to be successors of curriculum reform in trying to meet the principles of comprehensiveness. In fact, they may well be the opposite — a method of gaining and reinforcing pupil consent to newly-developed structures of curricular differentiation.

Once this fundamental problem is recognized, it seems to me important for those who wish to retain some vestige of comprehensive ideals that discussions about and strategies relating to assessment reform must be conducted in tandem with those sorts of discussions about curriculum content and entitlement which we failed to resolve, and therefore quietly dropped, in the 1970s. It seems to me vital, therefore, that if assessment reform is to make a positive contribution to the restoration or further development of the comprehensive experience, then the development of common motivation and loyalty must be linked to the development of common experience, belief and purpose also. Motivation, we should remember, is but a *means*. It is the *ends* of learning that are ultimately most central to the comprehensive experience. In this sense, we could do not better than heed and act on the words that are tucked away in a broadsheet jointly produced by the Centre for the Study of Comprehensive Schools, the National Profiling Network, and the School Curriculum Development Committee, which urge that 'records of achievement should reflect a curriculum of entitlement for all young people' (SCDC, 1986). This entitlement, I would add, should be a common one. With the clear harnessing of records of achievement to the establishment of such common entitlement, there would be a real possiblity that the new patterns of assessment would advance the socially progressive interests of comprehensive development, and not undermine them with a bag of motivational tricks designed to adjust young people to the experience of government-sponsored educational and social differentiation, or as forces for comprehensive educational improvement. It is important that teachers and schools make this choice by careful deliberation and not by hasty default.

The nature of that choice has considerable ramifications not just for pupils but for teachers too. Indeed, the very scope of teachers' professional choices and judgments, the areas in which they can be legitimately exercised are currently in the midst of political reconstruction. It is not simply that the centralization of educational decision-making is reducing the autonomy of teachers' judgments and responsibilities per se, in absolute terms. Rather, what is at stake in this period of assessment-led reform, is a significant redefinition of teachers' professional reponsibilities, of the areas in which they can exercise legitimate influence, and of the areas in which they can be held accountable for educational success or failure.

On the one hand, the movement towards a centrally developed and controlled national curriculum is eroding teachers' involvement in and responsiblity for decisions about the fundamental purposes of education, about what it is regarded as necessary and desirable for young people to learn. At the same time, teachers are also being made increasingly responsible for the technical means by which this centrally and politically determined *content* is to be delivered. They are being given a measure of control over, while also being held more responsible for the *process* and *structure* of the curriculum; over the motivational means for getting pupils to acquire the newly-decided curriculum contents.

In effect, what all this means is that teachers are being increasingly excluded from curriculum conception while being made more responsible for its efficient execution (Apple, 1986). Teachers, that is, are being made responsible and held responsible for the efficient technical delivery of pupil learning and behaviour; for the learning of contents and purposes over which teachers themselves have little control and in which they have little involvement. They are being made the technical executors of others' political will.

If, for any reason, the newly-constructed educational system with its academic, subject-based national curriculum and its restructured patterns of educational assessment and appraisal comes to be seen as having failed; if, for instance, improved 'standards' are not achieved, or extra jobs not secured, or levels of disruption and delinquency not reduced, it is not likely that the new national curriculum, the new set of centrally and governmentally-defined educational purposes will be blamed for this. We should anticipate little criticism that the newly defined 'basic' subjects at the heart of the national curriculum might perhaps be too conventionally academic, too intellectually remote, or insufficiently practical or stimulating for many pupils, for instance. It is unlikely that the Secretary of State will be left to carry that particular curriculum can.

Most likely, rather, it will be the teachers, the new generation of deskilled educational technicians, who will take the blame for their technical ineffeciency, for their failure to motivate, for their inability to deliver effective pupil learning and acceptable standards of behaviour. This, I believe, is the key issue on which the professionalism, status and perceived competence of teachers will rest in the 1990s. If the teaching profession is to avoid being politically scapegoated for its inability to deliver a new nationally decided, differentiated and subject-based curriculum, it must not remain content with debating its new technician-like responsibilities in assessment reform, but must actively contest the development of a national entitlement curriculum too.

At the heart of any such contestation, I believe, should be a strong, intellectually sound, socially sensitive and professionally responsible case for a broad and balanced entitlement curriculum, covering a wide range of educational experiences in which what is counted as 'basic' does not easily defer to political prejudice or academic tradition, but includes personal and social development, aesthetic understanding, environmental awareness, political literacy and so on too. This kind of breadth, by widening the possibilities of educational achievement and giving them equivalent status as 'basics', will assist the development of educational opportunity and achievement for *all* social groups in a way that would enhance the character of secondary education as a distinctively *comprehensive* one. It would restore comprehensive purpose to the centre of curriculum reform.

To do all this teachers themselves must have a strong and continuing professional input into the development of such a curriculum. And they should be wary of diversions from this essential task by lesser involvements in the more technical processes of assessment reform. Assessment reform is not a substitute for curriculum reform. The two, in fact, are already working very much together. A common pattern of assessment and motivation is being developed as support for an increasingly differentiated and subject-centred curriculum in which comprehensive vision has been lost. If comprehensive purpose is to be restored to the centre of the secondary curriculum, it is important that teachers regain and be helped to regain a key role in the construction of curriculum content, and not remain satisfied with assessment-led, motivationally inspired and technically-limited involvements in curriculum structure and curriculum process instead. That may be vital not just for the restoration and reconstruction of comprehensive purpose, but for the defence of teacher competence and professionalism too.

Notes

1. Note for example, the replacement of the School Certificate by 'O' levels, the implementation and expansion of the CSE, protracted discussions through the Waddell Committee and elsewhere about a possible system of common examining at 16+, the proliferation of new credentials in vocational education, and so on.
2. The list does not end here, of course. Others would include the expansion of the activities of the Assessment of Performance Unit into the monitoring of national standards; the increasing use of educational testing; the development of staff appraisal as a mandatory requirement of conditions of teacher service, the requirement through the 1980 Education Act that schools publish their examination results, the introduction of 'AS' levels as a way of broadening the sixth-form curriculum etc.
3. Here, there have been remarkable similarities between the observations of Sir Keith Joseph, formerly Secretary of State for Education and Science in an influential speech to the North of England Education Conference at Sheffield in January 1984, and of David Hargreaves, the man who was soon to become Chief Inspector of the Inner London Education Authority, in an equally significant review of secondary education in the ILEA (ILEA, 1984).
4. For evidence of this influence within early profile schemes, see HMI (1983a) and Goacher, (1983) for instance.
5. These are by no means the only sources on which I have drawn, however. My interpretation has also been influenced by other writing on crisis developments in the modern state (for example, Offe, 1984) and on the nature of the capitalist state in general (for example, McLennan, Held and Hall, 1984; Dale, 1982).
6. This proposition is explored more fully in the introduction to this volume.
7. More expanded explanations of the first two crisis phases — of administration

and reorganization, and curriculum and belief — can be found in the final chapter of *Two Cultures of Schooling* (Hargreaves, 1986a)

8 As for instance, in *The Early Leaving Report* (Ministry of Education, 1954), and*15–18* (The *Crowther Report*) (Central Advisory Council for Education, 1959).

9 See (The *Robbins Report*) (Central Advisory Council for Education, 1963).

10 *Children and Their Primary Schools* (*The Plowden Report*) (Central Advisory Council for Education, 1967)

11 In dealing with comprehensive reorganization and indeed the raising of the school leaving age, the Ministry of Education and later the Department of Education sanctioned school building projects occasioned by these initiatives only (see Hargreaves, 1986a, chapter 2, for detailed evidence on this point).

12 Within Marxism, there has been a great deal of discussion as to whether teaching is 'productive' or 'unproductive' labour. The point about education, however, as Habermas himself argues, is that it is neither directly productive nor unproductive, but *indirectly productive*. It has a loose and uncertain relationship with economic activity that is exceedingly difficult to trace. Consequently, when recession bites, a well-funded programme of state education can quickly come to be seen as a dispensable investment.

13 For a critique of *Teaching Quality* and of the evidence used to support the subject specialisation thesis within it see Hargreaves (1988).

14 This argument has been developed in a very different way by David Hargreaves in *The Challenge for the Comprehensive School* (1982), and has been used as an argument for making comprehensive schools the centre of community restoration.

References

APPLE, M. (1986) *Teachers and Texts*, London, Routledge and Kegan Paul.

BALOGH, J. (1982) *Profile Reports for School Leavers*, York, Longmans.

BENNETT, N. (1976) *Teaching Styles and Pupil Progress*, London, Open Books.

BOYSON, R. (1976) 'Maps, chaps and your hundred best books', *Times Educational Supplement*.

BURGESS, T. and ADAMS, E. (1985) *Records of Achievement at 16*, Windsor, NFER-Nelson.

CENTRAL ADVISORY COUNCIL FOR EDUCATION (1959) *15–18* (The Crowther Report), London, HMSO.

CENTRAL ADVISORY COUNCIL FOR EDUCATION (1963) *Higher Education* (The Robbins Report), London, HMSO.

CENTRAL ADVISORY COUNCIL FOR EDUCATION (1967) *Children and Their Primary Schools* (The Plowden Report), London. HMSO.

COX, C. B. and BOYSON, R. (1975) *Black Paper 1975*, London, J M Dent & Sons.

DALE, R. (1982) 'Education and the capitalist state: Contributions and contradictions' in APPLE, M. (Ed) *Cultural and Economic Reproductions in Education*, London, Routledge & Kegan Paul.

DEPARTMENT OF EDUCATION AND SCIENCE (1983) *Teaching Quality* (Cmnd 8836), London, HMSO.

DEPARTMENT OF EDUCATION AND SCIENCE (1984) *Records of Achievement: A Statement of Policy*, London, HMSO.

FOUCAULT, M. (1977) *Discipline and Punish*, Harmondsworth, Penguin.

GOACHER, B. (1983) *Recording Achievement at 16+*, York, Longmans for the Schools Council

GOACHER, B. (1984) *Recording Achievement at 16+*, York, Longmans for the Schools Council.

GRAY, J., MCPHERSON, A. F. and RAFFE, D. (1983) *Reconstructions of Secondary Education*, London, Routledge and Kegan Paul.

GRETTON, M. and JACKSON, P. (1976) *William Tyndale: Collapse of a School or a System*, London, Allen & Unwin.

HABERMAS, J. (1976) *Legitimation Crisis*, London, Heinemann.

HALPIN, D. (1980) 'Exploring the secret garden', *Curriculum*, 1, 2.

HARGREAVES, A. (1985) 'Motivation versus selection: Some dilemmas for records of personal achievement' in LANG, P. AND MARLAND, M. (Eds) *New Directions in Pastoral Care*, Oxford, Basil Blackwell.

HARGREAVES, A. (1986a) *Two Cultures of Schooling: The Case of Middle Schools*, Lewes, Falmer Press.

HARGREAVES, A. (1986b) 'Record breakers?' in BROADFOOT, P. (Ed) *Profiles and Records of Achievement*, Eastbourne, Holt-Saunders.

HARGREAVES, A. (1988) 'Educational assessment: A test for socialism' in LACY, C. and ROBERTS, R. (Eds) *Educational Development and Development Education*, London, World Wildlife Foundation, Kogan Page.

HARGREAVES, A. *et al* (1988) *Social and Personal Education: Choices and Challenges*, Oxford, Basil Blackwell.

HARGREAVES, A. (1988) 'Teaching quality: A sociological analysis', *Journal of Curriculum Studies*, 20, 3, pp. 211–31.

HARGREAVES, D. H. (1982) *The Challenge for the Comprehensive School*, London, Routledge & Kegan Paul.

HARRISON, A. (1982) *Review of Graded Tests*, Schools Council Examination Bulletin 41, London, Methuen Educational.

HARTLEY, D. (1986) 'Structural isomorphism and the management of consent in education', *Journal of Education Policy*, 1, 3.

HER MAJESTY'S INSPECTORATE (1977) *Curriculum 11–16*, London, HMSO.

HER MAJESTY'S INSPECTORATE (1979) *Aspects of Secondary Education*, London, HMSO.

HER MAJESTY'S INSPECTORATE (1982) *The New Teacher in School*, London, HMSO.

HER MAJESTY'S INSPECTORATE (1983a) *Records of Achievement at 16; Some Examples of Current Practice*, London, HMSO.

HER MAJESTY'S INSPECTORATE (1983b) *Curriculum 11–16: Towards a Statement of Entitlement*, London, HMSO.

HER MAJESTY'S INSPECTORATE (1983c) *9–13 Middle Schools: An Illustrative Survey*, London, HMSO.

HER MAJESTY'S INSPECTORATE (1985) *Curriculum 5–16*, London, HMSO.

HITCHCOCK, G. (1986) *Profiles and Profiling*, Harlow, Longmans.

INNER LONDON EDUCATION AUTHORITY (1984) *Improving Secondary Schools*, report of the Committee on the Curriculum and Organization of Secondary Schools London, ILEA.

JONES, J. (1983) *The Use Employers Make of Examination Results and Other Tests for Selection and Employment: A Criteria Report for Employers*, Reading, School of Education, University of Reading.

KOGAN, M. (1978) *The Politics of Educational Change*, London, Fontana.

MCLENNAN, G., HELD, D. and HALL, S. (1984) *State and Society in Contemporary Britain*, Oxford, Polity Press.

McKay, N., (1987) 'GCSE and the new vocationalism' in Horton, T. (Ed) *GCSE: Examining the New System*, London, Harper & Row.
Ministry of Education (1954) *The Early Leaving Report*, London, HMSO.
Moon, B. (Ed) (1984) *Comprehensive Schools: Challenge and Change*, Slough, NFER/Nelson.
Offe, C. (1984) *Contradictions of the Welfare State*, London, Hutchinson.
Popkewitz, T. (1986) 'Educational reform and its millenial quality: The 1980s', *Journal of Curriculum Studies*, 18, 3.
Radnor, H. (1987) *GCSE — The Impact of the Introduction of GCSE at LEA and School Level*, Final research report, Windsor.
Raffe, D. (1986) 'Unemployment and school motivation: The case of truancy', *Educational Review*, 38, 1.
Reid, W. A. (1978) *Thinking About the Curriculum*, London, Routledge & Kegan Paul.
School Curriculum Development Committee (1986) *Records of Achievement*, London, SCDC.
Simon, B. (1985) *Does Education Matter?*, London, Lawrence & Wishart.
Torrance, H. (1987) 'GCSE and school-based curriculum development' in Horton, T. (Ed) *GCSE: Examining the New System*, London, Harper & Row.
Williams, R. (1961) *The Long Revolution*, London, Chatto & Windus.
Willis, P. (1977) *Learning to Labour*, Farnborough, Saxon House.

Chapter 3

The Birth of the GCSE Examination

Roger Murphy

Introduction

Conceived in the 1960s and born in the mid- to late-1980s the General Certificate of Secondary Education (GCSE) examination took longer to be delivered than anyone could possibly have ever imagined. Indeed it looked at times as though this much called-for reform of the dual CSE and GCE 'O' level examination systems would never actually happen, as successive governments and Secretaries of State failed to make a definite decision to go ahead with the idea or drop it completely.

Certainly no analysis of recent policy and practice in British education could be complete without some scrutiny of the far-reaching implications of this lengthy saga, and the resulting examinations that have now completely replaced CSE and GCE 'O' level. Naturally there are many different ways in which this phenomenon can be analyzed and readers seeking to extend their own analysis beyond the areas covered in this chapter are referred to two recent collections of articles, analyzing a number of different aspects of the GCSE, edited by Gipps (1986) and Horton (1987), and a report discussing some aspects of its impact on LEAs and schools by Radnor (1987).

Impact on Schools

Perhaps the most interesting aspect of the GCSE phenomenon is the impact that it has had on classroom practice in schools. At a stage when schools have only recently completed the first examination for the new courses it is unfortunately too early to draw firm conclusions about what this has been. Furthermore there will clearly be very different responses from different teachers depending on the subject that they teach, the level of change demanded of them, their enthusiasm for those changes, and the resources and training made available to them to allow them to attempt to make the change. Radnor (ibid) has given an early indication of some of the overall trends and in particular has pointed up many shortcomings in the preparation and training that has occurred.

There are, of course, many different dimensions to the changes that could occur in the teaching of GCSE syllabuses — a move away from separate CSE and 'O' level teaching groups, changes in emphasis in teaching the subject in relation to skills, content or teaching style, greater emphasis on coursework with a challenge to set differentiated coursework tasks that allow all pupils to demonstrate what they know, understand and can do, are a few.

At the moment the most dominant impression emerging from secondary schools around the country is a fear of the unknown, moving into uncharted territory particularly with respect to the assessment arrangements, many of which are still being worked at. Alongside this have been persistent reports of a lack of sufficient training and resources to support the changes, difficulties with getting the necessary information from the examination groups, and problems with reconciling the GCSE with the national curriculum tests at 7, 11, 14 and 16, the Technical and Vocational Education Initiative (TVEI), Certificate of Prevocational Education (CPVE), 'AS' level, Records of Achievement and the many other somewhat disparate initiatives that have been demanding different changes from the same teachers all at the same time.

Central Control of the Curriculum

The examination boards have always had a fairly powerful control over the 14–18 curriculum in secondary schools, a level of control which the DES must often have envied as it has tried to encourage curriculum change from the centre. The GCSE has brought with it some very significant changes in this respect. The power in respect of curriculum influence has moved significantly towards the DES through the creation of national criteria, to which all GCSE syllabuses must conform, and the School Examinations Assessment Council, the new government-funded body which is charged with the responsibility, amongst other things, of approving all GCSE, 'AS' level and 'A' level syllabuses. The boards have therefore been left with a much less powerful role in relation to the curriculum and are now more concerned with putting into practice curriculum and assessment policies that have been laid down by the DES (Salter and Tapper, 1987).

Nuttall (1984) has pointed to the injection in the late 1970s of the idea of national criteria, for each of the twenty major GCSE subjects along with a set of general criteria to cover the others, as a key factor in determining the shape and implications of the eventual GCSE examinations. These criteria laid down, in considerable detail, requirements for individual syllabuses, including aspects of the subject that must, or must not, be included in them along with constraints on the way they should be assessed.

The use of the national criteria by the DES to force curriculum changes in certain areas of the curriculum can now be seen as a forerunner of the proposed National Curriculum. By limiting the choice of GCSE subjects that pupils can enter for, there is in the national criteria, and GCSE syllabuses that conform to them, a ready-made 14–16 National Curriculum. Although some of the curriculum changes imposed by this method may have been welcomed by many teachers as reinforcing desirable innovations in particular subjects, there have also been many cries of anguish from those forced to drop familiar approaches. Linked to this has been the fear that the criteria may prove in time to be inflexible to change and may inhibit rather than promote further curriculum changes.

Assessment for All?

One of the original aims of combining CSE and 'O' level examinations, which led to the call for a common examination in the 1960s, was a desire to prevent the divisive nature of separate syllabuses and schemes of assessment for pupils expected by their teachers to reach different levels of attainment. However GCSE moved, in the late stages of its development, a long way from many of the original ideals intended for a common examination at 16+. Along with the national criteria came a strong emphasis on differentiation, which involved ensuring that pupils were set assessment tasks (and by implication followed syllabuses) that were appropriate to allow them to show what they could do rather than what they could not do. As Gipps (1986) and others have argued this can easily be seen as bringing things back to the former dual examination situation with children needing to be grouped at an early stage in GCSE courses for separate schemes of study and assessment.

The other dilemma connected with considering the GCSE as being less divisive than CSE and 'O' level is the fact that the seven GCSE grades A–G have been equated with the old 'O' level grades, A, B and C and CSE grades 2, 3, 4 and 5. Thus however much anyone may wish to argue that the new examination is designed to be suitable for all pupils, the reality is that the second lowest grade (Grade F) is to be equated with CSE Grade 4, which by definition has always been fixed in terms of the performance of an average pupil. The examination is therefore ostensibly designed for approximately 60 per cent of pupils in schools, until such time as criteria can be developed as a basis for grade awarding *and* Sir Keith Joseph's dream of all pupils reaching the standard represented by the current CSE Grade 4 is achieved.

Rhetoric and Reality

Many things were claimed for GCSE in the early 1980s, which have proved to be either impossible, impractical or unlikely. As with all new products that are being marketed there is a temptation to oversell their potential, and Sir Keith Joseph could be thought to have fallen into this trap. The most striking example in this respect was the issue of criterion-referencing, which was announced to the House of Commons on 20 June 1984 as one of the four key features of the new examination, which was to be introduced into the GCSE syllabuses in the form of grade criteria, which were at that time being drafted by a series of working parties. Elsewhere (Murphy, 1986) I have explored in some detail the sequence of events that led to these grade criteria having to be abandoned, at least for the time being, due to the complexities involved in agreeing them and then, in turn, of incorporating them into the GCSE schemes of assessment.

Draft grade criteria have now been produced for many of the twenty subjects for which there were already national criteria. These grade criteria attempt to constitute a basis for fixing the standard of each GCSE grade in each of these twenty subjects. The ultimate aim, being to reach a situation whereby GCSE grades would assume a much clearer meaning than previous public examination grades, through being linked to 'benchmark targets', which are clearly specified attainments that every candidate who receives that grade must have demonstrated.This idea is a very ambitious one, for examinations which were not designed for that purpose, and may now have to be abandoned or else watered-down and replaced by some system of 'grade descriptors', which will indicate the typical (rather than actual) achievements of candidates receiving a selection of the GCSE grades in certain subjects.

As ambitious, in terms of previous experience with public examination, were the claims that were made for the new approach to differentiated assessment. Until the results of the first schemes of assessment in 1988 have been analyzed it will not be possible to see how fully this has been achieved, but in essence the idea is that the assessment provided should allow every pupil to positively demonstrate what they know, understand and can do. Thus even the pupils, who obtain the lowest of the seven grades, grade G, are supposed to acquire this through a positive assessment experience where they gain a high proportion of the marks on the assessment tasks they are given. Laudable though this aim is, it seems unlikely that such a major shift in examination practices can occur so quickly, especially when many GCSE examination papers bear a close resemblance to the former 'O' level and CSE papers. Further doubt must be attributed on the basis of the account of Nuttall (1987), who has revealed that the Open University team, who were involved in making the training videos for GCSE, had to abandon the idea of one on 'Differentiation', because when they went into schools with their cameras they 'could not find good examples of differentiated assessment to illustrate the concept'.

Perhaps most worrying of all in this respect is the fact that the very features of GCSE, which appear to be more akin to rhetoric than reality (i.e. criterion-based grading and differentiated assessment) are the very features of the examination that the present Secretary of State is proposing as the basis for tests at the ages of 7, 11, 14 and 16 that will accompany the new National Curriculum. Promising more than can be delivered in one examination system is one thing, but then going on to attempt to replicate the same promises elsewhere is quite another.

The Future of the Examination Boards

Along with the desire to reduce the number of syllabuses that were offered in examinations at 16+, the GCSE reform involved a major reduction in the number of examination boards involved in administering the system. The reorganization of more than twenty individual CSE and GCE boards into five examining groups can be interpreted in many different ways. Some have suggested that it is a step towards establishing a single national examining board. Scrimshaw (1987) argues that it was certainly an attempt to bring the boards into a position where they could more easily be controlled by central government.

The reorganization of the boards has not in any way diminished the level of competition between them, and the freedom of entry granted to individual schools and the right that each examining group has to fix its own examination fees has exacerbated what many will see as an unhelpful level of rivalry and suspicion between them.

There are many other features of life within the examination boards that are vitally important to a full understanding of the GCSE development. The grouping of GCE and CSE boards together within the same examining groups has led in many cases to the meeting of very different cultures. Administrators and board committee members from the different boards have brought to the groups very different assumptions, working methods, and assessment practices. These in turn have led to some protracted discussions about how GCSE should be implemented, in terms for instance of procedures for coursework assessment and moderation.

Some of the GCE boards have made very limited use of coursework in the past, whereas it has been a fairly central part of the assessments conducted within CSE examinations throughout their existence. The wider experience of coursework assessment amongst CSE boards has also extended to a wider, qualitatively different, experience of coursework moderation. Many CSE boards have operated systems of moderation that have relied heavily on teacher involvement, not only in initial marking but in elaborate systems of agreement trials and cross-moderation exercises. Such procedures contrast markedly with the more remote procedures of statistical moderation, which are based entirely on information gained from external examination papers, or the re-marking of samples of coursework by external moderators, who normally have little knowledge of the school they are moderating. Clearly such different approaches are based on very different examining philosophies, and in such circumstances it is hardly surprising that it has been so hard to reach agreement, about future strategies, between the newly-constituted groups of GCE and CSE boards.

It is understandable that board officers working under considerable pressure to put together the detailed procedures for GCSE, while still administering the final years of CSE and 'O' level, have been inclined to draw on the procedures with which they are already most familiar. This in many ways has limited the extent to which GCSE has moved very far from the methods used previously in CSE and 'O' level examining. As I have argued elsewhere (Murphy, 1987) the decision to entrust the administration of the new GCSE examination to the existing examination boards was perhaps one of the most significant steps that was taken in its development.

A final and not insubstantial feature of what is happening in the boards is the fact that within each of the examination groups there has had to be much restructuring of responsibilities, posts and resources and in some cases legal steps have been taken to merge the interests of several boards into a single new body. All of this has had a distracting effect on board staff who were already stretched in terms of delivering GCSE and all the supporting materials that were needed for it within the timescale allowed. Such factors are at least a partial explanation of the fact that some teachers were more than half way through teaching GCSE courses before they received from the boards some of the basic information about the course and the assessment procedures that they required. It has also been widely argued that even if the information about GCSE had been available in time, then there were still not enough resources for it to be properly disseminated, allowing teachers time for instance to assimilate it and make adequate plans for revised approaches to teaching and assessment. The boards themselves have not been excluded from the pressure caused by limited resources, and have frequently argued with the DES about the level of funding that has been provided for them to undertake all of the development work, training and publicity that has been required of them during the change over period. Much of this has been done inevitably on a 'shoe-string', and the results of this have shown through in the quality of some of the materials, the serious delays that have occurred in terms of meeting deadlines, including the date for issuing the first set of GCSE results, and the lack of adequate staff development activities for the board staff themselves to prepare them for the demands of a completely new system.

The Relevance of GCSE for the 1990s

There are many features of GCSE that have led to the suggestion that it would have had far greater relevance had it come to fruition in the 1960s or even the 1970s. In the very different social, economic and educational climate of the 1980s it does in many ways appear to be a bit of an anachronism.

The rise of unemployment and the increase in youth training and education post-16 have added fuel to the arguments for the abolition of examinations at 16. Alongside this have been arguments that the changing nature of the secondary school curriculum should lead to assessment being conducted across it rather than within the traditional single subject boundaries. The rise of profiling, records of achievement, graded assessment, and modular assessment have each in their way provided alternative models, which many schools have found more compatible with their own curriculum aims.

A broader analysis (Murphy and Pennycuick, 1985) of the assessment implications of several recent educational reports including the ILEA's

Hargreaves Report along with several other DES and HMI curriculum statements yielded a fairly consistent set of ideals for new assessment initiatives. According to these documents new assessment schemes should:

1 record information about a *much wider range* of the achievements of pupils than have been emphasized through a narrow approach to educational assessment in the past;
2 lead to *meaningful* and positive descriptions of what *all* pupils can do;
3 *promote* rather than inhibit curriculum development and reform;
4 enhance pupil *motivation* and teacher morale and thus lead to an overall improvement in educational standards;
5 lead to a more *harmonious* relationship between assessment methods, curriculum design and teaching methods within individual schools. (Murphy and Pennycuick, 1985)

Unfortunately there is little evidence at the present time that GCSE has been able to measure up, in any significant way, to any of these ideals. Of even greater concern is the fact that its very existence may well hinder the development of other initiatives that could do just that.

It is somewhat ironic that this reform of the 16+ public examination system is being accompanied by an unprecedented number of alternative assessment initiatives, most of which are designed on a completely different philosophy to examinations. 1988 is the first year of the new GCSE examination but it is also the year in which the DES has pledged to issue national guidelines to all schools, about a system within which all pupils will receive from their secondary schools a Record of Achievement, based largely if not solely on information derived from assessments conducted within that school reflecting a wider range of achievements than could ever be assessed by public examinations. Some would argue that GCSE results will form a useful part of those Records, but an alternative view is that the two systems cannot really co-exist, and ultimately a decision will have to be made between them (Murphy and Torrance, 1988).

GCSE is an idea of the 1960s born in the 1980s. Whether it will survive much beyond the early 1990s remains to be seen. Much will depend on the influence and impact of emerging changes in the secondary school curriculum, including the current interest in modular courses, and the extent to which Records of Achievement and other current assessment initiatives are successful in creating a genuine alternative to what remains a fairly conventional approach to assessment at 16+.

References

Gipps, C. (Ed) (1986) *The GCSE: An Uncommon Examination*, Bedford Way Papers, no 29, London, Institute of Education.

Horton, T. (Ed) (1987) *GCSE: Examining the New System*, London, Harper & Row.

Murphy, R. J. L. (1986) 'The emperor has no clothes: Grade criterion and the GCSE' in GIPPS, C. (Ed) *The GCSE: An Uncommon Examination*, Bedford Way Papers, no 29, London, Institute of Education.

MURPHY, R. J. L. (1987) 'A changing role for examination boards?' in HORTON, T. (Ed) *GCSE: Examining the New System*, London Harper & Row.

MURPHY, R. J. L. and PENNYCUICK, D. (1985) 'Evaluating current initiatives in educational assessment: Graded assessment and the GCSE', paper presented to the Nuffield Assessment Seminar Group, London, 15 November.

MURPHY, R. J. L. and TORRANCE, H. (1988) *The Changing Face of Educational Assessment*, Milton Keynes, Open University Press.

NUTTALL, D. L. (1984) 'Doomsday or a new dawn? The prospects for a common system of examination at 16+' in BROADFOOT, P. (Ed) *Selection, Certification and Control*, Lewes, Falmer Press.

NUTTALL, D. L. (1987) 'The current assessment scene' in *Action on Assessment in B-TEC* (Coombe Lodge Report), 19.

RADNOR, H. (1987) *GCSE — The Impact of the Introduction of GCSE at LEA and School Level*, final research report, Windsor, NFER.

SALTER, B. and TAPPER, T. (1987) 'Department of Education and Science — Steering a new course?' in HORTON, T. (Ed) *GCSE: Examining the New System*, London, Harper & Row.

SCRIMSHAW, P. (1987) 'Towards a conservative curriculum' in HORTON, T. (Ed) *GCSE: Examining the New System*, London, Harper & Row.

Chapter 4

TVEI: A Policy Hybrid?

Roger Dale, David Harris, Mark Loveys, Robert Moore, Chris Shilling, Pat Sikes, Mike Taylor, John Trevitt and Vicki Valsecchi

There are two major linked problems — both more or less well recognized — in talking about the Technical and Vocational Education Initiative (TVEI): the vagueness of its definition and the very wide diversity of its practice. In the press, for instance, TVEI has been variously described as a scheme where children receive a technological or business-based instruction as part of their curriculum and what they learn is placed in the context of the world of work as 'making schools and colleges more technically and vocationally oriented', as 'providing resources for job related training for 14–18-year-olds in which industrialists work with teachers in this development of courses' as a 'learn and earn' scheme, and as 'aimed at steering youngsters to the boom spheres of business and industry'.

The problems associated with this range of definitions are compounded by the diversity of TVEI practice. This very diversity means that it would be possible to find evidence to justify almost any argument about TVEI. On the basis of particular TVEI schemes it is as easy to refute criticisms of the Initiative as it is to expose its pretensions.

In view of these difficulties, what we intend to do in this chapter is to take one of the undeniable 'facts' about TVEI — that it is funded and ultimately controlled by the MSC — and examine some of its implications. We shall do this by asking rather different questions about the effects of TVEI, from those which have so far proved rather sterile and inconclusive. Most discussions about TVEI, for instance, have been about its effect on the curriculum — is it narrowing the curriculum, as many educators contend, or 'one of the most significant broadenings of the curriculum this century' as Lord Young argues? Again, the diversity of TVEI practice makes it extremely difficult to resolve such questions empirically. What is needed, then, is some progress towards *conceptualizing* TVEI more adequately.

One step towards this is the development of sensitizing concepts which present the possibility of going beyond the mere aggregation of descriptive accounts of different schemes based on different, and frequently tacit, purposes, methods and theories. Such sensitizing concepts would be an attempt at an initial focussing of enquiry, a medium for the possible grounding of theory. What we are proposing here, then, is delaying consideration of TVEI's impact on the *content* of schooling until we have considered the changes it signals in the *scope* of education policy. And we shall be examining in particular the effect of the hybridization of education and employment policy which TVEI represents.

In this first part of the chapter, then, we expand on the idea of TVEI as a hybrid,[1] comparing the two traditions which make it up in terms of their assumptions about the mandate and the capacity of the education system. In the second part of the chapter we attempt tentatively to indicate how these ideas contribute to an understanding of three important aspects of TVEI — its effects on gender stereotyping, the discourse of management it stimulates, and its effect on teachers.

Of course, there is a long history of attempts to bring education more closely into line with the apparent requirements of the economy. The roots of the efforts to reconcile 'secondary' and 'technical' education, and the consequences of the failure to do so have been very well charted by McCulloch (McCulloch, 1986; McCulloch *et al*, 1985). As he puts it, 'TVEI might be interpreted as in the tradition of the Bryce Report of 1895, the Spens Report of 1938, and the Crowther Report of 1959. All sought to reconcile technical with secondary education by stimulating a distinct kind of "secondary technical education" ' (McCulloch 1986, p 40.)

However, 'reconciliation' of these two strands of education has rather more limited connotations than those we wish to suggest are associated with potential changes in the scope of education policy created by the kind of hybrid TVEI represents. It is not so much a question of the reconciliation of these two unfortunately — and indefensibly — separate strands of secondary education. Rather, central to our concern are the outcome of that larger hybridization, and the different assumptions held in the two contributing traditions about the scope of education policy. By the scope of education policy we mean broadly what it is assumed a public education service should be, and is capable of, doing. That is to say, the scope of education policy is concerned with assumptions about the *mandate* for the education system and about its *capacity* to fulfil that mandate. This chapter tentatively compares MSC and DES assumptions about the scope of education policy and the consequences of their hybridization in TVEI.

Educational Mandates

Mandates for the education system are made up of conceptions of what it is desirable and legitimate for the education system to seek to bring about. At any one time there exist myriad mandates, giving different priority to the three major categories of targets to be achieved by the education system. These are succinctly set out in the White Paper *Working Together — Education and Training*: 'children go to schools so that they can develop their talents, become responsible citizens and be prepared for work' (paragraph 2.1). The co-existence of strong mandates separately (and often contradictorily) stressing each of the three main targets of education is a common, if not permanent, feature of education in this country, and an essential part of its dynamic (Dale, 1981). Over the past ten years, though, one of these mandates has been dominant, that contained in the 1977 Green Paper, *Education in Schools*. This document both prefigured and required the kind of hybridization of education-training for employment whose culmination is TVEI. Essentially that mandate called for a much greater emphasis on the preparation of workers and citizens, than on the development of individual talents.

This was a mandate for the education service prepared within the education service, albeit with unprecedentedly extensive and unprecedently welcome input from outside the education service. The MSC, then a relatively small organization, was not a significant factor in drawing up the mandate nor in the plans for its fulfilment. However, MSC was at that time beginning to work in adjacent areas, and there is considerable overlap between the *Education in Schools* mandate for education and MSC's developing approaches to the problems of training and youth employment. The Holland Committee, for instance, recommended the creation of the Youth Opportunities Programme to guarantee some form of work experience to all unemployed school leavers. It is significant that 'it was authoritatively rumoured at the time that a battle raged in Cabinet before the decision was made between the DES and the D(epartment) of E(mployment) about which of them should be given the money to provide for the young unemployed. We are told that DE won because it could guarantee to produce places very quickly on the ground. The DES could provide much less because it would have to make grants to local education authorities and simply exhort them to deliver' (Short, 1986, p. 42).

Thus, there is clear overlap in the mandates of the two organizations in respect of the education and training of young people. There are, though, distinct differences in their capacity to fulfil this mandate. This applies not just to the broad, overall conception of 'vocational education', but also to such issues within it as gender equality, the management of the curriculum, and teachers' careers too, which we shall be discussing below.

What we are suggesting, in effect, is that there are crucial differences between (and within) the political and administrative discourses of DES and MSC. The nature and consequences of these differences can be clarified by examining the two bodies' respective conceptualizations of the scope of a public education service.

Interpreting the Mandate

We have already pointed to some overlap in the education and training mandates of the DES and MSC. There are though, very important differences of interpretation and emphasis between the DES and MSC. These differences have two, linked, bases. The first lies in the different traditions of which they are part. In giving reasons why the MSC's work 'is still largely separate from that of the DES and the local authorities that maintain schools and employ teachers' William Taylor (1985) lists the following:

> Administratively, training has been linked with employment rather than education. Politically, governments have been somewhat less than satisfied with the way secondary schools have dealt with their older age groups. Financially, it is been difficult to earmark for particular purposes the funds made available to local authorities. But more fundamentally, the separation reflects the way in which history, economic circumstances and social structure have given us a heritage of values, attitudes and assumptions that constitute education and training as two separate metaphors, a heritage which continues to influence our thought and our practice.
>
> It is not difficult to identify the values conventionally associated with these two metaphors. Education is often depicted as soft, person-centred, moralized, academic, critical, contemplative, radical in attitude but traditional in form, theoretical, norm-referenced, enclosed, a consumption good rather than an investment. In contrast, training is represented as hard, task-centred, materialistic, practical, oriented towards action, criterion-referenced, pragmatic, innovative in structure but conservative in substance, unselective, open, a valuable national investment' (p. 109)

The second basis of the difference of interpretation and emphasis is the 'policy obligations' of the DES and MSC. These are perhaps best set out in the lists of objectives of the Department of Employment and of the DES which appear, symbolically, on the inside front and back covers, respectively, of the 1986 *Working Together* White Paper.

> **Objectives of the Department of Employment**
> The prime aim of the Department of Employment is to encourage the development of an enterprise economy. The way to reduce unemployment is through more businesses, more self-employment and greater wealth-creation, all leading to more jobs.
> The key aspects of the Department's work are to:
>
> 1 Promote enterprise and job creation in growth areas such as small firms, self-employment and tourism.
> 2 Help business to grow and jobs multiply by cutting "red tape"; improving industrial relations by ensuring a fair balance under the law and encouraging employee involvement.
> 3 Improve training arrangements so that young people get a better preparation for work, and adults obtain the skills they need to compete in the world.
> 4 Help the young and those out of work for some time find work, training or opportunities likely to lead to a job.

In addition to the nationwide network of High Street Jobcentres, there are over 30 training, employment and business help schemes. Among them are schemes for people employed, unemployed, skilled, unskilled, young or old.
The Department's many other activities include:

— helping unemployed people by the prompt payment of the benefit and allowances to which they are entitled
— helping protect the employment of individuals, including those disadvantaged on grounds of race, sex or disability
— helping maintain and improve health and safety at work.

The Department of Employment Group also comprises the Manpower Services Commission, the Health and Safety Executive and the Advisory Counciliation and Arbitration Service.

Objectives of the Department of Education and Science

The principal aim of the Department of Education and Science is to improve standards throughout the education service and to increase the value obtained for the substantial resources allocated to it by the taxpayer and the ratepayer.
In *schools*, the Department aims

— to promote agreement on the curriculum and ensure that it is broad and balanced for all pupils;
— to foster the application of what is learnt to real problems and situations;
— to stretch pupils of all abilities;
— to give parents more influence; and
— to enhance the powers of governing bodies.

In *non-advanced further education*, the Department aims

— to increase the responsiveness of the service to the needs of employers;
— to provide a sound education for young people and adults; and
— to secure an improved use of resources — and in particular a significant tightening of student: staff ratios.

In *higher education*, the Department aims

— to raise quality and standards while preserving the full breadth of educational provision;
— to make the system more responsive to the needs of the economy;
— to improve management systems in universities, polytechnics and colleges; and

> — generally to increase value for money by rationalization.
>
> The Department is also responsible for
>
> — *adult and continuing education*. The principal aim is to update the skills of the national workforce at all levels.
> — the *civil science base* financed by the University Grants Committee and the Research Councils. The principal aims are to promote excellence by greater concentration and selectivity of research activities and to stimulate commercial applications of new ideas.
> — *teachers*. The aim is to secure the supply of sufficient teachers of the quality needed to teach the agreed curricula and to update the skills of the existing teacher force.
>
> Throughout the education system — at all levels — the output of citizens competent in mathematics, science and technology must be increased. The DES — in cooperation with the other Government Departments concerned — is developing a range of policies to that end.

What we mean by policy obligations can be derived from these lists. For instance, while the DES is *obliged* to 'ensure a broad and balanced curriculum for all pupils', the DE(MSC) is not — though that is not to say that in its forays into education it will not seek to do so, as it claims to have done with TVEI. Similarly, it is not an obligation, let alone a prime aim, for the DES to encourage the development of an enterprise economy — though again it *may* choose to meet its aims in part by doing so. The main relevant difference between the two departments for our present purpose is that while the DES is obliged to pursue all three broad targets for education, the MSC is not; while education is an end in itself for the DES, for the MSC it can only be a means to achieving its (MSC's) own objectives. We are not suggesting either that every action of MSC and DES can be directly related to their policy obligations, or that either of them are entirely monolithic (we know that neither is), merely that they are subject to different fundamental pressures.

To return to the mandate contained in the 1976 Green Paper: its fulfilment provided two major problems for the education system. The first was that the system itself was identified in the Green Paper as one of the obstacles to the mandate's fulfilment. The degree of autonomy of the education system, schools and teachers, and the ways that autonomy was alleged to have been used, made the system as much part of the problem the new mandate addressed, as the key means of fulfilling it. The mandate indeed implied not only changes in the orientation of education policy, but changes in the way it was formulated and implemented too — not only changes in the content and purpose of education but also in the way those changes were devised and introduced into the system.

The formulation and implementation of policy — in particular, the inability of the DES to institute system-wide change — comprised the second major problem. The DES was not able to compel compliance, only to persuade and pressure in various ways (Ranson, 1985). It was this inability to fulfil the 1976 Green Paper mandate — together with massive rises in youth unemployment — which brought MSC, via Prime Ministerial initiative, into the educational system at school level for the first time in 1983.

The different policy obligations of the DES and MSC emerge clearly in their respective assumptions about the scope of education policy. Two such assumptions are especially important. The first concerns whether education policy is predominantly *strategic* — i.e. aimed at affecting the world outside education as much as directly affecting those in the system — or largely confined to bringing about changes within the education system for its own sake. The policy obligations of the MSC and DES clearly differ in this respect. The MSC's policy obligation has little to do with an intrinsic education policy. It must seek to use education to bring about changes in the world outside education. This orientation is nicely caught in the very first paragraph of the *Working Together* White Paper — 'We live in a world of determined, educated, trained and strongly motivated competitors. The competition they offer has taken more and more of our markets — both overseas and here at home.'This sets the tone for an education policy that is almost entirely strategic. The DES, on the other hand, can only look to such strategic considerations when they are congruent with its intrinsic obligations — and, of course, a great deal of the debate about meeting the *Education in Schools* mandate has been precisely about the degree of congruency that can, or should, be achieved between intrinsic and strategic considerations.

The second difference in DES and MSC assumptions about the scope of education policy is whether education policy is typically involved with structural (system-wide) *reform* or with more restricted, local *innovations* (Papagiannis *et al*, 1982). We would suggest that both tradition and policy obligation push MSC to the former and DES to the latter of these positions. As Taylor suggests, training has been regarded as requiring central direction and control, while there is a very strong tradition of decentralization — and variation — in the education system. Within the education system even the most far reaching attempt at structural reform — the introduction of comprehensive education — offered alternative models (based on existing local practice) to local authorities, rather than imposing one system nationwide. The most interesting tensions at the birth of TVEI were concerned with this very issue of whether the scheme was to be administered through LEAs or through a separate set of institutions. As we know, it we decided to administer it through LEAs and that decision was the origin of the peculiar administrative and ideological hybridity which now characterizes TVEI.

Capacity to Implement the Mandate

There are perhaps even greater potential differences between DES and MSC in terms of their capacity and *modus operandi* than there are in their traditions and policy obligations. In understanding TVEI, differences between DES and MSC in this area — and the way they are hybridized — are at least as important as differences in interpretation of the mandate. The capacity and modus operandi of the DES and MSC differ significantly in a number of ways.

1. The DES is a Department of State headed by a Cabinet Minister politically accountable through Parliament to the *electorate.* It operates according to a structured, bureaucratic rule-following model. The MSC, on the other hand, is a corporate body, made up of people representing particular *interests*, particularly the two sides of industry. This means both that MSC is a coalition of potentially competing interests, and that any decisions and actions it takes can be assumed already to have the approval of those they affect (insofar as they are represented on the commissions); those actions and decisions do not have to go through further consultative, participative discussion stages — which is one of the reasons that the MSC is able to act much more quickly than the DES. As the Director of the MSC puts it, 'MSC . . . is no advisory body, but a public board charged with executive responsibilities . . . When a commissioner commits himself/herself to a particular programme, policy, or line of action, he/she is also committing many more people and organizations in the world outside. This commitment . . . is the key reason why so many far-reaching developments have taken place so quickly under the commission's auspices . . .' (Holland, 1986, p. 88)
2. The MSC's operating model differs from the DES's. Rather than being bureaucratic and process-orientated, it is technocratic or even commercial. For the MSC, achieving results is the criterion of action, while the DES is bound by the need for accurate rule-following. The DES can only bring about major change by changing the rules, i.e. by introducing legislation; for the MSC it is a much more straightforward matter of changing the substance in the most immediately effective way.
3. Until relatively very recently, it had been assumed that DES could only operate through the local education authorities, whom it could not in any case compel to follow a particular path; perhaps the best known example of this is the failure of Shirley Williams as Secretary of State at the DES to get local authorities to spend for the state's purposes, the £7m she had earmarked for in-service training. The implications of this are clear from Clare Short's comment quoted above, and in the introduction of TVEI itself.
4. Certainly in the education area, MSC has operated more like a fire-brigade than a police force. It is essentially a crisis-management organization. It could withdraw altogether from education and has no built-in continuing commitment to the area. Thus not only is it able to introduce different kinds of programmes, it is also able to do so less

hampered by the ramifications they may have for the rest of the service or by the need to continue supporting them if they appear initially to be unsuccessful.

5 Associated with this is the different pattern of funding available to the two bodies. The MSC's funds are for particular programmes, typically contracted for by providing agencies on terms laid down by the MSC. Its budget is not immutably tied up in continuing financial obligations which take up almost all its resources, unlike the DES, with its major commitments in the area of school building and higher education, for instance. The DES has, then, been financially as well as constitutionally restricted in the kind of intervention it could make in the education service.

6 A further financial difference is that the DES needs (from the Secretary of State) approval *before* committing expenditure, whereas the MSC is accountable only *after* spending the money. The corollary of this however, is that the MSC has to do far more monitoring, auditing, etc. of projects *after* they're set up (and this has been a major source of irritation to teachers and schools in TVEI).

7 The MSC is much more likely to intervene from the supply-side, while the DES's tradition has been much more demand led funding. The MSC provides funds whose levels are known beforehand for specified programmes aimed at identified objectives, and subject to monitoring. The DES has traditionally been much more reactive (within its constitutional limits), responding to pressures and suggestions within the education system, rather than using fully what powers it has to steer the system.

8 Another difference in the mode of intervention lies in the source of the resources used. Though this is beginning to break down, certainly informally (as other chapters in this book demonstrate) DES assumptions have traditionally been that state education will be wholly state funded. MSC assumptions are quite different, and deliberately so. Efficiency of performance and cost-cutting through competition are much more important in determining which bodies will carry out the work than a commitment to state provision.

9 These various constitutional and financial differences combine in the different types of activity and intervention the two bodies make. This difference can be summarized as the difference between what Claus Offe calls 'allocative' and 'productive' types of state activity and it is worth expanding on the distinction a little. Offe's distinction is usefully summarized by Jessop:

> Allocation involves the use of state resources to secure the general framework of economic activity and/or to provide general public services in accordance with general constitutional or legislative codes which effect the prevailing balance of political forces. Production involves direct state-sponsored provision of material resources as a

> precondition of crisis-avoidance or crisis management where there is no general code that can be applied and decision rules must therefore be developed in order to determine more effective action by case. Offe then argues that, although rational-legal bureaucratic administration may be appropriate to the allocative activities of the state, it is inadequate to the demands of state productive activities insofar as they are orientated to the attainment of particular objectives rather than the general application of pregiven rules. (Jessop, 1982, pp. 110–1)

This distinction encapsulates much of the difference between the DES and the MSC, and the ramifications of MSC sponsorship, in terms of substance, style, purpose and method, that mark TVEI as a form of education policy at least as effectively as the funds it provides.

TVEI as a Hybrid

The hybrid that is TVEI is far from being sufficiently settled or organized to specify anything more than a range of broad patterns of practice. Indeed, it may never emerge as a clearly identifiable separate strain of education policy. The two sets of factors making up the hybrid combine in different ways in different circumstances, where existing patterns of practice (themselves largely in the education rather than employment tradition) appear to have been frequently influential. In this situation of flux, as many opportunities as constraints are likely to be found, with the combination of traditions providing greater freedom for teachers and schools in some areas, greater control over them in others.

TVEI does not, of course, represent a new issue as much as a new solution to a recurrent problem (see Reeder, 1979). What essentially distinguishes TVEI from previous attempts to bring education and employment closer together is not so much its influence on the mandate addressed by education policy makers — which, with greater or lesser variations has characterized all phases of the recurrent debate — as its influence on the *capacity* of the education system to meet that of the mandate. Rather than relying on exhortation, persuasion or even pressure — all of which connote action from *outside* — on the education system, in TVEI the employment interest has become a *partner* with the educational interest in *achieving* as well as devising a broadly agreed mandate. It is its operation in the spheres of both the mandate and the capacity of the education system that makes TVEI unique, and makes its analysis as a hybrid so potentially fruitful. We move now to the tentative application of these ideas.

Gender Stereotyping/Equal Opportunities for Girls and Boys

Equal opportunities is not a new concept in education. The MSC, however, has emphasized the issue by making equal opportunities for both sexes the first criterion for TVEI. Both the DES and MSC recognize that sex stereotyping does occur particularly in scientific, technical, and vocational areas and that girls suffer educational disadvantages in schools. But are their definitions of 'equal opportunities' the same and do their basic assumptions about the scope of education differ?

Neither the DES nor the MSC have issued clear policy statements or guidelines for the implementation of equal opportunities. Therefore the following analysis draws on inferences from selected DES documents which refer to some aspect of female disadvantage in schools.

As early as 1973, the DES recognized a need to study the extent to which 'curricular differences and customs contributed to inequality of opportunity for girls and boys and to indicate whether changes in schools were necessary.' DES Educational Survey 21 (*Curricular Differences for Boys and Girls*) concluded that:

> If all secondary schools were to carry out an analysis of both content and organization of the curriculum from the first year onwards and ensure that choices made later were based, as nearly as practicable, on a real equality of access to experience and to guidance, that would be one step towards eradicating prejudice about the roles of men and women which *frustrate individual development* . . . (our emphasis)

The DES issued Joint Circular 20 (1976) proposed to 'draw to the attention of local education authorities and other bodies responsible for the provision of education, the new duties and current practices and arrangements in the light of the (1975 Sex Discrimination) Act'. It also cited both *Curricular Differences for Boys and Girls* and the White Paper, *Equality for Women* (September 1974) as additional points of reference. Whilst the primary purpose of the Circular was to aid in clarifying the legal implications of the 1975 Act, in steering away from detailed interpretations of its provisions, it reflected certain attitudes towards equal opportunities.

Firstly it underlined the limitations of the Secretary of State:

> While he will not hesitate to use his powers to stop any particular act of discrimination, he does not control curriculum and it is important for teachers with the support of local education authorities, to take a hard look – at the organization of the curriculum and to consider whether the materials and techniques they use, and the guidance they give, especially in the early years, *inhibit free choice* later. (our emphasis)

The implementation of equal opportunities was therefore first and foremost the responsibility of the local authorities and teachers.

Secondly while avoiding positive definitions of equal opportunities the Circular makes the statement that:

> Equal opportunities does not necessarily imply and may well be incompatible with, the maintenance of any particular balance of sexes in the intake of a school or the make-up of a class.

It further states that the Act does not 'prohibit the continuation of separate facilities for boys and girls where these are considered appropriate provided that the facilities afforded to each sex can justifiably be regarded as equal'.

Careers education and guidance given by teachers is subject to the provisions of the Act. The DES underlined the obligation of local authorities to provide such guidance with discrimination and with 'regard to the recommendations of the survey by HM Inspectors', *Careers Education in Secondary Schools*, (Education Survey 18) that curriculum in schools should enable boys and girls to *keep subject options open.*

The 1976 Circular, typical of most DES documents, was clearly *suggestive* rather than overtly *directive*, placing responsibility for implementation at local level. Whilst containing no real definition of equal opportunities, it resisted gender balance as a possible indication. No extra expenditure was seen to be necessary in order to comply with the 1975 Act.

More recent DES reports have made some reference to equal opportunities. The Green Paper, *Education in Schools*, (1977), states that 'distinctions between what boys study and what girls study are disappearing.' In common with earlier DES publications it did not provide guidelines. It did, however, acknowledge that equal opportunities does not necessarily mean identical classroom provision for boys and girls. Further it recognized the necessity that, in translating their aims into day-to-day practice, schools should not by their assumptions, decisions, or choice of teaching materials *limit the educational opportunities* offered to girls.

This report referred to science as an integral part of education while that same year HMI working paper, *Curriculum 11 — 16*, indicated that there were 'considerable differences between schools in the patterns of choice girls make in science and these are very difficult to explain solely in terms of factors operating outside the influence of the school'. This statement inspired later reports in specific subject areas including *Girls and Science* (1980), and the APU's *Girls in Physics* (1985). Whilst these show great sensitivity to the complexities of the issues they still fail to stress the need for developing positive strategies to encourage girls and do not provide guidelines and directives to achieve that aim.

As MSC involvement in education is so recent, the body of existing documentation is limited. Their general approach to education is exemplified by TVEI. As a relatively new creation, with its own networks and funding procedures not directly responsible to Parliament, MSC can take, and has taken, an interventionist stance.

Whilst the MSC has also failed to issue clear policy statements with guidelines for the implementation of equal opportunities, the first criterion of TVEI is that:

> Equal opportunities should be available to young people of both sexes and they should normally be educated together on courses within each project. Care *should be taken to avoid sex stereotyping*. (our emphasis)

'Good careers advice and educational counselling will be essential.' Though these statements in themselves are vague, many programmes have interpreted this to mean there should ideally be an equal number of girls and boys in all course areas of TVEI. If this is indeed the intention of the MSC, it not only goes beyond DES definition but contradicts it. It is certainly true that various TVEI programmes were severely reprimanded for continued sex stereotyping based, at least in part, on statistics on gender uptake in subject areas. They were strongly advised to 'do something about it' — the inherent threat in the withdrawal of funds.

This would appear to imply that the MSC, at least initially, assumed that schools, and specifically TVEI programmes in schools could and should (via their project coordinators) be able to 'do something' to redress gender balance in technical and vocational areas of the curriculum. This was not a suggestion but a directive — a requirement.

What we see here, then, can be interpreted as as displaying the difference between MSC and DES assumptions about the scope of educational policy. The differences are especially clear with respect to the different mandates contained within their respective political and administrative discourses as they apply to gender differentiation. In essence, for MSC closing off particular subjects to either gender is a potential obstacle to the development of an enterprise economy; for DES it is a potential obstacle to the full development of the individual's capacity. Thus we see the MSC introducing a set of *requirements* applicable to all schools, and placing as much emphasis on extra-educational factors as on the effect on individuals (through its highlighting of the gender stereotyping of *subjects*, as well as of providing equal opportunity), and the latter *reacting* to circumstances, with a set of *suggestions* aimed at equalizing the basis of *individual* pupil choice.

However, when it comes to assumptions about the capacity of the education service to bring about more equal opportunities for males and females, there is more common ground between the two bodies. They both identify the problem as one of *socialization*, the DES because that is central to its conception of what schools can do about the problem, the MSC because strategies that would attack the crucial labour market end of the problem effectively have so far proved difficult to find (cf. the experience of attempts to achieve equal opportunities on YTS). Hence the most common explanation of gender differentiation is in terms of differences in *socialization* between boys and girls. Although the school is often seen as reinforcing these differences, it can also be regarded as an agency of change which provides an alternative source of values and expectations to those which the students meet in their cultural community. Essentially this means providing an *alternative form of socialization*.

A problem with socialization arguments in general is that they see the individual as simply the *passive* recipient of outside influences and as lacking autonomy in decision-making. An alternative (but not necessarily contradictory) approach is to see the individual as making independent decisions upon the basis of an evaluation of what is realistically possible under given conditions. For instance, young women starting work tend to have as great an interest in a career and in promotion as young men with equivalent qualifications and positions, but fail to actively pursue career development (for example, by following courses for professional qualifications) because they perceive opportunities as biased in favour of men. Consequently *the problem* can be seen as not so much one of girls holding the 'wrong' values, as of *sexism* in the institutions and communities in which they move. Thus girls' decisions often reflect their *evaluations of what is possible* rather than a *failure to conceive* of alternative, non-traditional options.

None of this is intended to suggest that socialization is *not* important and that attitudes (of parents, teachers and boys as well as girls themselves) should not be addressed. Rather, the point is that these two aspects of the individual, recipient of received values and attitudes *and* active decision-maker, need to be seen together and as interacting, and that both MSC and assumptions about the capacity of the education service limit them to concentrating on the former.

The Discourse of Management

The introductory sentence to the aims and criteria of the TVEI states that the initiative is intended to 'explore and test ways of organizing and managing the education of 14–18 year old young people' (MSC, 1983). What follows is then offered as the guiding principles upon which participating education authorities are to construct their respective submissions (and so their schemes) in a variety of combinations allowed within the scope of the MSC's rubric.

As we stated at the beginning of this chapter, observing the implementation of schemes in more than one authority reveals a sufficiently wide variation in forms of organization, option structures, and methods of 'delivery', to make it almost impossible to offer a universal description of what is distinctively a TVEI component in the overall provision of secondary schooling and further education. One reason for this is the ambiguity contained within the aims and criteria which do not provide any definitive specifications for either curriculum innovation, pedagogic approach, or administrative procedure. However, if we shift the focus of enquiry away from the content of individual schemes on to changes in the structural relations that operate in and around the participating institutions, the somewhat neglected significance of the above quotation enables us to raise three broad yet important issues.

Firstly we need to distinguish more clearly between the *levels* of educational management that are intended to be addressed through TVEI. Organizational and managerial concerns have differing emphases in the various locations of educational provision and will raise different questions for the class teacher than for senior staff and for LEA officers, amongst others. Secondly, we also need to be clear as to what *aspects* of the education of 14–18-year-olds are to be affected by such implied management reforms. It seems likely that the TVEI will not only affect the nature of course structures and contents, but also the relationships between teachers and students, teachers and school administrations, schools and education authorities, and, not least, LEAs and government agencies. Thirdly, we need to identify the actual 'ways' that are being tested and explored in pursuit of the aims of the Initiative. These issues place emphasis upon a different aspect of the TVEI phenomenon than the more commonly-associated interest in the experience and involvement of the students themselves. Despite frequent reference to the idea of students managing their own learning processes, the environment in which this might occur must itself be structured and managed in order to meet the criteria for whatever learning outcomes may be previously established.

So, in accepting that the underlying principle of TVEI is to alter the significance of the institutional education experience of 14–18-year-olds we must also accept that the meaning of educational practices too, has to be changed for those responsible in the administration and maintenance of educational institutions. This has posed something of a problem, for much of the information that circulates generally about TVEI amongst administrators and practising educationalists, formally or otherwise, has been received with the suspicion that the Initiative offers a powerful threat to the perceived professional autonomy of personnel in schools, colleges and local education authorities. The perceived monolithic facelessness of the MSC is, for many, an important factor in the generation of professional paranoia. On more practical levels, however, so-called innovatory forms of assessment, accreditation, student-teacher relationships and curriculum initiatives, together with possible reorganization of curricular hierarchies and the devaluation of subject specialisms, seem to offer, for some, unprecedented opportunities for career enhancement. For others, they threaten a disestablishment of professional security, and for most, a confused and sometimes despairing resignation that the role of secondary (and tertiary) education is becoming further eroded in a political climate that prioritizes economically productive efficacy over a broader and more rounded development of the young individual.

In responding to TVEI, teachers are likely to position themselves within their occupational environments according to their individual philosophies of educational practice. It is probable these would also take into account the advantages and disadvantages to their own and others' interests. However, the (self-) evaluation process that leads to such positioning will largely depend upon the quality and quantity of information that is known, acquired or made available with regard to the environmental changes occurring in particular locations. In respect to programmes like the TVEI, such kinds of information will vary according to the degree of proximity to and involvement in the implementation processes as they occur within individual institutions and at different levels of administration. Furthermore, both individual and institutional orientations towards TVEI in general can and do alter, positively and negatively, as fluctuations in the supply and quality of information occur during the period of involvement.

Because of the MSC's dominant position in respect to funding and, less obviously, regulating TVEI programmes, it is tempting to regard them as the key source of information. However, it would be more accurate to say they are the initiators of new or modified orientations to educational provision and, once schemes are in operation, they become the 'interpreters' of individual scheme viability. They approach this task through various mechanisms of feedback, including national and local evaluations, negotiations with education authority officers and, more importantly, through the appointment of regional advisors who, in 'partnership' with authority personnel monitor the progress of schemes and offer guidance on the suitability of TVEI submissions and particular options, forms of organization and pattern of relationships within them.

However, despite the apparent confidence of MSC personnel and the sometimes blustering rhetoric of the Commission's governmental sponsors, the MSC actually treads a slippery path in its involvement at the local levels of implementation. No matter how experienced their management, they cannot possibly have as sophisticated a grasp of local educational affairs as area administrators and senior staff. This is the major reason that scheme specifications cannot be provided on a national basis, for what may be appropriate and viable in one school could be anathema to another, even within the same authority. Instead, the aims and criteria must remain couched in a language of high generality allowing a diversity of local responses to be mediated, regulated and consolidated by the MSC TVEI Unit through the interpretative role of the regional advisors.

Theirs is a delicate task of discursive diplomacy where a new vocabulary of the vocationalist ethos is insinuated into the conventional rhetorics of educational policy-making and implementation. And this seems to be done in a way that does not immediately threaten the identities and autonomy of established educationalists, yet provides a basis for transformation which appears to articulate with conventionally established educational perspectives at all levels.

Thus, for example, 'participation' becomes a neutral, though evocative, key term in communicative processes all the way from the MSC/DES relationship down through every level of implementation to the teacher-pupil relationship. Indeed, it is at this level where such implied change has its most potent implications. One regional advisor is on record as stating that 'the really major thing that's happening is that the teacher's role is changing', and that statement is then powerfully linked to what are identified as the three major factors underlying the TVEI — curriculum development, institutional development and assessment development — all of them terms familiar to educationalists at large.

But, what is actually suggested is that curriculum development, of which staff development in the form of off-site higher education courses is a central factor, has diverged from and outstripped the development of assessment methods and procedures. Because of its predominantly academic bias, its influence on teachers depreciates recognition and accreditation of pupils' experiential knowledge. At the same time the institutional structures that have evolved from this in the secondary sector have produced strongly insulated, examination-oriented subject specialisms which tend to exclude large numbers of school children from acquiring broader certification of their achievements, and to produce not only an ill-equipped future workforce, but also a disillusioned, alienated and aimless citizenry.

Partly as a result of this we have seen the importation of successfully established course and institutional structures from the further education sector — principally those offered by the RSA, City and Guilds of London Institute and the Business and Technician Education Council (B/TEC). These provide experientially-based syllabi organized in modular structures that can be variously combined, integrated, assessed and, most importantly, accredited more broadly in ways not dependent on academic exactitude and excellence. The task of the MSC is, in their own words, to 'strike a balance between curriculum, assessment and institutional developments' and on the basis of that equilibrium to ensure that 'staff development is tied to school practices'.

The implications of these statements for the future role of teachers, subordinated, it would appear, to curriculum development, is worthy of careful consideration. A close monitoring of the ways in which TVEI is discussed and negotiated will not only give some indication of the levels of 'management' to which TVEI is targeted, but also the differing forms of that management within affected schools. In the process, the manner in which the MSC involves itself in local initiatives allows some insight into what they see as the 'ways' of managing change as well as changing management.

Effect on Teachers

Altering the scope of educational policy involves assumptions about and has implications for secondary school teachers' perceptions and experiences of their subjective and objective careers (see Sikes, 1986). It is teachers who implement and realize TVEI and the nature and extent of its 'success' or 'failure' depend, to a considerable degree, upon them and upon their response. At a structural level this is shaped by the political influence of the teaching profession as a whole, at an institutional level by their level of professional autonomy, and at a personal level by their commitment and capacity, and sense of their own career prospects. Quite crucially, all these features are affected by the hybridization of education in TVEI.

Thus, while only a minority of teachers are actively involved in teaching or administering TVEI schemes, the very existence and extensiveness of TVEI has (at least potentially) changed the position of all secondary schools, and of all teachers working within them.

These changes can be usefully divided into those relating to the context and to the content of teachers' work. Our observations of TVEI in practice suggest that while the content has tended to remain a more purely 'educational' strain, the contexts in which teachers involved in TVEI work have become much more hybridized as a consequence of such factors as categorical funding, increased and more specific accountability, more extensive and intrusive monitoring, together with quite novel expectations about inter-institutional arrangements and about the greater speed at which change can be brought about.

For instance being seen to 'satisfy' the MSC involves evaluation. Supplying statistics, being observed and interviewed, answering questionnaires and distributing them to students, all impinge on teachers' work experience. Even those not personally involved in teaching TVEI sessions are likely to have been touched in some way by certain evaluation processes and procedures:

> There's so much evaluation — 'fill this in', 'fill that in', 'the kids have got to do this questionnaire this afternoon' — all kids mind you not just TVEI ones, God! Is it worth it I ask? (non-TVEI teacher)

> Sometimes it's like living in a goldfish bowl. You fill in these forms about whatever and then you're (the evaluator) there in the lesson. I must say I haven't had anything like it since I was on teaching practice. (TVEI teacher)

And evaluation requirements are only one organizational change. In some TVEI schools consortia arrangements have necessitated alterations to the structure of the school day, either in terms of the number and timing of periods or/and in starting and finishing times. There have also sometimes been quite radical timetabling and option blocking changes. As the changes affect everyone in the school they have made people aware of TVEI — and some see it as being a major source of disruption:

> I think it's a case of the tail wagging the dog. We've had to alter the timetable, alter the school day, periodically we have to provide these statistics, then there's your comments for the profile, and for how many pupils? That's the thing, fifteen in the first year, thirty in the second, isn't it? And there's the discipline issues. What do you do with pupils from another school who misbehave here? You need to get a policy on that one. (teacher, TVEI school)

Looking at the various elements of TVEI it is clear that it has introduced little or nothing new in some schools. A main and salient difference is the *speed* with which the MSC demands that things are moved and implemented. Right from the start the pressure has been on — to prepare submissions, to set up organizational structures, to write syllabuses. This speed is consistent with the MSC's market/business orientation. It is however foreign to education. Time or the lack of it has been a constant source of tension.

> The MSC want everything done yesterday. We could have made a much better job of the submission if there'd been a proper period to prepare it in. Instead there was, I think, a week. (headteacher, TVEI school)

Although there are continual complaints that it is unrealistic to expect schools to respond so immediately, it does seem that the pace of response has quickened, and some feel this to be a positive:

> I'll say this for the MSC they've got us buzzing. You get things done and put through much more effectively, and that can't be a bad thing. (teacher, TVEI school)

More specifically, the intervention of the MSC through TVEI demands that teachers broaden their scope and orient the content of what they teach towards the practical and applied, and alter their pedagogical style by placing greater emphasis on experiential and discovery-based learning. The implication is that if this is done all will be well, or at least better than before.

Some teachers have resented being *required* to do what they believe they were already doing, by choice. Their feeling is that the MSC as an employment, rather than educationally-oriented, concern has revealed its ignorance of what actually has been happening in schools — and of what is feasible. Others question the whole appropriateness of specifically applied content and instructional styles in schools.

TVEI has had considerable impact in subject areas where practical work has always been the norm. Within many schools, these subject areas have been marginal and low status, seen as being more suited to students who are not academically oriented or able. This low status, non-academic image has also frequently been attached to those who teach in these areas. One consequence of this is that relatively few needle- or wood-work teachers for example, are found in senior management posts (see Hilsum and Start, 1974), although this may, in some cases, be due to their own career perceptions and preferences as much as to their expectations of and experiences in achieving promotional posts (see Sikes, 1986). Thus, from being in a situation where they often had to scrounge, ferret, hoard and work with inadequate and inappropriate materials and equipment, some teachers now find themselves with what is frequently quite literally an embarassment of riches — and often with enhanced promotion prospects as well.

The contrast between TVEI and 'non-TVEI' departments within a school more generally, is particularly marked at a time when, as in recent years, there has been so little money available. Quite understandably teachers have felt strongly about this — the following quotes are typical:

> It reflects a view of the purpose of education that I'm not happy with

> because it moves away from the liberal and humanistic towards the vocational and pragmatic. Schools should be about education and spending X number of pounds on CNC lathes and paying for lecturers to come in and instruct the kids how to use them, or sending the kids down 'tech isn't, in my view, education. (art teacher, TVEI school)

> I do benefit from TVEI and it's nice after scrimping and making do for so long to be able to do things properly for a while. It won't last, I know that, but I'm taking advantage while I can. We've been the cinderella subject for so long and while I understand and sympathize with the others I'd be lying if I didn't think well, we've always got the difficult kids, the less able, the disruptive and to some extent we still do but it's nice to have a bit of what you might call compensation. (CDT teacher, TVEI school)

The changes that teachers have perceived and experienced in the context of their work, then, tend to involve being guided into a more vocational direction. However, the terms in which they talk about the 'classroom' benefits of TVEI and its impact on the content of their work, are rather more traditionally 'educational'. Many headteachers went into TVEI hoping that the resources and financing that it provides would enable them to improve the quality of education for all their pupils. Teachers have shared this view —

> TVEI has given me the chance to do the sorts of things that I've been wanting to do for ages but couldn't because the resources weren't available. (TVEI teacher)

> We can work with classes that are the right sort of size. You can do so much more and you can experiment and try things out that you can then use with other classes. (TVEI teacher)

> Well the equipment's there and it's used across the school. In my opinion everyone's benefitting. (TVEI headteacher)

Taking advantage of the financial opportunities available to improve the quality of the educational experience of all students is only one way in which teachers have utilized TVEI. Some schools have taken advantage of the divisive potential of TVEI to divert able or less able or disruptive students into particular courses, which inevitably has significant consequences for the teachers expected to work with these various groups. This is an example of how TVEI has been incorporated into existing traditions — in some cases the tradition of practical applied work for the less able or anti-academic, in others, the tradition that the 'brighter' students get the best facilities and resources.

To date, teachers seem to have incorporated TVEI and MSC requirements into their jobs largely through a process of strategic compromise. It is, though, a compromise with, rather than a complete absorption of, TVEI. The content of teachers' work is not unaffected, and not only superficially affected, by their participation in TVEI. The clearest illustration of this is the way in which teachers have taken up and use language (or jargon) and concepts which have originated from or been sponsored and propagated by, the MSC. Examples include: 'Delivery' — the realization of a programme/scheme agreed between various parties, and 'Ownership' — which occurs when some body, be that an LEA, a school, or a teacher or a student internalizes and/or adopts and takes responsibility for something — such as a TVEI scheme, an experimental approach to teaching, or their own learning. This linguistic spread is an important means by which the MSC have consolidated their coverage (see Sikes, 1986; and also Torrance, 1986).

Over the years, initiatives and innovations have tended to have a limited effect in schools (see Rudduck, 1986) although they have been significant for the subjective and objective career experiences of *some* teachers. TVEI (and other MSC interventions, see Sikes, 1987) differs from other curricular and organizational innovations and developments because it challenges fundamental traditions and basic assumptions about the nature and purpose of education, educationalists, and educational institutions (see Pyart, 1985, p. 324). It has opened up what goes on in classrooms and workshops to national rather than just local surveillance; it has challenged the traditional rhythm and pacing of educational development; it has required rather than suggested; and it has threatened traditional subject status hierarchies. Far from reacting passively to this however, many teachers have taken advantage of the situation to enhance their own positions. They have done this with regard to their professional development, by taking and creating opportunities to attend in-service training courses; they have cultivated TVEI related 'specialities' which have been valuable currency in the promotion stakes; and they have made full use of the extra resources and opportunities associated with TVEI to put their ideas and dreams into practice, thereby enhancing their job satisfaction. There are, of course, those for whom TVEI has had negative implications. TVEI is the product of an MSC philosophy oriented towards 'enterprise', adapt and survive or go to the wall. The DES, on the other hand, takes a more traditional stance. How teachers experience the hybridization therefore depends to some extent on how far they are opportunistic entrepreneurs, or traditionalists.

Conclusion

In this chapter we have argued that the key to understanding TVEI lies not so much in accumulating more and more descriptive evidence (which is likely to be varied and inconclusive) of schemes in operation, but in developing systematic, theoretically informed, ways of approaching the collection and interpretation of that evidence. We have suggested that one such way of approaching TVEI is to see it as a hybrid produced by the enforced conjunction of MSC and the education service in its administration and implementation. We have agreed that seeing TVEI in this way sheds light on both its limits and its possibilities, and we have sought to demonstrate this by examining three of its key features. Thus, in the area of equalizing opportunities, we contrasted the DES tradition of *encouraging equal opportunities* for the realization of *personal potential*, with the MSC's *requirement* to *take steps* to mitigate the *gender stereotyping* of school subjects. In looking at how schools, local authorities and teachers have interpreted and managed the impact of TVEI, we have suggested that it is crucial to register how the implementation of a programmme largely drawn in one tradition in institutions is shaped by and for the other tradition. We have concluded that neither complete central determination nor local freedom are ever likely to be operative. Rather the weighting of the two traditions, exactly what kind of hybrid they become, is determined neither by their origins, nor by the environment in which they develop, nor by any predictable or necessary relationship between them, but by continuing negotiation carried out from the starting point of 'where the schools are' at any particular point.

Note

1 Education has, of course, been part of other social policy hybrids. The development of nursery provision from a joint health-education concern (and a Health Department responsibility) to the current emphasis on pre-school *education*, is one example. Another is the education-social work hybrid that was popular in the 1960s; this required changes in both the boundaries and the authority of the school. These were not forthcoming and the hybrid withered. Both these examples — of successful and of unsuccessful education related hybrid policy — clearly relate to conceptions about the scope of education.

References

DALE, R. (1981) 'Education and the capitalist state: Contributions and contradictions' in APPLE, M. W. (Ed) *Economic and Cultural Reproductions in Education*, London, Routledge & Kegan Paul.

DEPARTMENT of EDUCATION and SCIENCE (1977) *Education in Schools: A Consultative Document*, London, HMSO.

DEPARTMENT of EDUCATION and SCIENCE (1977) *Curriculum 11–16*, London, HMSO.

DEPARTMENT of EDUCATION and SCIENCE (1986) *Working Together — Education and Training*, London, HMSO.

HILSUM, S. and START, K. B. (1974) *Promotion and Careers in Teaching*, Windsor, NFER.

HOLLAND, G. (1986) 'The MSC' in RANSON, S. and TOMLINSON, J. (Eds) *The Changing Government of Education*, London, Institute of Local Government Studies.

JESSOP, B. (1982) *The Capitalist State*, Oxford, Martin Robertson.

MCCULLOCH, G. (1986) 'Policy, politics and education: The politics of the Technical and Vocational Education Initiative', *Journal of Education Policy*, 1, 1.

MCCULLOCH, G., JENKINS, E. and LAYTON, D. (1985) *Technological Revolution? The Politics of School Science and Technology in England and Wales Since 1945*, Lewes, Falmer Press.

Papagiannis, G. J., Kees, S. and Bickel, R. N. (1982) 'Toward a political economy of educational innovation', *Review of Educational Research*, 52, 2, pp 245–90.

Pyart, B. (1985) 'An overview of TVEI' *School Organization*, 5, 4,

Ranson, S. (1985) 'Contradictions in the government of educational change,' *Political Studies*, 33, 1,

Reeder, D. (1979) 'A recurring debate: Education and industry', in Bernbaum, G. (ed) *Schooling in Decline*, London: Macmillan.

Rudduck, J. (1986) *Understanding Curriculum Change*. Inaugural professional lecture, University of Sheffield, 19/2/86.

Short, C. (1986) 'The MSC and special measures for unemployment' in Renn, C. and Fairley, J. (Eds) *Challenging the MSC on Jobs, Education and Training*, London, Pluto Press.

Sikes, P. J. (1986) *The Mid-Career Teacher: Adaptation and Motivation in a Contracting Secondary School System*, University of Leeds, unpublished PhD thesis.

Sikes, P. J. (1987) 'Teachers and the MSC' in Barton, L. and Walker, S. (Eds) *Changing Policy, Changing Teachers*, Milton Keynes, Open University Press.

Taylor, W. (1985) 'Productivity and educational values', in Worswick G. D. N. (Ed) *Education and Economic Performance*, Aldershot, Gower.

Torrance, H. (1986) 'Expanding school-based assessment: Issues, problems and future possibilities; *Research Papers in Education*, 1. 1.

Chapter 5

The Certificate of Prevocational Education

Hilary Radnor, Stephen Ball and David Burrell

On 11 January 1985 the Joint Board of Pre-Vocational Education officially launched the Certificate of Prevocational Education (CPVE). The press release stated:

> The Certificate of Prevocational Education will be a national qualification of prevocational education for young people aged 16 and above who undertake an approved one-year full time programme of study and related activities.
>
> The Joint Board believes that the new CPVE scheme will go a long way towards meeting demands from employers, educationalists and the government for a course which will equip young people with the flexible skills and competencies required by today's employment market.

The press conference for the CPVE, to begin in the autumn of 1985, was a public declaration by the Business and Technician Education Council (BTEC) and the City and Guilds of London Institute (CGLI) of their achievement at becoming the validating body, recognized by the Government for issuing certificates to this particular target group. The number of students involved is estimated at around 100,000 who will be able to follow CPVE courses in schools, sixth-form college and colleges of further education.

In the first two sections of this chapter we consider three simple questions. Examinations already exist for this target group so why was the CPVE considered necessary? How did it come about that BTEC and CGLI became the validating body? Why were the GCE and CSE bodies, who are also involved in examinations for this age group, virtually excluded?

Section 1 CPVE: An Historical Account

The bulge in the birthrate (1947–64) and the trend towards a longer educational life led to an expansion of post-16 education. This trend towards staying on at school could be equated with the reduced opportunities available for young people to take up low-skill jobs. The DES have certainly recognized the fact that young people who did not intend to go on to higher education were, in increasing numbers, choosing to continue their education for at least one more year. As early as 1963 the Robbins Report recommended that '. . . courses should be made available for all those who are qualified by ability and attainment to pursue them and who wish to do so'. Both schools and colleges of further education responded to this expansion. The percentage staying on into the sixth-form increased from 11.7 per cent in 1961 to 20.8 per cent in 1973. By the mid-70s the traditional sixth-form, in the school sector, consisting of students committed to academic study, had given way to a much more diverse student body, a substantial portion of whom wanted to take non-'A' level courses. In many schools and colleges this led to an opening up of the sixth-form and some degree of curricular change and examination restructuring to provide courses for these students. However, this restructuring did nothing to alter the basic academic orientation of sixth-form studies. Edwards (1983) makes the point that 'It can be argued that the sixth form curriculum illustrates with particular vividness a general failure to reconstruct the content of secondary education as its organization has been transformed' (p. 64). The GCE and CSE boards, responding as they saw it to the needs of these students, piloted an experimental examination — the Certificate of Extended Education (CEE) — which began in 1972. In contrast, within the further education sector, similar groups of young people were taking mainly technical, engineering, commercial and secretarial courses. The CEE clearly represented a further extension of the academic definition of the sixth-form, 'it was apparently still possible to ignore their substantial 'fringes' and so continue to regard sixth-forms as being *essentially* the selective route to highly selective forms of higher education' (ibid p. 65).

In 1976 the Schools Council proposed that the CEE examination should be firmly established and validated. In response to this proposal the DES set up a Committee of Enquiry in 1978 chaired by Professor Kevin Keohane. This Committee reported in 1979 and recommended that 'A CEE examination but with important differences from the pilot examination should be officially introduced.' The proposed differences were intended to help candidates to be more effectively prepared for employment. They recommended compulsory tests of proficiency in English and maths, leaving schools free to devise courses leading to any individually-selected package of examination subjects. The Committee urged, however, that schools and colleges should give careful consideration to ways in which they could help these young people to prepare for employment. This would include the offer of some vocationally-oriented CEE studies. They also urged the examining boards 'to develop CEE syllabuses relevant to the world of work with titles that adequately describe their contents to employers looking at examination certificates'. The report seemed to reflect a compromise between strong student and parental pressure for academic style subject courses and pressure from the Labour government and industrialists for more 'relevant' education.

Meanwhile, however, within the FE sector, the Further Education

Curriculum Review and Development Unit, which was attached to the DES in Elizabeth House, was assessing the needs for post–16 students who were attending FE colleges. Their brief was to examine existing courses to see to what extent the range of provision reflected student need and to indicate their views on the appropriate bases, components and balance of curricula for this group and relevant teaching, learning and assessment methods. The result of this review was the publication in June 1979 of *A Basis for Choice*. In *A Basis for Choice* the FEU suggested that the general objectives for a basic post-16 pre-employment course should consist of core, vocational and job-specific studies.

The basic contrast in approach and root assumptions between the FE sector and the school sector is evidenced in the difference between CEE and the curriculum design outlined in *A Basis for Choice*. *A Basis for Choice* advocated a definite curriculum structure and laid down a set of criteria to be provided in a variety of courses with a definite course-employment link. CEE permitted teachers themselves to choose the curriculum structure dependent only on the choice of the individual package of examination subjects. Course-employment links were not defined. It is important to note the general political and educational context in which these constrasting proposals were set. In the late 1970s schools were facing fierce criticism from two directions. In Williams' (1961) terms, the 'old humanists' were fiercely criticizing what they saw as declining standards, increased social disorder and the untoward influence of 'trendy left wing teachers', while the 'industrial-trainers' were bemoaning the lack of vocational preparation in schools and the anti-industrial bias of teachers. Both lobbies were agreed that teachers were at fault. Bowes and Whitty (1983), discussing the development of 16+ examinations in this period, make the point that 'the theme that the teaching profession should be made more accountable to those outside it clearly influenced the development of the examination reform proposals' (p. 236). In this situation, a proposal supporting CSE board courses based on considerable teacher control of curriculum and assessment seemed unlikely to carry the day. In addition the 'educational bureaucrats' in the DES (Salter and Tapper, 1981) seemed determined to rationalize the 17+ courses available to non 'A' level sixth-form students. In October 1980 the DES published a consultative paper *Examinations 16–18* setting out, among other things, the conclusion reached in 'Proposals for a Certificate of Education in the light of the proposals in *A Basis for Choice*'. The paper clearly came down on the side of *A Basis for Choice*. Paragraph 11 states:

> The government have considered whether in any case the Keohane proposals for a CEE offer a sound foundation for the development of pre-vocational courses. In their judgement, the proposals for a single subject examination with no required core of syllabus content apart from the communication and numerical skills assessed in English and Mathematics tests are not fully appropriate to the needs of the target group. While not uncritical of aspects of the proposals in *A Basis for Choice*, they consider that these come closer to what is required.

They go on to state their opposition to the introduction of separate patterns of provision for those in schools and FE and state their belief in the idea that the target group in both sectors can be best served by 'provision more akin to traditional FE practice developed in the light of the recommendations in *A Basis for Choice*'.

The consultative paper gave the go-ahead for the development of a pre-vocational examination broadly along the lines recommended in *A Basis for Choice*, i.e. one that could be taken by young people attending either schools or colleges. It suggested that one of the FE examination/validating bodies might be invited to undertake the coordination of arrangements for the new examination. It was indicated that the CEE was only to be allowed to continue until a new examination was set up and GCE and CSE boards should not be engaged in the development of prevocational examination courses but should concentrate on the development of a single system of examinations at 16+. We will return to the implications and effects of this in the next section.

Following the publication of *A Basis for Choice*, the FEU did a feasibility study, to 'test and where necessary, reshape the core', with a group of eight colleges. In general terms the extent and nature of the common core was found to be acceptable and realistic. In September 1980, the FEU tested the criteria of ABC as part of a validating process. They did this in association with the City and Guilds of London Institute who, as a validating body, had the means of developing the machinery for piloting and validating *A Basis for Choice*. In the light of the consultative paper *Examinations 16–18* a request was made through the Schools Council to arrange for a number of schools to be associated with the pilot study. The report *ABC in Action* was published in September 1981. The pilot showed that it was possible to validate the criteria of ABC.

The next question was who should be directly responsible for validating the new course. The CGLI saw themselves as ideally placed to undertake the role of validating body for a new system of national awards. In their response to the DES consultative document *Examination 16–18* they state, paragraph 4:

> . . . we would point out that the Further Education Curriculum Development and Review Unit in its recommendations to the Department of Education and Science in July 1980, proposed that the Institute should be invited to undertake the role of validating body for a new system of national awards. The Institute should welcome the opportunity to fill this role as now envisaged and believes that it is ideally placed to establish a national and credible system.

They go on to claim that their network of consultative and policy committees which enables them to consult with all sectors of industry at national and regional level would help to ensure wide recognition of the resulting qualification. They further claim strong links with not only FE institutions but schools and sixth-form colleges and indicate that they would be prepared to develop links with the Schools Council and GCE/CSE boards by reconstituting their advisory committees. They put forward an economic argument for 'evolving from the existing system' as opposed to setting up an entirely new body. Such claims must have carried powerful credence in the context of general government education policy and they provide, almost at a stroke, a significant curricular reorientation for schools at least for the reference grouping within which non-'A' level post-16 courses would be set. The interests of the GCE and CSE boards were clearly under threat.

The Schools Council, another potential loser in this reorientation, responded to the consultative document with doubts about the role of CGLI and BTEC '. . . It therefore wishes to raise serious questions about the arrangements proposed for validation' and a counter-claim based on the Council's own experience of curriculum development.

> The Council therefore welcomes the opportunity to contribute to the development of suitable machinery for planning, coordinating and validating the new examinations, and looks forward to playing a creative part in this work, from the start.

However, this counter claim for part responsibility for, and control over, 17+ examining carried little weight. In May 1982 *17+ A New Qualification* was published. This was a statement that set out government policy on the introduction of a new range of prevocational courses. 'These courses will be offered in schools and colleges of further education and will lead to a national certificate at 17+.' This statement clearly indicated that the DES did not consider *single subject* examinations as suitable for the needs of this group of students and that the proliferation of prevocational courses on offer only served to confuse employers and needed to be rationalized into a single system leading to a nationally recognized qualification that was provisionally entitled 'the Certificate of Prevocational Education'. The concept of CPVE was thus established. How this qualification was to be administered was stated in paragraph 30.

> It would be unrealistic to expect one examining/validating body to secure the cooperation of other such bodies and coordinate their activities.

This appeared to refute CGLI's imperialist claims to administer the validation of the CPVE. The paragraph goes on to say:

> On the other hand an entirely new and fully representative examining authority for the CPVE would be cumbersome and would take time to establish itself. The solution which meets all the requirements, and which the Secretaries of State have decided to adopt is to invite the examining and validating bodies listed in para 27 above (CGLI, BEC, TEC, RSA, GCE and CSE) in conjunction with local authority associations to undertake the administration of CPVE as a joint enterprize through a small consortium under an independent chairman appointed by the Secretaries of State and with the help of a chief executive and a permanent staff. Such a consortium would minimize

> the risk of having different qualifications competing for the same candidates, provide a way of building on existing expertise and avoid the creation of an entirely new body which might be slow to gain acceptance.

At first sight this would appear to be a compromise proposal involving a sharing of influence between the FE and schools sectors and the contending examination bodies. However, this proved not to be the case: in practice, CGLI and BTEC succeeded in gaining control of the validation process, and together they effectively dominate the Joint Board as *Better Schools* published March 1985, Paragraph 112 indicates:

> The Government has promoted the establishment of a new qualification, the CPVE, for those young people who stay on full time in either schools or colleges for one year after the compulsory period and who are not pursuing CSE or 'O' level (or in due course GCSE) qualifications with a reasonable hope of success, and do not have a clear vocational aim in view. The CPVE is administered by a Joint Board of the two principal examining and validating bodies for prevocational education — CGLI/BTEC — on which the other examining bodies, in schools as well as in further education, together with employers and LEAs, are represented; it is intended to replace a range of existing courses including the prevocational courses of the CGLI, B/TEC and the Royal Society of Arts and the Certificate of Extended Education offered by most CSE and GCE boards.'

Although in 1982 the government had considered it 'unrealistic for one examining board to secure the cooperation of others', by 1985 two examining boards, CGLI and BTEC, had convinced the government that they could deliver the goods.

B/TEC and CGLI certainly have the sort of validating experience which would have enabled them to put the government's plan for CPVE into action within the time frame that DES desired. The Secretary of State issued an invitation to CGLI and B/TEC to set up a Joint Board under the chairmanship of Sir Edwin Nixon, CBE (Chief Executive, IBM (UK) Ltd), to develop the new award. In the first instance there was no representation on this Board of any other examination boards. The GCE and CSE examination boards and the RSA (validating body for commerce and clerical qualifications) were excluded. However, these bodies made representations to the Secretary of State. Mr. Bill Frearson, the Chairman of the Study Conference of Regional Examining Boards (CSE Boards), along with a representative from the GCE boards and the RSA had an interview with Sir Keith Joseph. At the end of that meeting, which lasted 1 hour and 20 minutes, Sir Keith agreed that they would have a place on the Joint Boards. So the Joint Board eventually consisted of thirteen members: five B/TEC, five CGLI, one GCE, one CSE, one RSA, plus the Chairman.

The Board operates on a 'consensus' basis, the chairman deciding to act on issues that appear to have the majority of the Board behind it. B/TEC and CGLI have a built-in majority and when the Joint Board issued its consultative document (May 1984) on the CPVE, its style and tone were remarkably similar to the structure and format of B/TEC general and CGLI foundation courses. The CPVE emerged as a rationalization of existing FE practice in the prevocational area drawing, in particular, on the CGLI Foundation and Vocational Preparation (365) courses and the B/TEC general course. The earlier references to consensus of interest and partnership between school and FE sectors were firmly overtaken in the planning work of the Joint Board.

Section 2 An Explanation for CPVE

As Whitty (1985) has pointed out, public examinations are an arena of critical ideological and political dispute in education. Examination agencies are particularly significant as a 'recontextualizing context' in the sense that they operate to mediate, organize and package a selection of that knowledge which is 'produced' in universities, industry and elsewhere (the primary contexts) in such a way that it is 'appropriate' for reproduction in schools and colleges (secondary contexts).

In the present case, the secondary context is schools and colleges of further education. We are interested here specifically in schools. The primary context consists of two competing sets of agencies and interest groups where knowledge is produced — the universities (academic knowledge), stated crudely as the *old humanists* in Williams' (1965) terms and industry (technical knowledge), the *industrial trainers* in Williams' terms. More specifically, the old humanist lobby is here represented by the GCE and CSE examinations boards, the industrial training lobby by the FEU and CGLI, B/TEC and RSA examination boards.

Bernstein (1982) makes the point that:

> When a text is appropriated by recontexualizing agents, operating in positions of this field, the text usually undergoes a transformation prior to its relocation. The form of this transformation is regulated by a *principle of decontextualizing*. This process refers to the change in the text as it is first *delocated* and then *relocated*. This process ensures that the text is no longer the same text. (p. 352)

Here the terrain of the conflict between the opposing lobbies and agencies is the definition and control of the curriculum relating to the examining of students at 17+. Two contrasting 'modalities' and 'voices' are in competition. In *A Basis for Choice* the industrial trainers are offering an integrated, skills oriented, prevocational course, linked, on the basis of definitive criteria, to employment. The old humanist tradition is embodied in the single subject CEE courses which build upon and extend the academic curriculum of the secondary school.

Figure 1

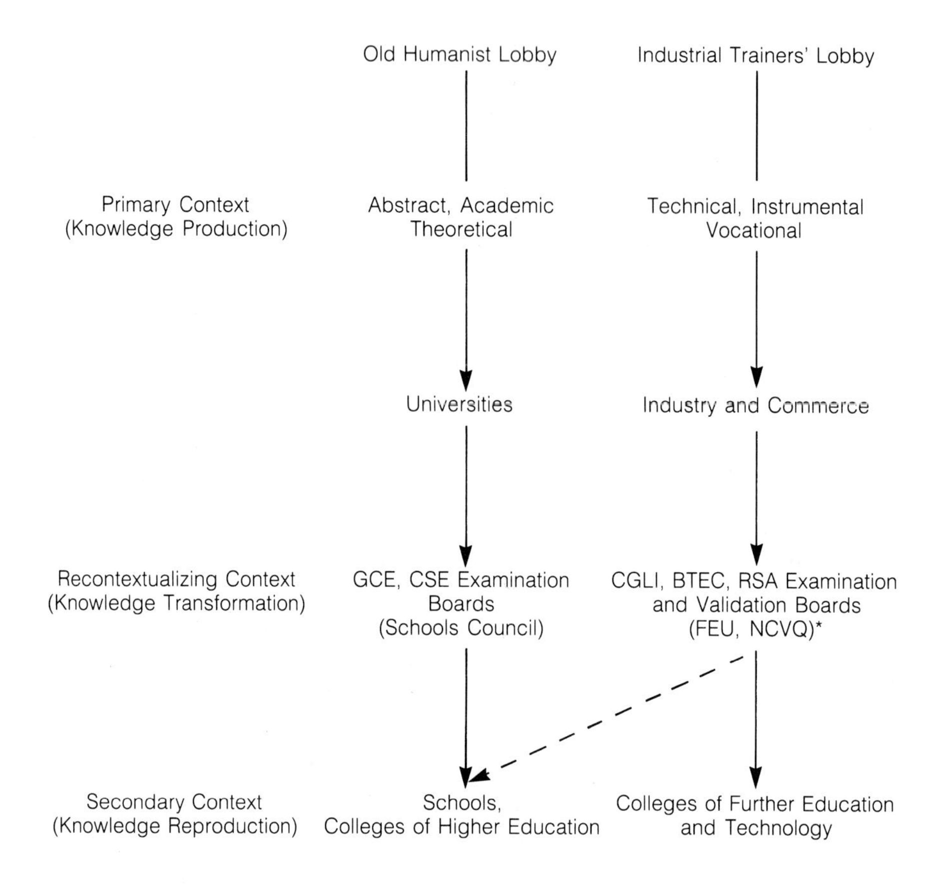

*NCVQ = National Council for Vocational Qualifications. An agency set up by Kenneth Baker to oversee and advise on the restructuring of vocational qualifications and to establish patterns of progression between qualifications.

The government and DES decision of 1980 to support the development of prevocational courses and latterly to phase out CEEs entirely, clearly indicates a shift in the balance of power between the academic lobby and the industrial lobby in this sphere. However, it is all too easy to oversimplify the causes and origins of this shift. Indeed it is possible to identify a number of institutional, commercial and political factors at work in this sector of the examinations field. What we find is considerable disunity and conflict within the educational state and a complex, internecine struggle for control over a key area of the school curriculum. What we offer below are some tentative interpretations of the CPVE issue.

1 In the most immediate sense, the emergence of the CPVE is part of an institutional and commercial struggle between rival examination agencies for control of, or division of, the school examination market. The whole vocational education debate and the pressure being put on schools since 1976 to take more account of the needs of industry, along with the rapid increase in 'non-'A'-level' sixth formers have produced an opportunity for B/TEC and CGLI in particular to expand their sphere of influence into schools and to capture a greater share of the school examination market. Both the school boards (CSE and GCE) and the FE boards (B/TEC, CGLI, RSA, etc.) were already being hit financially by the effects of falling rolls. The market was shrinking, the overall number of entries in decline. The DES draft circular (1986) *Providing for Quality: The Pattern of Organization to Age 19* warns that numbers in the 16 to 19 age group will drop from a high of 2.4m in 1983 to 1.6m in 1995. the overall decline in student numbers and the expansion of the FE boards clearly threatens the interests and the commercial viability of the CSE boards and in the long term the GCE boards, which have had between them virtually unchallenged control of school examining for twenty years. In simple commercial terms the CPVE represents a significant financial loss for the CSE boards whose CEE examinations are being phased out. Hence, attempts are being made by some boards (SREB, SEREB) to pilot versions of the CPVE based around existing CEE syllabuses in competition with joint board courses which use B/TEC general and CGLI 365 components. Hence, also the explorations of some CSE boards for the new roles in the examining field; to provide expertise for course submissions; to offer in-service training; to develop profiles and Record of Achievement schemes. Hence, also the hastily arranged rash of mergers between GCE and CSE boards (for example, SREB and Oxford), although these mergers are also responses to the introduction of GCSE. The GCE and CSE boards are attempting to adapt themselves to a new market situation. Thus the commercial competitive aspect of the 1980 decision is important.

2a But this commercial battle can also be viewed in another way. Are market forces being used to 'discipline' and make the examination agencies more 'accountable'? And, in line with the overall ideological thrust of the Conservative government, is a free market in school examining being created? Certainly the groundwork is being laid for a future 'pick and mix' curriculum which will allow the creation of one-off, tailor-made curriculum packages suited to the 'needs' of individual schools and pupils. As elsewhere in government policy there is an emphasis on consumer choice and cost efficiency and the effect is both an insertion of the values of capitalism deeper into the schooling process and the increasing commodification of knowledge itself. Even the new GCSE examination consortia cannot agree among themselves a standard entrance fee, and budget priced examining may be a real possibility in the new system. Schools could choose between courses on the grounds of cost rather than educational criteria.

2b Looking at this commercial argument another way, for the vocational FE examination boards the CPVE is a considerable 'beach-head' in the schools. It is a possible basis for influencing the whole curriculum and the basic modality of the 'knowledge culture' of schools. Set alongside Lord Young's Technical and Vocational Education Initiative (TVEI) it may be a second front in the battle to vocationalize the secondary curriculum (or certain parts of it). This may go a long way in explaining the DES's willingness to go with the CPVE as against CEEs. B/TEC and CGLI certainly have aspirations to expand their influence in schools (B/TEC-CGLI, 1986) and both have recently begun to develop and offer courses for 14–16-year-olds. CGLI appears to take the hardest line, and makes the hardest sell, in relation to the 14–16 curriculum. In their response to the FEU document *Progressing from Vocational Preparation* (1982), they refer to 'obtaining acceptance of an alternative to the traditional academically-based route into adult life'; and describe phase 1, aged 14–16, as 'providing a general educational basis of skills and an understanding of the adult and working world'. The FEU are less forthright. But the introduction to *Progressing* suggests that:

> . . . whilst the validity of some university examinations has been regularly and openly criticized over the last decade or so, it is interesting (but perhaps not surprising) to note how little schools and colleges through their curricula, have contributed to the concept of quality of work. (p. 6).

The possibility arises of linking CPVE to TVEI courses and CGLI and B/TEC awards to bring into existence a differentiated or segmented school curriculum. The concept of two distinct curricula and separate 'routes' through school is firmly established in the FEU literature. The tensions and divergence of interests between the constituent members are certainly in evidence in the proceedings of the Joint Board. The CSE representative on the Joint Board described, in an interview, a key incident in Joint Board meetings.

> . . . at the moment within the Joint Board there are quite a number of rifts now appearing. At the meeting held on 28 November the RSA and SREB put forward a submission to the Joint Board for CPVE. I've always been under the impression that, as far as the examining boards are concerned, we would be able to accredit and certificate these examinations or these courses under licence from the Joint Board and that's precisely what the RSA and SREB thought of doing. And after half-an-hour into the debate which was allowed by the Chairman who, on that particular day was Donald Fisher, CEO for Hertfordshire, a very much more amenable man than possibly the permanent chairman who doesn't allow a great deal of discussion — it was pretty obvious that the members of CGLI and B/TEC were not going to move from the stand that they have made all along the line. That they were given authority from the DES to deal with CPVE and that we are just members of the Board and virtually from the way things have happened have got very little part to play.

However, the work of the Joint Board, a cooperative effort between the vocational examination baords, also brings into focus the continuing commercial rivalry between these boards. Two instances from interviews illustrate these tensions.

> Now the RSA have said that unless the CPVE come more into line on what the original proposals were, they will continue to offer RSA examinations and will not take part in CPVE. Now that is a devastating statement to make because the RSA, being very much a leader in the commercial examination field without doubt, over 600,000 candidates entering per year, that is going to be a bitter blow to the Joint Board.

And:

> What B/TEC have done now is produce another B/TEC exam and it is interesting that last week, at Joint Board, the Chairman, obviously representing the RSA, asked why B/TEC has introduced another type of certificate at 17+ that is not subsumed into CPVE. And it was pretty obvious that Mrs Elliot, the Joint Board Secretary — who is also in charge of education examinations at B/TEC — she was very embarrassed by the question and found great difficulty in answering it. Even the DES assessor stated that it was most unfortunate that this kind of press release of a new kind of B/TEC examination had been published. And I think I would be right in saying that a great number of students and a great number of institutions that have relied on B/TEC have now seen the answer to their problem — we won't take the CPVE we'll take the new B/TEC.

In this free-for-all market situation, the GCE and CSE boards also feel entitled, despite disapproval from the DES, to continue to offer single subject CEEs at 16+. The struggle for entry fees and control of this particular area of the school curriculum is likely to continue to develop.

3 In addition to the commercial and economic aspects of the struggle over the CPVE, two more straightforwardly political issues can be added in. The eclipse of the CSE boards in this area can be linked to the increasing distrust of the boards and their procedures during the late 1970s. Rightly or wrongly, the CSE boards were implicated in the Black Paper and Great Debate critiques of declining standards and increasing political indoctrination in secondary schools. Both aspects of the critique were identified with the growth of Mode 3 examining, specifically in the increased level of teacher influence in the examination process generally, not least in the CSE field. As Whitty (1985) has argued, the CSE boards have come to be tarred as ideologically unsound:

> the Mode 3 issue became during the 1970s a symbol around which broader struggles over the future content and control of the school examination system, and even society itself, could be fought out. (p. 123)

Thus, in the DES attempt to abolish CEEs, the CSE boards had their comeuppance. Alongside the development of GCSE, the 'dangerous' autonomy of the CSE boards and their teacher representatives would be done away with once and for all. The problem with such an interpretation is that it demands that we accept a high degree of Machiavellian planning within the offices of the DES. Another political scenario makes similar demands. Rather than seeing CPVE as a 'second front' to the TVEI assault on the secondary curriculum, it could be interpreted as a counter thrust, a belated attempt on the part of the DES, through their FEU agency, to stake their own claims in the vocationalizing process. There is certainly a peculiar degree of discoordination between the CPVE and TVEI. At the school level these initiatives are often in direct competition for staff time, commitment and energy. But where TVEI has the clout of money attached to it, CPVE has none. For the DES it is a form of curriculum development on the cheap. However, there is a considerable amount of liaison between the MSC and FEU, particularly in relation to YTS. And the setting up of the National Council for Vocational Qualifications (NCVQ) has raised questions about the future role and scope of the FEU. Plans to advertise for a new, permanent Unit Director have been shelved and a DES review is to be conducted. (Like B/TEC the NCVQ will be set up as a company limited by guarantee, intended, after three years, to be self-financing. It is likely to be driven by a much stronger commercial logic than the FEU ever was.) Also the DES-MSC rivalry sometimes suggested in press reports seems less realistic in the light of the recent reshuffle of top level civil servants in the DES and the upgrading of Geoffrey Holland, the MSC Director, to the equivalent of Second Permanent Secretary (*Times Higher Education Supplement* 15 September 1986, p. 3). Nonetheless, the CPVE may emerge as the foundation for a national framework for vocational qualifications, but that will depend on the outcome of the work of the new National Council for Vocational Qualifications.

However, as always in the examination of education policy formation the question which is begged is 'how does policy translate into practice?' In this case the potential for change in schools is considerable. Edwards (1983) suggests that 'the recent and rapid blurring of the boundary between schools and further education may be an organization change with potentially much greater impact on the sixth-form curriculum than the transition from selective to non-selective schools' (p. 67). Certainly, important aspects of the curriculum (content and structure), the pedagogy and the assessment of the CPVE sit uneasily within the existing structures and practices of the secondary school. In section 3 of this chapter we consider some of the problems created by these mismatches and examine the extent of acceptance and resistance to change involved in the resolution of these problems. The barriers to change analysis offered by Gross, Giaquinta and Berstein (1971) will be employed to illustrate the ways in which policy demands get reinterpreted at school level.

Section 3 CPVE in Practice

In the previous section of the chapter we suggested that the CPVE represented part of a planned incursion by vocational examination boards into the school curriculum and was also an aspect of DES and government sponsorship of FEU curriculum, design and planning for certain groups of school based students. As such the CPVE must clearly face implementation problems. It confronts teachers imbued in the logic and assumptions, the modality and voice, of an academic single-subject, externally-examined curriculum with the logic and assumptions, the modality and voice, of a very differently organized, further education curriculum. Specifically, in Bernstein's (1971) terms, the CPVE carries a whole set of profound challenges to the existing basic three message systems of the curriculum: content (what counts as valid knowledge), pedagogy (what counts as a valid realization of knowledge) and assessment (what counts as valid evaluation of knowledge). Radical changes from the classical collection code curriculum are involved. These are embodied in what Dale (1986) calls the 'new FE' ideology, and he says 'that ideology represents a major challenge to the professional and academic interests that have been the dominant influence on the secondary school curriculum and of the education experiences of most young people in school' (p. 38). Furthermore, 'it is a means of working through the practical curricular, pedagogic and assessment implications of (an) attempted shift from the expressive to the instrumental, the intrinsic to the extrinsic' (p. 38).

Employing Bernstein's analysis, as far as content is concerned, two changes underpinning the CPVE are significant. First, there is the role played by vocational studies and work-related knowledge. There is a deliberate attempt to articulate school work with the world of work. The work experience placements also have a role to play in this. Academic knowledge for its own sake is not encouraged. Thus mathematics is transformed into numeracy, English becomes communication and social studies becomes industrial, environmental and social studies. There is also a shift from the purely cognitive to enactive forms of, or presentations, of knowledge, that is from knowledge to skills (objective and transferrable rather than specific task skills) (Cohen, 1984). Finally, there is an important change in the relationships between knowledge components: a change from strong boundaries between subjects, to weak boundaries, from a collection to an integrated code. The emphasis is upon integration.

> The core and vocational studies must occupy a minimum of 75 per cent of the course time, and these two components should be co-ordinated and integrated so that students see them as a coherent whole rather than as separate subjects. (CPVE Blue Book).

But while the new industrial training curriculum threatens the insulation of the old humanist curriculum, it also introduces in practice, if not in principle, a new insulation between the curriculum types. CPVE students experience strong boundaries between their prevocational curriculum and the academic curriculum and thus between future possibilities and life chances available to them as opposed to 'A' level students.

In the area of pedagogy two proposals stand out. First, there are the concepts of negotiated learning, active learning and experiential learning and the shift in the balance of power that these suggest in the control of the curriculum. Students are to be involved in decisions about their learning. The teachers must give up some aspects of their accustomed role in the classroom. In other words there is an apparent shift in the relations of power.

> Activity-based learning also provides the basis for encouraging student self-development and increasing autonomy. To achieve this it must be based on the needs, interests and resources of the students themselves. (CPVE Blue Book).

Second, and related to the integration of subjects, is the use of team-teaching. Teachers are encouraged to collaborate with colleagues in teams to plan, teach and evaluate CPVE work. In the area of assessment, again there are a series of related proposals. There is a change from assessment by examination to forms of profiling and the use of records of achievement. This is a change from the assessment of failure, what students do not know, to the recording of success, what they do know or can do. It is also a shift of emphasis from summative to formative evaluation. And what is more, the teachers would be responsible for designing their own forms of formative assessment.

> Schools and colleges must design suitable procedures for formative assessment, and for the review of student performance. The Joint Board will not impose standard procedures for formative assessment locally. (CPVE BLUE book).

Assessment in the form of the construction of a profile is also related to student counselling. Once again there is a potential shift in the balance of power relations between student and teacher, whereby students are to be involved in forming and discussing their assessment. It is no longer something that is done to them. In this the terms of assessment are also changed, from a language of grades and marks to one of abilities, skills and attitudes. There is more of the student as person available for evaluation, so that people rather than just performances are at stake. Such changes Atkinson, Dickinson and Erben (1986) suggest, amount to weak classification and strong framing, and underline the training as opposed to educational objectives of the course. Emphasis is upon formation of the person as worker. In substance (if not status) the CPVE is not an add-on innovation, it challenges many entrenched aspects of the role and methods of the sixth-form teacher. It requires a change in style, in relationships and in planning. It is quite at odds with other pressures towards greater emphasis on single-subject expertise. How then did the teachers respond? How did they handle the changes required of them? What difficulties and problems did they face?

In the six pilot schools (three comprehensives and three sixth-form colleges) monitored in our study of the CPVE a set of clear and interrelated implementation difficulties were identified. (For more detail see Radnor, Ball and Burrell, 1986). These difficulties, or barriers to change, were either a product of mismatch between the organization and structure of the CPVE and the existing organization and structure of the school curriculum, or of the processes of change involved. The barriers are summarized briefly here under five headings drawn from the work of Gross, Giaquinta and Bernstein (1971).

Lack of Clarity

It is necessary to recognize the existence of different degrees of involvement and investment in CPVE among the teachers putatively engaged in planning and teaching it. In most cases there was a small core group knowledgeable about, and interested in the CPVE with a sizeable time commitment to it and a much larger peripheral group who had minor time commitment and concomitantly less personal investment and interest. They had a sketchy understanding of what CPVE was about or patently misunderstood it. As a result their teaching and planning often failed to live up to or basically contradicted the spirit and intentions of the CPVE.

> It's been a problem because there hasn't been much consultation with the other elements of the course. Design has tended this term to work very much just as Design. We haven't been given the opportunity to find out what's going on in English or maths or science; and I think a lot of the staff feel there should perhaps be more consultation in future. (case study 5)

Those without experience of this approach could find the vague

> framework and guidelines on shaping course activities within this framework very worrying. The freedom offered, the use of students' experiences and interest as resources, needed considerable adaptability and support . . . Preparation prior to the start of the pilot year had evidently not been sufficient for all teachers involved in teaching on the course to be clear about their own roles and contribution to the course. (case study 6)

The CPVE is complex, and its complexity is quite alien to 'O' and 'A' level teaching. The pilot year was denoted by a great deal of ad-hocery at the Joint Board and the SREB. Documents were late and sometimes contradictory. The unrest, distrust and declining morale of teachers and the virtually non-existent in-service support meant that the CPVE was seen by many as yet another irritating diversion from their main teaching responsibilities. Teachers were being left to cope, virtually unaided, with one aspect of what is perhaps the most profound change in orientation in British education since the introduction of secondary education for all.

However, two pilot institutions undertook general staff development exercises in the form of 'awareness of CPVE' sessions, others arranged course team meetings on a regular basis, but attendance was sometimes a problem for the peripheral staff. Some support for other meetings came from the regional curriculum board and local authority initiatives. But the viability of these appeared to depend heavily on the commitment of core staff. In some cases the pilot teachers became acknowledged experts in their area, although they had started out themselves as explorers without a guide.

Teachers' Lack of Skills and Knowledge

Following from the above many teachers on the periphery of the course were unclear about, or totally ignorant of, the meaning of proposed changes like integration, team-teaching, negotiated learning and profiling.

> The need for more team teaching was recognized and for timetabled opportunities for teachers to plan activities in a mutually supportive way. No slots had been allocated to this, this year a linkage between subjects had reflected more on the personalities and capacities of the individual teachers. (case study 6)
>
> *Q.* Do you do negotiated learning?
>
> *A.* No. I'm not really absolutely certain what it is and how. (case study 5)

> Negotiated learning? I mean 'negotiated' is one of those things I've not really sussed out what it actually means: you know, it's a word that's bandied around a bit. It's a nice bit of jargon. (case study 5)

Again it is important to point to the speed of the change, the lack of in-service support and the incoherence of the documents underpinning the change.

Furthermore, the need to satisfy CEE requirements and get through the syllabuses in the time allocated affected the teachers' willingness to experiment with new teaching strategies and concepts like negotiation. The dilemmas faced by the peripherally involved need to be recognized.

It is understandable that teachers with a minor teaching commitment in the CPVE should see themselves as essentially in a service role. They are not being offered either incentive or opportunity to aquaint themselves with or retrain themselves for new teaching strategies. In addition, as several respondents pointed out, the CPVE was not the only change they were confronted with. There were clearly problems of *innovation overload* in some institutions. A whole range of internally and externally-initiated changes were being struggled with. And in some cases, like the GCSE, the demands being made pulled in an exactly opposite direction from the CPVE. The GCSE is underpinned by a strongly articulated rhetoric of subject specialism and academic standards. The CPVE stresses integrated and vocational knowledge. Teachers thus experienced *innovation incoherence.* In this way the conflicts and compromises involved in policy-masking in the educational state have their consequences in the school. Many coped by diverting their constructive energies in one direction and satisfying other demands. Nonetheless, there were others who found the CPVE less alien and less daunting, especially some of the sixth-form college staff. Some had had experience which gave them a better preparation for CPVE work.

> I've worked in FE and at a technical college and therefore I have some experience of, for instance, the B/TEC and BEC type structure, which is essentially core and option module based. And within my own experience therefore I've got some past knowledge to rely on. Maybe other people might have a more difficult problem in adjusting. (case study 3)

> There is going to be a lot of resistance from the old style grammar school teacher (of which we still have many). They are going to find the attitude change a difficult one to make. Not too devastating for me because I was primary trained — and it does make a difference — and my own degree was an OU so I did 11 subjects. I'm more used to the integrated approach. (case study 4)

New and different skills and qualities are being encouraged and rewarded by courses like the CPVE. In practical career terms the hegemony of 'the academic' is challenged.

The Unavailability of Required Instructional Materials

Two main issues arise here. First, the lack of resources must be underlined again.

> CEEs have been quite traditionally taught and I don't think anything

> has happened to change that. You can't negotiate quickly without a resource-based faculty behind it. And that doesn't exist.
>
> Look we need a thousand pounds kick-off just to float CPVE. But nobody put in for any money. From the word go it wasn't funded. We had to go around the faculties begging for paper to write on. (case study 5)
>
> Obviously a number of publications are actually being made at the moment. I think a number of publishers are trying to jump on the CPVE band-wagon. There are a number of things we've actually been looking at or actually had samples sent to us, but the cost is rather prohibitive, twenty pounds for a booklet or whatever. I think somebody has got to make sure that people know that CPVE cannot be a success unless it is allocated time and money. And at the moment it isn't. (case study 3)

The paucity of funding for the CPVE meant that at times even basic teaching materials were not readily available. However, in the different institutions the level of capitation for the course differed. Simple financial calculations are clearly becoming increasingly important as constraints upon course planning and curriculum development. A commercial logic of cost-effectiveness is insinuating into or usurping educational decision-making.

Second, there is a very little in the way of commercially-published material available to support CPVE teaching and curriculum development. Understandably the speed of the change and the uncertainty of its status has meant that publishers are loath to leap into the field. Material may become available but the home grown nature of the programmes does not provide a ready made market.

The Incompatibility of Organizational Arrangements with the Innovation

Here we must acknowledge the particular demands made by the CPVE in terms of curriculum structure, timetabling and staffing, as well as more general incompatibilities in terms of institutional ethos.

> CEE has always been the last thing to timetable, and so staffing tends to be fragmentary . . . there wasn't the perception from the timetabling people to see the potential damage that that sort of fragmentation could have created. (case study 5)

For both reasons of organization and ethos several of the institutions were clearly struggling with the notion of integration. All of the factors identified previously tend to conspire against the planning and investment of time needed to achieve integration.

> Integration this year has largely been down to individual teachers working together on an ad-hoc basis. One area that has proved

successful in this regard is the 'mini-enterprize' which has drawn together aspects of craft/production/design with economic literacy/business studies/numeracy. (case study 6)

. . . when I came at the beginning of the year, I think the structure was a little bit loose, to be honest — you probably picked that up already; and it was a little bit unclear exactly how the whole thing dovetailed really — there was no blueprint. (case study 5)

I would have thought to date a minimum has been achieved when you take the whole team of teachers involved in CPVE, but if you look towards the breakdown of that team into smaller groups, its remarkable that faculties are talking together for the first time in their lives. (case study 4)

I have one period a week which means I have sixteen other periods to teach and some of those are O-level lessons, and I think proportionally, the amount of time I have devoted to CPVE this term has been more than the proportion that my timetable really demanded. Its not really possible to integrate much at all. To what extent integration takes place because the staff involved have some idea of the overall aims and objectives of the course I can't really say. (case study 6)

The picture is not one of entrenched opposition or totally insuperable obstacles, rather progress is being made against a background of difficulties. this is one grinding-edge of conflict or incompatibility between the dominant 'old humanist' tradition and the assertive 'industrial training' lobby.

In all the institutions, except one, single subject specialist teaching was the established norm. Even in the exceptional case the CPVE seems to have fared no better in becoming integrated.

. . . there was agreement that the school as a whole was finding the integration element difficult, and that this would be priority next year. It was the intention that cross-curricular assignments should be discussed between faculties on a fortnightly basis, but for a number of reasons this had not been possible. Individual timetables added to the difficulty of integration with the onus on the student to see the cohesion. (case study 4)

The problems of CEE-CPVE compatibility can also be raised here. In the six institutions combinations of CEE courses with other vocational and additional studies components were being used as the basis of the CPVE. The CEE courses tended to require and encourage both a single-subject emphasis and a concentration on the use of traditional didactic teaching methods. The teachers working in these parts of the course clearly felt that their main responsibilities lay in getting as many students as possible through the relevant CEE. This focus on the CEE was probably strengthened further by continued uncertainties about the certification status of the CPVE. The award of the Certificate, and for what, seemed to be a matter of doubt for many of the teachers involved. The constraints of the CEE syllabuses were a major contributory factor in the failure to achieve pedagogic change in these sections of the CPVE, although it was apparent that these constraints were felt more sharply in some subjects (for example, Mathematics) and were taken more seriously by some teachers. It seemed possible to achieve greater flexibility from the CEE boards if efforts were made but again contradictory messages were received by the schools. In some cases the CEEs left little room for manoeuvre, integration and pedagogic innovation were simply shoved aside by the need to get through the material. This hardly created a useful basis on which to initiate group discussions on cooperation or teaching method.

In contrast, at least one institution, a sixth-form college, had prior experience of enquiry-based and activity-based learning in its courses and this expertise could be employed in CPVE work. But even here a drift back to more traditional styles of teaching was evident as the years progressed in order to accommodate the content requirements of CEEs.

> I tried various methods but came back to exposition because I needed to get through a CEE and was frightened I wouldn't get through the course otherwise. I don't approve of it, but what can I do. (case study 1)

> The CEE course demanded a lot of written projects and assignments and the CPVE students had problems completing these projects. Although the teachers gave the students opportunities to learn through oral work often this had to be curtailed because assessment was on written work. (case study 1)

> . . . the blue book is so content bound that you haven't really got any choice but to require specialist input,the thing becomes segmented . . . The trouble with CEE is it's so academic. You know, the maths that's in it. It's way beyond the basic core aims and objectives of CPVE. (case study 5)

Clearly also there were difficulties involved for those teachers who were moving between traditionally-taught lessons and CPVE lessons and the wide range of students in the CPVE courses created further difficulties in both choice of methods and selection of materials.

> Those staff who worked on the City and Guilds 365 course during 1983/4 learned a great deal about appropriate teaching strategies as a result of that experience. Other members of staff are trying to open up their teaching but (a) find it difficult to adapt from the methods they use with A-levels groups, and (b) feel constrained by a lack of appropriate teaching materials. (case study 3)

This second comment links back to (3) above.

The use of profiles was also a problem for some teachers.

> I think it's the mechanical method of recording, it's just because it's

> alien. Normally when we write reports on the students it's a continuous piece of prose and write what we've observed. Whereas calculating whether they have gained individual skills is, I think, probably more valuable to the student but more difficult to do. (case study 3)

In some cases it also turned out that the students themselves constituted a barrier to change. They were also moving from a long experience of single subject didactic teaching into a new set of working methods and new responsibilities. They felt threatened and sometimes resentful.

> One or two have felt dissatisfied in that they are so used to having a single subject oriented curriculum that they have found that its been rather vague and they haven't quite seen a through-line on it, I think, and a couple of them have got a bit upset about that. They couldn't quite see what they were achieving or what they were heading towards, and we've had to spend time talking them through exactly what the purpose of the course is and what they are intended to achieve. (case study 4)

> There are some students who had some reservations when they first came onto the course, there's no doubt about that . . . They have actually commented on both the team teaching approach,and the integration and the difference in style of teaching, in the sense that it is primarily not chalk and talk method, it's actually getting the students involved, it's getting the students to help one another. (case study 3)

Students, like some staff needed to be convinced that the new approaches were possible and that they worked. Fear of the unknown is a powerful source of resistance. Many of the CPVE students had returned to the sixth-form primarily to repeat 'O' levels and found themselves press-ganged into the new course. As a result some left, others experienced considerable incoherence and chaos, lack of teacher interest and worries about the exchange value of the Certificate. However, many of those who held on had positive comments to make about the CPVE by the end of the year. (see Final Project Report *The Student Response*).

Lack of Staff Motivation

Our research never specifically aimed to collect data on teacher motivation. What data are available arose incidentally. The main point to make is that the core-periphery factor is a major basis of differentiating between teachers. To reiterate, many of the core staff were very enthusiastic about CPVE work. For some the course had provided a new career impetus and a change in direction. Others clearly enjoyed the new relationships involved and the break from traditional practices that the course presaged. However some, but by no means all, of the periphery teachers were clearly sceptical about the CPVE and were only reluctantly taking part, limiting their involvement to a service role. The importance of the distinction is that the lack of motivation among a few could serve to undermine the joint planning, the integration, vocationalization and team-teaching that were being attempted. If the CPVE is to be implemented realistically it requires almost unprecedented levels of teamwork. Some people were choosing to be be involved, in one school requests for involvement exceeded teaching requirements, but others were just timetabled in.

> . . . to be honest, when I first started, I saw it written in there on my timetable, I didn't have a clue . . . I always get my fourth year lessons done, my fifth year lessons planned out, so I know what I'm doing with them and then CPVE is sort of tacked on the end. (case study 5)

> Quite frankly, I find the amount of work to digest as regards CPVE a little daunting, and if given the opportunity, I'd sooner let somebody else do it, and devote my time to areas I feel perhaps more valuable. We've had a lot of things in this school this term, the TVEI work particularly, and I think that has been successful because it's got money behind it, organisation and some 'punch' to it, whereas the CPVE work has got no 'punch' to it. The literature's there, but there isn't the time, there isn't the money, there isn't the in-service training, and it's all rather half-hearted I feel. (case study 6)

This can be contrasted with the comment from case study 3.

> The entire CPVE team has devoted their entire lunch hour and their next free lesson, that is a two-hour slot, in two consecutive weeks. And that type of commitment will come across to anyone who knows anything about the teaching timetable.

The difficulties, the other barriers to change, the ad hocery, the uncertainties, and the contradictory messages which were associated with the pilot year certainly took its toll with some staff and some were very much less keen to take on the CPVE for a second year. As noted already the very nature of the CPVE makes motivation a crucial issue.

Much of the planning and implementation for the CPVE took place during the period of teachers' industrial action. Meetings were often difficult to arrange, goodwill was at a premium. Furthermore, many of the teachers involved in CPVE work recognized the contradictions involved in the continuing government attacks upon and attempts to 'discipline and punish' teachers on the one hand, and the expectation that they would take major professional responsibility for planning, developing and implementing courses like the CPVE, TVEI and GCSE. In one sense, it is within this contradiction that their freedom of manoeuvre, in accommodation and non-implementation, lay.

It should also be noted that some teachers involved held to differing degrees ideological doubt about the CPVE. They were unsure of its value to students and felt that it may have been sold to the students on unrealistic promises. More fundamentally some teachers were suspicious of the political implications of CPVE. Some suggested that it was part of a government strategy to 'babysit' potentially unemployed youngsters and massage the gross unemployment figures, others that the students were being 'softened up' for work. That the CPVE was intended to produce quiescent, compliant, uncritical workers.

> . . . there's great danger in the CPVE becoming one of the pieces of the jigsaw which is based on some political ideology which says that there are certain skills that are needed out in the economy and some of our schools aren't giving those to kids therefore schools need to take on that function and give those kids those skills so that they can go out into the economy and get a job. I'd be worried about schools trying to fulfill that function (a) because I don't think they can and (b) because I wouldn't want schools to be involved in that sort of political manoeuvring. (case study 5)

However, there was little evidence of widespread penetration of what Cohen calls the 'ideology of new vocationalism'. The basic rightness and appropriateness of changes like the CPVE was rarely questioned. Difficulties were articulated as technical or bureaucratic problems related to practice or in relation to personal preferences and dissatisfactions.

Conclusion

Despite the barriers to change some of the pilot schools produced exciting and innovative courses. The picture is not of entrenched opposition or totally insuperable obstacles, rather of change produced against a background of difficulties. Some teachers found that the CPVE provided them with a career and/or morale boost. Others found the CPVE innovations spilling over into their other teaching. But there has also been a great deal of accommodation, in certain repects the CPVE has been moulded to fit an existing modality and voice. The degree of relative autonomy still available to teachers and the 'loose-coupling' (Weick, 1976) in school organization allows considerable reinterpretation of the messages and expectations contained in the planning and setting up of the CPVE. In addition, many of the barriers to change we identified have an inherent structural basis or arise from the contradictory demands for change that schools are facing from their various audiences. Policy messages from the educational state are often confused and confusing. The barriers seem unlikely to go away although CPVE teachers may become more skilled in circumventing them. Clearly, to a great extent the political future of the CPVE lies in the conflicts and struggles between the competing examining bodies but its educational possibilities reside in the determination and commitment of a few hardy pioneers in schools. Despite continuing criticism from politicans we found a good deal of willingness to change and as noted there is little coherent critique or substantive opposition in the schools. Ideologically the place of vocational courses is well-established. The industrial training lobby is undoubtedly gaining ground against the old humanists, the educational bureaucrats are forcing the pace of policy change and in the process building a powerful new educational state infrastructure. In all this activity 'public educators' seem decidedly thin on the ground.

In simplistic and economic terms, we might be tempted to interpret the introduction of the CPVE as an unqualified victory for the industrial trainers; yet another example of the direct impact of the 'needs of corporate capitalism' upon the examination system and the school curriculum. Certainly it would be unrealistic to suggest that this shift in emphasis in the school curriculum was totally unrelated to the effects of the accumulation crisis currently being experienced by major fractions of British capital. However, Whitty (1985) argues against 'the temptation to explain developments in terms of all-embracing but uni-dimensional theories of causation' (p. 137). As the discussions of policy-formation and school practice indicate, a more complex and less neat and tidy argument which interweaves economic, political and ideological elements, is required.

The examination agencies are, of necessity, driven by their own commercial logic. Falling rolls puts pressure on these agencies as it does on schools, they are fighting to retain their market share. Clearly though, some agencies represent views of the curriculum which are more in line with current government policies than others, although as we have noted these policies are by no means of a piece. The relationship between the agencies, their relationships with the educational state, with industry, with universities and with schools are constituted by ongoing conflicts over 'what is to count as education'. The outcomes for school practice are by no means foregone or predictable. The concerns and needs of capital are clearly evidenced in the political processes of policy-formation but their influence in schools is refracted and mediated in a variety of ways. Whitty (ibid), again makes the point that:

> it seems implausible that all settlements within the ideological and political spheres are somehow equally functional for capital and that the differences between possible settlements are totally irrelevant to the capacity of the state to carry out its long-term function on behalf of capital. This depends upon the relationship of any particular settlement to the outcomes of other struggles within the apparatus of the state. (p. 144)

Clearly the pressure from 'industrial trainers' for a thorough-going vocational reform of the secondary curriculum does not go uncontested; the universities and the GCSE boards only give ground reluctantly. And indeed the current attempts at reform are only the last in a long series of skirmishes, stretching back into the nineteenth century, over the constitution of the secondary curriculum. These have thus far invariably ended in the reassertion of the 'old humanist', academic tradition. The 14 to 19 curriculum may be seen to be increasingly thoroughly penetrated by the 'industrial training' lobby and by the interests of capital, but by no means all of the political, commercial and ideological changes in this field align with the macro-economic needs of capitalism. Furthermore, those needs are often articulated in very different ways by different groups and interests.

If we look generally at the outcomes of settlements in the examination arena it may be that the overall effect is one which does tie the processes of schooling more directly into the reproduction of the social and technical relations of production by separating out a specific academic route, through the GCSE, from a specific vocational route through TVEI, the CPVE and YTS. However, as the case study materials indicate, the reality of such an outcome, indeed the degree of vocationalization entailed in courses like the CPVE, embodies a number of unwarranted assumptions about implementation. In practical terms such courses may be much less closely tied to the 'lived realities of industry' than would appear from their rhetorics.

References

Atkinson, P., Dickinson, H. and Erben, M. (1986) 'The Classification and Control of Vocational Training for Young People' in Walker, S. and Barton, L. (Eds) *Youth Unemployment and Schooling*, Milton Keynes, Open University Press.

Bernstein, B. (1971) 'On the Classification and Framing of Educational Knowledge' in Young, M. F. D. (Ed) *Knowledge and Control*, London, Collier-Macmillan.

Bernstein, B. (1982) 'Codes, Modalities and the Process of Cultural Production: a model' in Apple, M. (Ed) *Cultural and Economic Reproduction in Education*, London, Routledge & Kegan Paul.

Edwards, A. D. (1983) 'An elite tranformed: Continuity and change in 16–19 policy' in Ahier, J. and Flude, M. (Eds) *Contemporary Education Policy*, Beckenham, Croom Helm.

Further Education Unit (1979) *A Basis for Choice*, London, FEU.

Further Education Unit (1981) *ABC in Action*, London, FEU.

Further Education Unit (1982) *Progressing from Vocational Preparation*, London, FEU.

Gross, N., Giaquinta, J. A. and Bernstein, M. (1971) *Implementing Organisational Innovation*, New York, Harper & Row.

Radnor, H., Ball, S. J. and Burrell, D. (1986) *Final Report of the CPVE Research Study*, SREB, University of Sussex.

Russell, T. J. (1981) *Curriculum Control*, London, FEU.

Salter, B. and Tapper, T. (1981) *Education, Politics and the State*, London, Grant McIntyre.

Weick, K. (1976) 'Educational organisations as loosely coupled systems', *Administrative Science Quarterly*, 21, pp 1–9.

Whitty, G. (1985) *Sociology and School Knowledge*: Curriculum Theory, Research and Policy: London, Methuen.

Williams, R. (1961) *The Long Revolution*, Harmondsworth, Penguin.

Chapter 6

The Lower Attaining Pupils Programme: Myths and Messages

Penelope Weston and John Harland

The Lower Attaining Pupils Programme (LAPP) was launched by the Secretary of State for Education and Science, Sir Keith Joseph, in July 1982, with the aim of providing a more effective education with a practical slant for those pupils in the fourth and fifth year for whom existing examinations were not designed. All English LEAs were invited to submit bids for inclusion in a programme of pilot curriculum development projects. Over sixty LEAs responded and thirteen were chosen. Of these, nine began work with pupils in 1983/84; four preferred to use 1983/84 as a preparatory year. In 1985/86 a further four LEAs joined the Programme. Two of the original projects formed part of the EC's initiative on the transition from school to adult life.

LAPP can be viewed as the first major national curriculum project to be managed directly by the DES. Predating the legislation enabling the government to sponsor initiatives through Education Support Grants, LAPP was funded to the tune of £2m per annum from the Urban Aid Programme, which falls under the remit of the Department of the Environment. This source provided up to 75 per cent of the funds for each project (with contributions from the EC for two projects), leaving the LEA to find the remainder. Across the initial thirteen projects there have been wide differences in the funds requested and received, ranging from £70,000 for one LEA to over £500,000 for another (1984/85 figures).

Such diversity is a salient feature of the Programme. For instance, unlike TVEI, none of the projects adopted the title 'LAPP'. Instead, a variety of less pejorative titles were coined to denote each local project (for example, 'New Learning Initiative', 'Alternative Curriculum Strategies', or just 'DES Project'). Similarly, the Programme includes many different approaches to the definition, identification and selection of pupils for the projects. Examples of targeting the project through setting, banding, option systems, discrete groups, or across the ability range can all be found within the Programme, sometimes in combination within one school. The variety extends to the curriculum developments undertaken for the projects. Collectively, projects demonstrate a broad array of such current initiatives as profiling, records of achievement, modular courses, experiential learning, oracy, residential and other off-site experiences, problem-solving, Instrumental Enrichment, base tutor systems and so on. Individual LEAs and schools vary enormously in the way they have selected or emphasized such developments. There is diversity, too, in the organization and scale of projects: some have accentuated the role of an LEA central team, while others have focussed on school-based 'bottom-up' development; one LEA selected a single school, another involved them all.

Finally, several forms of evaluation are evident in the Programme. In addition to the local evaluation that was required, some projects have encouraged teachers to conduct their own evaluation and review. HMI have published a report (DES, 1986a), based on their own survey of the projects, and EC rapporteurs have been working in the two EC-linked initiatives. In 1984 the National Foundation for Educational Research (NFER) was contracted to undertake the national evaluation of the Programme.

During the course of this evaluation we have tried to come to terms with broader questions of purpose and policy, while carrying out enquiries which were primarily concerned with practical problems of curriculum change in school and classroom. From the outset, anxieties have been expressed about the purpose behind a government-funded programme aimed primarily at one segment of the secondary school population — that is, pupils for whom existing examinations were not designed. What were the implications of fixing on such a group, who were they, and just what curricular priorities were envisaged for them?

Newspaper headlines announcing the initiative had little difficulty in identifying the group: this was a programme for 'the bottom 40 per cent'. This expression did not in fact appear in the text of Sir Keith Joseph's speech (DES, 1982a), but it could be derived by inference from his reference to existing examinations, and it touched on decisions that were being made during 1982 about the proposed GCSE. The Waddell Committee (1978) had assumed that the new 16+ exam would be designed for the top 60 per cent of the ability range (based on the intended populations for GCE and CSE) and this assumption fed forwards into initial planning for the GCSE, although it was to be challenged as preparations for the launch approached. So in 1982 an obvious question for the Secretary of State, faced with pressure to act on the 16+ issue, concerned the fate of the other 40 per cent. What new deal could be offered to them?

While the educational world was about ripe for another of its periodic attempts to 'do something' about disaffected school leavers (ten years on from ROSLA, twenty from the Newsom Committee), the educational climate, as well as the economic, social and political climate, had changed markedly since those days. Educational thinking about the nature of achievement and effective learning strategies had moved on, too, as several major reports had made clear. Hargreaves (ILEA 1984) had broadened the concept of legitimate educational achievement; the Bullock Report (DES, 1975) had emphasized the significance of language for the learning process in all subjects; and the Cockcroft Report

(DES, 1982b) had given weight to the application of 'practicality' and 'relevance' — ideas which had gathered momentum through the years of the great debate. Bearing these developments in mind, it is possible to present LAPP as a positive initiative by the government to provide material support and encouragement for reformers at all levels of the system who were anxious to devise purposeful and much-needed solutions for a longstanding and urgent educational problem: the failure of the system to provide much experience of success for large numbers of the school population, particularly in their last years of schooling.

Not everyone saw it like this. In his paper on tertiary tripartism, Stewart Ranson (1984) argued that circumstances were enabling the government to realize their plan to rationalize and stratify the system. Once changes had been made to the 16–19 area, it was suggested, it would be easier to move in on the compulsory sector. The case was put by a 'senior official':

> If we can achieve things with the new 17+ examination, that will give us an important lever to vocationalize or re-vocationalize the last years of public schooling. That will be a very important and significant step indeed.

For Ranson and others (for example Simon, 1985; and Reid and Holt, 1986) LAPP could be be construed as an example of what they they were concerned about. Was it not a centrally-directed programme, with a strongly 'vocational' flavour, for one segment or 'stratum' of the school population? Such an initiative, it was suggested, accentuates and legitimates existing divisions (by providing 'more appropriate' curricula for these pupils), thus making it defensible to maintain the established, subject-based curriculum for the mainstream 60 per cent.

How, then, should the initiative be interpreted? As part of a concerted move towards centralism, stratification and vocationalism? Or as a form of positive discrimination from the centre in favour of those teachers and planners who were trying to challenge accepted definitions of what is counted as valid and valued educational achievement, and to enable more pupils to experience success? In practice such stark polarizations are likely to be misleading, because there is seldom a 'simple', monolithic view from the centre. Indeed, the participants in the process, in Whitehall, town hall and school are all subject to a variety of pressures and principles which influence the way they interpret the messages of policy makers. In addition to local priorities, underlying educational assumptions play their part in this process. It could be argued, for example, that there is a degree of ambivalence at every level of the system over what should be done about the secondary curriculum. The ideas which have shaped it (for example about the nature of subjects and the importance of public examinations) have also shaped the experience of today's teachers, and indeed of most senior figures in education, who have all experienced success within this system. An equally potent ambivalence — this time about the value of vocationally-oriented courses — has permeated repeated attempts to offer more relevent learning experiences to the upper secondary school population. Launching a centrally-devised innovation into this kind of environment is always likely to be a risky business with uncertain outcomes, even if the purpose is clear and widely agreed, and the objectives well-defined. Far more complex interactions can be expected when the initiative itself is experimental in character — as LAPP undoubtedly was.

It is this last point which provides the impetus for this chapter. We feel that, rather than starting by trying to tie down LAPP with a label, it is more interesting and illuminating to examine the agenda provided by the government and see how this has been treated in practice. In our experience over the last three years the Programme has provided a good opportunity to observe policy in formation, in the interactions between the participants at all levels. In this initiative the process has been more than usually open to view, as LEAs and schools have continued to test definitions of what the Programme implied, and how much scope there was for local initiative in developing a particular version of it.

So what messages were being given about LAPP by its initiators, how have these been interpreted, and how has the process been managed? To address these questions we shall look more closely at two concepts which have assumed growing importance as the Programme, and government's broader educational policy, have developed: differentiation and 'the practical slant'. We shall then consider briefly the nature of the relationship between the 'partners' in LAPP, and what we can learn from this about the role of central government in curriculum development initiatives.

Hearing the Messages: Differentiation

Differentiation has become a loaded word in the last few years, acquiring layers of meaning formerly carried by several separate and well-established terms associated with longstanding debates about the nature of the common school and its curriculum. While the word itself was not used in the initial statements about the Lower Attaining Pupils Programme, the whole initiative reflected a concern about schools' relative failure to adapt their curriculum to the needs of all pupils. It is therefore crucial to our understanding of the programme to clarify how the various participants have in practice interpreted the concept of differentiation, which more recently has been directly associated with LAPP in *Better Schools*:

> there should be careful differentiation: what is taught and how it is taught need to be matched to pupils' abilities and aptitudes. It is of the greatest importance to stimulate and challenge all pupils, including the most and least able: within teaching groups as well as schools the range of ability is often wide . . . Such differences need to be reflected in classroom practice. The government is supporting development work to promote this principle through the Lower Attaining Pupils' Programme which investigates how differentiation is best developed

> and applied across the curriculum for pupils within the chosen target group. It is thus closely concerned with teaching approaches. (DES, 1985, paragraph 45)

This statement leaves a number of questions about differentiation unanswered; for example there is no indication of the extent or nature of the differences in content ('what is taught') or process ('how it is taught') that might be appropriate for different pupils (or groups of pupils), nor of who would make these decisions. But it is perhaps worth noting, first, that the definition refers twice to differences *between pupils* within groups, as well as between groups or schools, implying that the 'matching' needs to be carried out at this individual level; secondly, differentiation is explicity related to 'teaching approaches'.

To other commentators, however, such distinctions are mere hair-splitting. Brian Simon (1986) is unequivocal in his interpretation:

> Differentiation implies the imposition of different curricula for different groups of pupils — or it means nothing.

This definition accords with what others have called segmentation of the system; a useful term in that it implies chopping it into chunks which are clearly distinct from each other (Ringer, 1979). Some would go further, seeing differentiation as a code word for the reintroduction of selection. Indeed, the term is currently being stretched in a number of directions within education, and has been the subject of lengthy debate in relation to the GCSE. In the present context, however, it is important to begin by pinning down the definitions which have been offered by those associated with the central management of the programme, as well as considering how it has been interpreted within the LEAs. In looking at these definitions there are two key issues to consider. First, how did those responsible for LAPP define the 'target group'? Did the definition offered convey the idea of a separable group of pupils for whom a distinctive curriculum should be provided? Second, what evidence is there, in government-backed statements about LAPP, of the interpretation of differentiation (hinted at in the statement from *Better Schools*) which concerned *individuals'* learning needs (rather than with curricula for groups, or horses for courses)?

We would want to suggest that from the outset there have been moves to challenge assumptions and broaden definitions on both these issues, and that this questioning can be seen in guidelines emanating from central policy makers as well as in some LEA proposals. At the same time, ideology and pragmatic considerations have tended to reinforce, at all levels, the stereotype which the initiative's title suggest, of special courses for an identifiable group.

The only public guidance for project planners came from Sir Keith Joseph's speech to the Council of Local Education Authorities (CLEA) in July 1982 (DES, 1982a) and the letter to LEAs which was based on this. Nothing was said in these documents about whether or not the group were to be segregated from their peers, although the importance of planning their curriculum 'as a whole' was stressed. On the other hand it was emphasized that 'all pupils should be able to take their full part in the general life of their school, and all pupils should have access to the general range of opportunities to learn', which left many questions open. Nor were definitions of the target group at all clear cut, and intentionally so:

> I do not want to make too rigid a distinction between groups of pupils: any definition is bound to be arbitrary . . . It is no part of my intention to suggest that we should be seeking to draw sharp boundaries within secondary education between those young people who are the most successful in conventional academic terms and those who are the least successful in those same terms. (paragraph 4)

The group for whom 'we have still not got the mixture right' were defined as 'those pupils who are usually described as lower attainers: broadly the group for whom existing public examinations at 16+ are not designed'.

Perhaps partly because some LEAs and schools defined the group narrowly (both in terms of the criteria used and the numbers of pupils included), the Inspectorate was asked by the Secretary of State to address the conference of project directors in May 1984. In suggesting how the target group might be defined, the HMI lecture stated:

> A major problem is that the term '40 per cent' can suggest *ceilings* of achievement and so *limit* expectations of both teachers and pupils themselves. Furthermore, the reasons for pupils' lower than average performance can vary considerably and overlap with one another.

The target group could therefore include not only

1 those of below average ability, but also . . .
2 those whose low attainments are not necessarily due to low ability or particular learning difficulties, and . . .
3 those other pupils whose low attainments might be improved by access to more effective styles of teaching and learning (DES, 1984)

In intention, at least, then, government thinking about the nature of the target group, informed by HMI reflections, was less closed and unidimensional (that is, dependent only on 'ability') than appearances might suggest. However, the root question posed by the Programme's critics still remains: was it being suggested that the solution to these difficulties required the separation of groups of pupils with these characteristics from their peers, in order to give them a distinctive and 'appropiate' curriculum, as Brian Simon's definition of differentiation implies?

Evidence from early public statements and from the kind of projects which were selected for funding suggests that the question was left open; separating out a target group for a distinctive curriculum experience was one of many approaches that could be, and has been, tried. More recent statements by HMI in their own interim report on the programme (DES, 1986a) maintain an open mind about the value of this and other approaches to curriculum organization:

> . . . there was little evidence to suggest that any one form of pastoral or curricular organisation was in itself necessarily more effective than any other in achieving the aims of the programme. (paragraph 129)

It seems that at the outset questions about pupil selection and curriculum organization were left open to experiment for sound pragmatic reasons: in the light of inconclusive evidence from research and from previous HMI investigations about how the work of 'less successful' pupils should be organized, there was much to be gained from encouraging as wide a variety of approaches as possible to curricular organization among the projects selected for funding.

Since the criteria for LEA selection were not made public it is difficult to tell how far such a policy was deliberately followed through during the selection process, but in practice the Programme certainly includes projects with widely differing curricular structures for their 'project' pupils. There are some schools which selected one or more discrete groups of project pupils provided them with their own 'base room' and a team of teachers, and encouraged the team to develop an appropriate curriculum to meet their needs, unconstrained by the demands of the rest of the age group (echoes of the 'freedom' from examinations which the early secondary modern schools were encouraged to enjoy). While acknowledging the risks of 'sink group' labelling, some project teachers would defend this approach as appropriate for a pilot project working for radical change in difficult circumstances. The great majority of schools, however, have devised some kind of compromise in the curriculum structure: project pupils follow project activities or a project course (such as City and Guilds 365) for up to half their week; or a wider range of pupils can choose a variable number of project options through the existing system. Alternatively, project work may be undertaken in certain teachers' classes, with no structural change to the curriculum. Pupils may or may not be aware that they are involved in a project. There are many variants and some school planners have shown considerable ingenuity in circumventing or adapting their own structures to meet pupils' needs. Moreover, priorities have changed over time. In some projects interest has shifted from structure to strategies — towards incorporating ideas developed for project pupils within a much wider range of teaching groups. In many instances decisions about structure are increasingly tied up with school and LEA policy on 16+ accreditation, a point to which we will return in the last section.

Whatever decision schools reached about the curriculum structure for their project, it has become increasingly clear that there were further expectations about how the learning needs of individual pupils should be diagnosed and provided for. Since its emergence in *Better Schools* as one of the four marks of the acceptable curriculum (broad, balanced, relevant and differentiated), differentiation has been a key issue to consider in evaluating the success of LAPP. In their own writing, the Inspectorate have equated differentiation with proper provision for *individual* learning. In this sense, as Jim Campbell has noted in his contribution on the primary sector, it corresponds closely with the established idea of 'matching' learning to the needs of the pupil. In their survey of the programme (DES, 1986a), HMI were concerned that:

> many schools had not carried out a sufficiently detailed and systematic analysis of individual pupils' characteristics and educational needs . . . Where pupils tended to be regarded as a homogeneous group there was insufficient differentiation to take account of differences in needs and attainment. (paragraph 16)

In the paragraph specifically relating to differentiation the point was re-emphasized:

> individual pupils' needs were not identified in detail or regularly reviewed in most schools. Curriculum development was therefore aimed at groups: programmes devised for individual pupils and consequent differentiation of work had not materialized. (paragraph 28)

There are clear messages here not only about the apparent shortcomings of the projects — on which we would reserve judgment at this stage — but about the nature of the problem they should be addressing. In the view of the Inspectorate, success in raising attainment required close attention to this kind of individual-level differentiation. So perhaps practitioners should stop seeing differentiation as a loaded 'codeword', and reinterpret it as a label for one form of good practice. From this point of view, the aim of differentiation would be to take full account of differences between learners *within* a group — differences of motivation, previous experience, as well as more specific (or general) abilities — in planning and reviewing what is learned. Certainly this would be an interpretation which many project teachers would readily support. It was also endorsed during 1986 in a ministerial statement (DES, 1986b):

> All good teachers accept the need to identify and meet pupils' individual needs — they know that pupils learn in different ways and at different speeds, and will reach different levels of attainment. Differentiation is an essential element of good professional practice. Differentiation requires us to match what is taught and how it is taught to pupils' abilities and aptitudes, because that approach is most likely to help all pupils to develop those abilities and aptitudes to their full potential. (paragraph 14)

The writer acknowledged that the concept had not always been interpreted in this way, but doubts and fears about differentiation as a form of discrimination against certain groups of pupils were seen as outmoded:

> It raises moral scruples among those who (looking backwards rather than forwards) see differentiation as a threat to less able pupils. (paragraph 13)

So differentiation should be seen, it was argued, not as an 'immoral principle but a highly moral one' because it 'seeks to do justice to each pupil'. As in *Better Schools*, the Lower Attaining Pupils Programme was instanced as having lessons to teach on differentiation, in terms of meeting pupils' needs. However, it is important to note that the discussion about individuals' needs was explicity linked to, and presented as inseparable from, considerations about curriculum organization and pupil grouping ('with some regard to their abilitiies and aptitudes, whether by setting or banding or in other ways'). Statements of this kind were likely to reinforce the concerns of some and the convictions of others that differentiation does and should imply different curricula for different groups of pupils:

> What differentiation should mean . . . is *not* an attenuated version of the programmes of the ablest in each subject, but with the hardest bits left out. It should mean a set of curricula designed to meet *their* needs, challenge and stretch them but enable them to feel a genuine sense of success at the end of their compulsory schooling and have the confidence as well as the knowledge to continue to learn, and enjoy learning — formally and informally, full or part-time — throughout their adult life. (paragraph 15)

This restatement of the government's interpretation of differentiation presented the two strands we have been considering — segmented curricula for 'target groups' and the diagnostic approach to learning — as complementary rather than alternative strategies. Experience with LAPP suggests that up to now Inspectorate comments have emphasized the importance of the diagnostic approach while reserving judgment on the effect of differing forms of curriculum organisation. Explicit support for more discrete forms of pupil grouping and distinctive curricula has been most evident in the decisions made by some LAPP LEAs and schools. Of course, continued government funding for such projects could be seen by some as a kind of endorsement of the 'segmented' approach. But if official statements were restrained, other opinion shapers were less reticent; John Clare's case for a 'third stream' with 'a more practical and vocationally oriented curriculum' was clearly spelled out in a *Panorama* programme and in print (Clare, 1986). In any case, although they might listen to messages from the centre, practitioners who favoured discrete groups could equally well have been acting mainly in response to local pressures on the school, as rolls fell and the demand for examination performance rose. In difficult times, organizationally simple solutions have their attractions. An initiative such as LAPP, simply by focussing on a subset of the age group, may in practice tend to accentuate the tendencies schools already have, faced with the 16+ accreditation barrier, to provide different curricula for different groups of pupils.

Hearing the Messages: The 'Practical Slant'

Some of the same issues and problems of interpretation arise in connection with the other key LAPP principle we want to examine; that the education offered to project pupils should have a 'practical slant'. Was this to be understood as merely a re-presentation of ROSLA rationale with a neo-vocational twist, or as shorthand for a more fundamental shift to a less didactic pedagogy and a greater involvement of pupils in the management of their own learning?

Back to Sir Keith Joseph's 1982 speech. His concern for 'a practical slant' could be fairly easily dismissed as precisely what the 'neo-vocational' agenda would require — for example in maths, where the Cockcroft Report (DES, 1982b) was applauded for providing a foundation list of topics 'designed especially for lower-attaining pupils and based on the practical needs of adult and working life'. But something a little more open-ended was suggested in the next paragraph: 'there is a strong case for giving a practical slant to much of the teaching for all pupils as they approach school-leaving age (and before then too)'. This theme was taken further in the early HMI paper:

> Overall, 'practical' means applicable to real situations, capable of being put into practice; it goes beyond business and industry (important as they are for all pupils to understand) to all aspects of life, including moral, imaginative and interpersonal aspects . . . It can be applied to learning which helps pupils to make sense of their own feelings or of the variety of experiences they meet in their personal lives . . . More practical, less theoretical teaching and learning approaches can, and should, be developed in most if not all courses — for example problem solving in science, practical design in CDT or the use of cameras, tape recorders and the local environment in English, history, art etc . . . The contrast between the 'practical' and the 'academic' can be seriously misleading. It is not necessarily the present curriculum but the form in which it is delivered which lacks interest, relevance and a direct impact on pupils' lives. (DES, 1984)

This gloss on the guidelines, representing HMI commentary rather than DES statement, picked up and expanded ideas introduced in the speech which relate to different areas of the school curriculum, and only indirectly to the 'world of work'. The stress in both documents was on how to enable pupils to learn, to 'achieve', in a variety of contexts and modes. Interestingly, such tension as has arisen between the centre — represented by the HMI — and some project staff has centred on Inspectorate concern that insufficient attention was being given to 'academic attainment' — that is, improved performance as an outcome of new approaches in the broad areas of English, maths and science. The Inspectorate also considered that there was insufficient emphasis in some projects on aesthetic experience. So while projects have undoubtedly been encouraged to experiment with out-of-school learning experiences of various kinds, some of which have a work-related emphasis, concern and comment from the centre has increasingly focussed on the character of the learning process and teaching approaches adopted for project pupils.

Of course, there were pointers and messages in Sir Keith's speech for those who had concluded that a vocationally-driven curriculum was what the programme was all about. Indeed, one of the selected projects chose as its title 'Prevocational and Technical' project (PVT), and schools in a number of LEAs have adopted the 'prevocational' framework of the City and Guilds courses and certification schemes for their projects. The determination to give 'their' pupils a fair chance in a harsh world has led a number of project leaders to record with some satisfaction the jobs won by ex-project pupils. By contrast, in other projects such vocational activities and emphases are incidental to the central purpose which may be to develop oracy within the 'mainstream' curriculum as well as in contacts with adults outside school; or to transform approaches to learning through changes in assessment. Or the project may be used as a lever for wider changes within the school or the LEA, particularly where it has the informed support of the senior management.

There is no doubt that it is *hard* to translate HMI-speak about 'the practical' into a reality that will enable pupils who, for whatever reason, have become accustomed to expecting relative failure in school to achieve success which they and others will recognize as valid in their own and the school's terms. From the evidence coming in from interviews with teachers and pupils, and from a survey of project teachers' views, this has begun to happen in a variety of contexts. On the other hand, longstanding conventions about the kind of course which is appropriate for Newsom/ROSLA/LAPP pupils may carry more weight in shaping teachers' understanding of the 'practical slant', especially when these conventions can be readily reworked to fit what are seen to be current priorities about fitting pupils for the world of work (or unemployment). It seems likely that long-term change in learning/teaching approaches will only happen where the lessons learned through the project are applied further down the school as well as across the age group, so that strategies for successful learning become the concern and property of the whole school community, rather than quick-fire remedies for the last two years of failure. Only a clear indication from the decision-makers at all levels that change of this order is needed in order to address the learning problems the Programme was explicitly set up to tackle, and sufficient resources, support and encouragement from school management and the LEA team, will be likely to persuade teachers that the risk and effort are worthwhile.

Managing LAPP: The Issue of Central Control

Ambivalence about educational reforms that seek to challenge the prevailing assumptions about secondary education can be identified in recent years at all levels of the system. Perhaps this is part of the reason why successive governments have felt the need to obtain a tighter grip from the centre on the schooling system and in particular on the management of the curriculum. But it would be naive to assume that 'centralism' of this sort implies or is based on a single DES view, or to fail to take account of the effect of short-term shifts in political priorities. And the implementation of such a policy is, of course, far from simple. Much has been made of the declining influence of the LEAs in a period of financial restraint. But Shipman (1985) has pointed out that, as well as demonstrating considerable sophistication in the way they have *responded* to national pressures and intervention, a number of LEAs have themselves *initiated* curriculum change, in some cases on an extensive and long-term scale. It has also been suggested that one of the reasons that the LEAs in the end did not fight against the decision to close the Schools Council was that they had 'come of age' in the curriculum development business, and had come to feel that the process should in most cases be managed locally (Briault, 1985). Shipman stresses the tensions that exist *within* LEAs, as well as between them and central government, and clearly LEAs differ markedly in their ability to seize the initative even in responding to (or anticipating) DES overtures. But it seems important to recognize the complexity of the relationship between local and central government and the diverse interests that shape policy-making within the LEA. The relationships between schools and the LEA, and indeed between schools and the national government, also raise important questions about the management and control of policy.

It should have become clear that a fair degree of diversity has been permitted or encouraged within LAPP. This suggests a light, rather than a heavy, hand at the centre. Whether or not by deliberate design, the central management of the programme over the last three years has for the most part been characterized by a distinctly low profile approach. Indeed, in the view of some of the participants within the LEAs more clearly defined central direction and goal setting at the outset would have strengthened the impact of the Programme and simplified the task of local authorities. On the other hand there were some advantages in avoiding the limelight and the consequent pressure to conform to a set of media expectations. The contrast with the development of TVEI, which took place over the same period, is marked. This may have something to do with the differing styles and traditions of the DES and the MSC, as suggested by Dale and his colleagues (chapter 4), as well as to obvious discrepancies in the scale of funding and important, if more elusive, differences of clientele for the two initiatives. For those who are interested in the *process* of centralization — the series of moves made by central government to shift the balance of power within the 'partnership' — the history of LAPP provides an intriguing case study: an early prototype of the now familiar central curriculum initiative.

Pointers to a centralizing tendency were freshly to hand when LAPP was launched — particularly Sir Keith Joseph's decision to close the Schools Council (April 1982). But at that time — before the Secondary Examinations Council, TVEI and ESGs — expectations were rather different, as Sir Keith's speech to CLEA in July 1982 suggests. In terms of intentions there is no doubt that LAPP was put forward as an important central initiative, not least in financial terms; in announcing the government contribution of some £2m a year he remarked:

> By the standards of the past, this is a large financial contribution towards development in a single aspect of the work of schools and LEAs. (DES, 1982a)

It was also clear that the then relatively unfamiliar process of inviting LEA bids left selection of projects and therefore ultimate control with the DES. But in addition to the usual emphasis on partnership, the tone and content of the speech left much of the definition of projects to the LEAs and even to schools — not only about how the task should be tackled but how much of the financial cake to bid for. The message coming through the speech points to the government exercising what it saw as its legitimate leadership role by setting a priority and providing resources and some guidelines — the rest was up to its 'partners'. In other words while this was explicitly a central *initiative*, only a very limited framework of central *control* or direction was implied.

Three aspects of the task illustrate this argument. First, the allocation and management of funding. From the perspective of 1986, the financial contribution no longer looks very large, although over sixty LEAs considered it worth bidding for. How 'significant' has the central funding proved? One of the many factors that makes this difficult to evaluate is that, because of the way the LEA bids were set up, the scale of funding requested by each varied widely. There was only an overall ceiling for the programme — none for individual projects (this policy has changed for the four LEAs which joined the Programme in 1985/86). Two projects are part-funded by the EC under the Transition Initiative. So in financial terms, central funding was much more 'significant' in some projects than others. As with ESG schemes,LEAs were expected to contribute directly 25 per cent of the costs, but some LEAs emphasize that their direct contribution has been much larger than this, indeed larger than the amount they have received from the LAPP funds. Recent studies the NFER team have undertaken into the resourcing of projects have given some indication of the extent to which projects have also relied on existing resources within the LEA and school — what one project leader has called the 'silent costs' of the initiative. As important for LEAs as the scale of the central funding has been the way in which it has been administered. The fact that the money comes from the Urban Aid programme has created additional complexities for the DES and for LEAs, in the management and timing of the contributions. For whatever combination of reasons, much of the ongoing responsibility for the management and control of funding, within the framework agreed with the DES, has been devolved to the LEAs. The contrast with standard MSC procedures which have been applied to TVEI shows up clearly for project leaders who, in everyday terms, may have little to remind them of the fact of central funding.

Secondly, administrative control. The programme is managed by a very small team of administrators within the DES, all of whom have other responsibilities, and may be moved to other work during the lifetime of the programme in accordance with normal civil service practice. One of the interesting aspects of DES/LEA relationships within LAPP is that despite these constraints, the DES team have got to know project leaders and local evaluators quite well over this period, and have felt it important to make a number of visits to project schools to 'see for themselves'. There has thus been an important opportunity to learn at first hand, and sometimes fairly directly, about the frustrations of this kind of curriculum development, as well as its more positive aspects. But, given the constraints on time and manpower, such contacts and strategic discussions about LAPP have to be fitted in with the ordinary requirements of administration and the process of negotiating agreements about various aspects of the programme among the 'partners' of the education system. From the LEA side, frustrations and difficulties have arisen mostly from the *differing timescales* of central funding and local budgetting and policy making. An image which often crops up is of LEA (or school) as a super tanker which takes a long time to turn round, whereas central funding deals in short-run initiatives. Political and administrative constraints at the centre have meant that decisions may come too late for local staffing and budgetting schedules, and only LEAs which already have well-established policy making structures are in a position to take full advantage of the extra fillip which centrally funded initiatives of this kind can provide.

Thirdly, the 'steering' of the initiative. As we have seen, there is very little evidence, in intention or practice, that the then Secretary of State or the DES wanted to run a 'top-down' initiative. This was just as well, since it is difficult to see how it could have been done from within the existing resources. It was hardly the job of the administrative team. Professional advice about the progress of LAPP is provided by HMI, both in the Programme's steering group and through the reports and feedback from the monitoring programme carried out since 1984 by a small national team supported by locally based HMI. But it is important to emphasize that, in keeping with their normal practice, the role of the HMI, including those based in Elizabeth House, is advisory: they are not involved in directing or managing LAPP in any way, and do not constitute some kind of curriculum development group for the initiative. While the influence of Inspectorate advice and suggestion, on local steering committees, at post-inspection feedback sessions and in speeches and the published report should not be underestimated, it is primarily reponsive. Care is taken to emphasize the distinctive role of the Inspectorate, and to distinguish it from that of the administrative team. At the local level, too, established understandings and conventions are carefully maintained: as one senior HMI put it, any attempt to 'direct' the project would be bitterly resented. In summary, there are messages around for project leaders who wish to hear them, and no shortage of advice for those who seek it; in some cases where there is a difference of view with the Department communication will be more direct. But messages, as we have seen, may themelves be ambivalent, and can undergo a subtle process of change between central and local agents.

In practice there has therefore been considerable scope for LEAs to develop projects as they thought best, and to use their initiative in relating LAPP to other current projects or policies within the authority, though progress in this respect has varied widely. What is much more difficult to assess is the degree of indirect control that central government is able to exercise simply from its agenda-setting position as a curriculum development funder. In this instance, we suggest, the significance of that kind of influence has only emerged slowly as the various voices at the centre have begun to indicate, largely by defining what is not considered appropriate, the limits of experimentation. Nevertheless, the launching of the initiative in itself played its part in providing some new terms of reference for the developing debate about the 14–16 curriculum in the comprehensive school.

Setting LAPP in Context

We started by posing questions about the purposes behind the launch of LAPP and suggesting that the initiative was particularly susceptible to redefinition at the local level as the projects developed. We have suggested that a degree of consensus at the centre about the Programme's priorities emerged only slowly, and that ambivalence at all levels about such key concepts as differentiation and practicality meant that widely divergent interpretations continued to coexist within the Programme. Such divergence could be seen as an appropriate response to the spirit of experimentation in which the pilot projects had been launched. But was there after all an underlying message from the centre which the Programme was intended to convey? And, if so, how effectively could it be delivered, given the limited scale and scope of the central executive for LAPP at the DES?

In trying to reach an answer to the initial questions about the aims behind LAPP it is important to recognize that the context itself changes over time. While Sir Keith Joseph apparently had a very real concern to improve the lot of the 'target group', and this shaped his original ideas about LAPP, he might have seen the task rather differently if he had been launching it three years later. For instance while the need to provide opportunities for success to those whom the system had failed remained as urgent as ever, changes in the definition of the potential GCSE population (which Sir Keith had supported) meant that the exam-related bottom 40 per cent label for the 'target group' was already obsolete. Other developments were helping to change the context for LAPP. Apart from the festering sores of the teachers' dispute there were plenty of positive moves from the centre for LEAs to react to: the burgeoning of other centrally initiated 14–16 projects, particularly the GCSE and TVEI, rapid shifts in 16–19 schemes and — of crucial importance in this context — a potential realignment on 16+ accreditation foreshadowed in the draft report of the Johnson Committee (DES, 1986c).

Any one LEA or school taking part in the Programme would have to take account of all these influences in formulating and developing their LAPP project. Indeed the references to LAPP in such a key document as *Better Schools* located the initiative firmly within overall policy for secondary education. While for much of the time the signals from LAPP headquarters (if indeed that is an appropriate metaphor) might be relatively weak by the time they reached the school, they could be reinforced or reinterpreted when taken in conjuction with messages about other developments. It would be difficult, for example, for schools to have remained unaware of the growing emphasis, received through various channels, on the 'can do' approach to learning and assessment and the pressure for careful specification of assessment criteria, both of which have also been stressed within LAPP statements. More fundamentally, it has become increasingly clear that all schools now have to learn how to accommodate centrally issued directives on curriculum and assesssment.

While it probably remains true that the Programme has allowed LEAs more than usual scope to develop their projects in line with local priorities, pressures and constraints, it would be naive not to recognize the amount of central influence that could be exercised indirectly on projects through these various routes. It is particularly important to acknowledge the importance of one powerful assumption which many would consider inherent in LAPP and which in many projects has not really been challenged: that there is some underlying continuum of ability or attainment upon which pupils can be placed. This idea makes it meaningful to distinguish pupils with 'lower' and 'higher' levels of attainment. While there might still be debate about the appropriate cut-off point for the 'target group' in a given context, as long as this assumption holds, the 'bottom 40 per cent' remains an intelligible concept. Some heads have even presented the case for a 'whole school' approach for their project within this conceptual framework, arguing that their entire school population falls within a nationally-defined bottom 40 per cent.

The significance of LAPP in underwriting this kind of thinking has particular relevance for the reshaping of 16+ accreditation structures that may now be imminent. Is the GCSE really for all? How many teachers are deciding that it is too difficult for their least able/bottom 40 per cent/LAPP pupils, and opting for some other form of accreditation? There is no shortage of alternative offerings, from national bodies such as CGLI/BTEC and RSA, from regional consortia linked to examining groups and from the LEAs. While these schemes can be in practice be combined in various ways with the GCSE, it is also possible for them to be viewed as a package deal, an appropriate alternative framework for a certain 'target group' within the school. As the examination bodies and accrediting agencies jockey for position and bid for custom, in the way in which Ball and his colleagues describe in their account of the CPVE (chapter 5), it is to be hoped that decision makers in every sector of education are aware of the possible outcomes. Recent educational history in the UK suggests that segmented accreditation means segmented curricula. Such an outcome may well not be any part of the intention behind LAPP, and it may prove an inaccurate prediction of how things will develop, but it would be consonant with the way some projects have matched their interpretation of official thinking on the Programme to their own local contexts.

The point of myths is that they continue to convey potent ideas. In redirecting attention and resources to areas of relative failure in schools the LAPP initiative has encouraged skilful and experienced teachers to experiment with approaches to learning which could be beneficial for all pupils. It is understandable that a funded programme should be fairly closely focussed so that the effort of pilot projects is not dissipated. But in this instance it was not so much a question of setting a focus as of selecting a particular lens. By talking about a 'target group' for this Lower Attaining Pupils Programme (generally now agreed to be a most unfortunate title), the initiators inevitably evoked a whole way of thinking about pupils' ability and attainment that carried with it well established assumptions about how courses should be planned and pupils grouped. Such groupings might be presented by schools as purely pragmatic arrangements to facilitate the desired changes, but as always organizational decisions convey other messages to those whom they affect. The image which LAPP can acquire on the ground as a scheme for the Rems, basket-weavers, DES kids, Joeys or even 'Achievers' can be hard to dislodge.

Conclusion

LAPP was set up as an experimental Programme which would come up with practicable strategies for improving motivation and attainment. Whether, for example, this should involve decisions about pupil grouping as well as changes in teaching approaches was itself part of the agenda, a practical question to be considered. So despite the central funding and management, the Programme fitted in with the tradition of relative autonomy, in which LEAs and schools were used to deciding their own educational priorities. As the Programme progressed, guidelines and recommendations were provided from the centre to indicate how such concepts as differentiation and practicality might be applied to further the aims of the initiative. But there were several problems. It was not entirely clear that, even at the centre, there was one accepted interpretation of these concepts. In some respects the public guidelines were radical in the demands they made for change in the way teachers organized and monitored pupils' learning. But they were only guidelines; there was no way a particular approach could be imposed from the centre. Financial and administrative levers could only operate slowly and with limited effect in steering the initiative in a given direction. In practice, project proposals, and the way in which these had been developed within schools, often appeared to be a response more to local pressures and priorities than to promptings from the centre. And in some cases these local influences and constraints underwrote a narrow interpretation of differentiation and practicality that was nearer than anything in official documents about the

Programme to the 'tripartite' philosophy for education which some have attributed to central policy makers.

References

BRIAULT, E. (1985) 'The other paymaster: The view from the local authorities' in PLASKOW, M. (Ed) *Life and Death of the Schools Council*, Lewes, Falmer Press.

CLARE, J. (1986) 'Streamed for failure in the name of equality and socialism', *The Listener*, 5 June.

DEPARTMENT OF EDUCATION AND SCIENCE (1975) *A Language for Life* (The Bullock Report), London, HMSO.

DEPARTMENT OF EDUCATION AND SCIENCE (1982a) Sir Keith Joseph: speech to the Council for Local Education Authorities, July.

DEPARTMENT OF EDUCATION AND SCIENCE (1982b) *Mathematics Counts* (The Cockcroft Report), report of the Committee of Enquiry into Mathematics in Secondary Schools.

DEPARTMENT OF EDUCATION AND SCIENCE (1984) conference for LAPP project staff, May.

DEPARTMENT OF EDUCATION AND SCIENCE (1985) *Better Schools* (Cmnd 9469), London, HMSO.

DEPARTMENT OF EDUCATION AND SCIENCE (1986a) *Report by HM Inspectors on a Survey of the Lower Attaining Pupils Programme: The First Two Years*, London, HMSO.

DEPARTMENT OF EDUCATION AND SCIENCE (1986b) Minister of State's speech to the PAT annual conference, Manchester, 29 July.

DEPARTMENT OF EDUCATION AND SCIENCE (1986c) *Report of the Working Party on Conference for Pre-vocational Courses pre-16* (Chairman: R. J. Johnson), Welsh Office, HMSO.

INNER LONDON EDUCATION AUTHORITY (1984) *Improving Secondary Schools* (report of the Committee on the Curriculum and Organization of Secondary Schools) London, ILEA (The Hargreaves Report).

NUTTALL, D. (1984) 'Doomsday or a new dawn? The prospects for a common system of examining' in BROADFOOT, P. (Ed) *Selection, Certification and Control*, Lewes, Falmer Press.

RANSON, S. (1984) 'Towards a tertiary tripartism: New codes of social control and the 17+' in BROADFOOT, P. (Ed) *Selection, Certification and Control*, Lewes, Falmer Press.

REID, W. A. and HOLT, M. (1986) 'Structure and ideology in upper secondary education' in HARTNETT, A. and NAISH, M. (Eds) *Education and Society Today*, Lewes, Falmer Press.

RINGER, F. K. (1979) *Education and Society in Modern Europe*, Bloomington, Indiana University Press.

SHIPMAN, M. (1985) 'Local education authorities and the curriculum' in RAGGATT, P. and WEINER, G. (Eds) *Curriculum and assessment: Some Policy Issues*, Oxford, Pergamon/Open University.

SIMON, B. (1985) *Does Education Matter?*, London, Lawrence and Wishart.

SIMON, B. (1986) Imposing differentiation in schools', *Education Today and Tomorrow*, London, 37, 3.

Chapter 7

Assisting Whom? Benefits and Costs of the Assisted Places Scheme

Geoff Whitty, John Fitz and Tony Edwards

The Assisted Places Scheme has helped to make the relationship between state and private education a major party political issue once again. In some people's minds it has raised the spectre of an increasingly privatized education service and some of the Scheme's supporters have begun to regard it as a precursor of a full-fledged voucher system. However, although the Scheme was linked to other measures to widen parental choice, it was intially conceived largely as something more akin to a 'scholarship ladder' for bright children from families of modest means, whom it was felt would be inadequately stretched in neighbourhood comprehensive schools. It has therefore also revived long-standing arguments about the academic costs associated with comprehensive education and the social costs associated with academic selection.

The Scheme was established under Section 17 of the 1980 Education Act, and the first pupils to participate in it entered their schools in the following September. Its announcement was the first significant act of education policy by the Thatcher government after the 1979 election, much of its detail having already been worked out by representatives of the Conservative party and the private sector. The central justification for the Scheme was that it would make it possible for 'bright children from less affluent homes' to attend independent schools of proven academic worth from which they would otherwise have been excluded by their parents' inability to pay.

In 1985–86, £33.8m of government money was paid to independent schools to reduce or waive the fees charged to parents of academically eligible children, and to pay certain incidental expenses arising from the taking-up of places. By this fifth year of the Scheme's existence, 21,412 children hold assisted places in 226 of the most prestigious English schools. Their government-assisted presence there is justified as an extension of parental choice, a restoration of academic opportunities to many children who would not be fully stretched in schools which have to cope with a full range of ability, and a protection both for those individuals and for the nation's resources of talent against the levelling-down effects attributed to comprehensive reorganization. Opponents of the Scheme see it as an unnecessary and offensive declaration by the government that the public sector is incapable of providing for very able children, and as a government-sponsored withdrawal of middle-class support from schools so evidently identified as being second-best.[1]

Origins and Concerns of the Research Project

Our initial interest in studying the Scheme lay in the relationship between certain claims made by its advocates and critics, and its actual operation and effects. Much of the preparatory work for the project therefore involved identifying and collating conflicting claims from propaganda produced by the various interest groups involved, from Parliamentary debates, from press accounts of the controversy surrounding the Scheme's inception, and from interviews with leading participants. Some of the conflicting expectations reflected irreconcilable philosophical differences which cannot be subjected to empirical testing. Thus, much of the debate expressed predefined positions on the relative claims of freedom and equality to inform the structuring of society. Even if it were possible to reach some conclusions about the extent to which either of these 'goods' was being enhanced by the Scheme, no research could adjudicate between their respective merits. In such cases we sought to locate supporting and opposing arguments within the context of these broader philosophical positions, and within the ideological repertoires of the various political parties.[2]

Other claims, however, took the form of more specific predictions about the outcomes of the Scheme. In broad terms, advocates of the Scheme tended to insist that the only relevant criteria for judging its success or failure were the benefits it brought to the individual participants, while critics concentrated on its systemic consequences and its effects on individuals remaining in the maintained sector. Despite such complications, some of the claims made by supporters and critics of the Scheme (and hence some of its costs and benefits) did seem directly susceptible to empirical investigation, viz:

1. The most obvious example was the degree to which places in the Scheme were taken up and whether it was reaching its target group. For example, while supporters claimed that 'able children from our poorest homes would once again have the opportunity of attending academically-excellent schools', sceptics suspected that only a very small proportion of places would go to 'the sons and daughters of Andy Capp', all previous experience suggesting that the places would be monopolised by the middle classes.[3]
2. It also seemed feasible to undertake the more difficult task of studying some of the Scheme's effects both on the schools participating in it, and on state primary and secondary schools around them. In particular, certain claims made about the Scheme required investigation of its effects on the intakes to different types of secondary school, and any backwash effect it might have on local primary schools.

3 At the point of entry to secondary schools, it was important to explore whether parents' perceptions of the Scheme were related to the prevailing patterns of state provision in their areas. The Scheme was initially presented as being of particular importance in inner city areas with neighbourhood comprehensive schools and in areas without maintained grammar schools.
4 We also needed to investigate the claim that assisted-place pupils would gain tangible benefits (individually or as a group) in relation to their peers in the state sector. While advocates of the Scheme have insisted that it complements the state sector by providing academic opportunities difficult to maintain in schools catering for the majority, its critics have argued that it represents an unjustifiable expenditure of public money without any check that the pupils given assisted places needed to move out of the public sector to obtain those opportunities.[4]
5 Finally, although ultimately this will be a longer term undertaking, we wanted to examine the claim frequently made by the Scheme's critics that it would bring about a systemic change in the relationship between the state and private sectors, to the detriment of the state sector and the pupils remaining in it.

These then were the major considerations that shaped our decisions about what evidence to collect. In collecting that evidence, we worked at three levels — nationally, in selected areas with high concentrations of assisted places, and in individual schools. We tried to focus down on individual pupils and parents affected by the Scheme while maintaining in view its broader contexts.[5]

The National Study

At the national level, we conducted two kinds of enquiry. The first was an attempt to locate the Scheme in its historical and sociological context. The second focused on the statistical distribution and take-up of places during the Scheme's implementation. Only brief summaries of these studies can be given here:

(i) The historical analysis related the Scheme to previous attempts to link the public and private sectors, while the sociological analysis explored its relationship to other aspects of contemporary social policy. We also undertook a more detailed study of its origins within the private sector, its appearance as a Conservative party policy commitment in 1976–77, and its formulation as a workable scheme (in unusually short time) following the Conservative election victory of May 1979. This was based upon detailed interviews with the Scheme's various architects in the independent sector, the Conservative party and the Civil Service, together with archive research which included the analysis of an important collection of primary source material made available to us in the course of the project. Of particular interest here was the extent to which the Scheme could be 'read' as manifesting some of the main themes in the new educational ideology constructed by the Right during the 1970s, and so as a prime example of an ideologically-derived 'policy preference' rather than as a pragmatic response to the pressure of events.[6] Given the Scheme's attractions as an inexpensive way of displaying simultaneously the new government's commitments to preserving academic standards, extending parental choice, and rewarding the 'deserving', it was tempting to see it entirely in this way.

In practice, however, our documentary and other evidence did not reveal universal enthusiasm for it within the Conservative party, nor any contributions to its formulation from those (in and around the Centre for Policy Studies or the Institute for Economic Affairs) who were actively engaged in reconstructing the party's ideological base. As advocated from within the private sector, the Scheme was closely aligned with two major themes in the Black Paper reappraisal of progressive assumptions — the incompatibility of equality with equality of opportunity, and the reduction in opportunities open to able working-class children brought about by the 'destruction' of grammar schools. A successful articulation between independence and a grammar school education was critical to the appeal of the Assisted Places Scheme. It was in those terms that the Direct Grant Schools Joint Committee framed its own proposals, first for improving the 'direct-grant system' (1970–72) and then for 'restoring the direct-grant principle' after the old system was ended by the Labour government in 1976. We have examined in detail the interaction between this pressure group, its supporters elsewhere in the private sector, its political allies in the Conservative party, and the DES officials presented in May 1979 with a scheme for which much of the groundwork had already been done. In the process of implementation, the 'national network of independent schools' envisaged by its main political architect, Stuart Sexton, was considerably scaled down, and there were prolonged negotiations over the selection of sufficiently meritorious schools from 290 firm applications, the appropriate proportion of assisted pupils to be recruited from the public sector, and the income-scales needed to match assistance to need. The parties to the negotiations concluded that the participating schools should remain entirely independent and that the administrative (and monitoring) role of the DES should be light. In order to defend the Scheme against an incoming Labour government, it was to be embodied in statute and involve contractual relationships between the DES and individual participating schools.

(ii) The distribution of assisted places is highly significant in relation to the expectation that priority would be given to inner-city areas without selective maintained schools, that the nature of local provision in the public sector would be carefully considered in determining allocations, and that there would be rough equality of provision between regions and between boys and girls. Our analysis, which draws upon school-by-school statistics held by the DES which are far more detailed than the summary statistics published annually by the DES and by the Independent Schools Joint Council, indicates that:

(a) The Scheme has been considerably constrained by the location of the philanthropic activities of individuals and merchant companies long ago. Furthermore, a predominance within the Scheme of former direct grant schools and of a dozen former LEA-grammar schools was inevitable, given the necessary emphasis on high academic standards and the absence of public assistance for meeting the costs of boarding education (see table 1).

(b) There has been a consequently heavy concentration of assisted places where such schools are most numerous — in and around the cities of London, Bristol, Manchester, Liverpool and Newcastle — and little or no provision in some other heavily populated areas less well endowed by history (see table 2). An equitable distribution of places around the country was impossible, short of creating new independent schools or enticing far more voluntary-aided grammar and ex-grammar schools out of the maintained sector than actually made that move. As table 2 shows, marginal adjustments to the allocation of places since 1981 have done nothing to reduce these inequalities.

(c) Amongst the boys' schools, patterns of take-up have reinforced the dominance of day schools. Of the eighteen boys' schools which have recruited less than 70 per cent of their quota of places 1981–85, fifteen are boarding schools, including twelve in membership of the Headmasters' Conference. While there were 1387 boarders among the 1985 assisted place holders (6.5 per cent), two-thirds of them receiving some help from their schools, the continued government refusal to include boarding costs among the 'incidental expenses' it was willing to repay has contributed to the low take-up of places at many of the prestigious 'public' schools whose participation in the Scheme was energetically sought in 1979–80. Some of these — for example, Stowe, Tonbridge and Charterhouse — have so few places that their participation can hardly have even symbolic value.

(d) An initially lower allocation of places to girls (due mainly to the smaller average size of girls' schools) has been made more unequal by lower rates of take-up, with girls constituting about 42 per cent of assisted place holders. Lack of take-up in the case

Table 1: Allocation and take-up of places by type of school (England)

	Schools		**% Places Allocated**		**Actual % of all APs 1985**
	No.	*%*	*1981*	*1985*	
Former direct grant	116	51.3	66.3	63.0	65.2
Former LEA-aided	12	5.3	8.7	9.7	9.4
HMC boarding	50	22.1	8.9	9.4	8.5
HMC day (not ex-DG)	14	6.2	5.1	5.2	5.5
Other boarding	14	6.2	3.7	3.7	3.3
Other day	20	8.8	8.6	8.1	8.0

Table 2: Examples of local allocation and take-up of places (England)

	Schools	**11–13 Places**		**No AP Pupils 1985**	
		1981	*1985*	*Total no*	*% Total*
Outer London	24	477	406	1919	9.2
Inner London	19	470	460	2186	10.5
Liverpool, Birkenhead	10	300	346	1523	7.3
Manchester, Stockport	9	236	228	1150	5.5
Bristol, Bath	13	199	218	1126	5.4
Newcastle-upon-Tyne	5	157	145	660	3.2
Birmingham, Wolverhampton	3	122	117	595	2.8
Nottingham	3	45	70	300	1.4
Bradford	3	58	63	276	1.3
Leeds	2	75	55	273	1.3
Sheffield	1	40	16	80	0.4
Leicester	0	–	–	–	–
Sunderland	0	–	–	–	–

of girls' schools has not been restricted to the boarding schools and, of the twenty girls' schools which have reported less than 70 per cent take-up of places, fifteen are day schools (including thirteen ex-direct grant schools).

(e) While the majority of boys' day schools have far exceeded the minimum quota of assisted place holders drawn from the maintained sector (60 per cent), a significant minority of schools (mainly girls' schools and boys' boarding schools) has consistently failed to meet this quota. The prospect of reductions in their total allocations has not always proved an effective deterrent.

(f) The national take-up of assisted places has risen from 77 per cent in 1981 to 95 per cent in 1985. However, 20 per cent of sixth-form places were unfilled in 1985, despite the removal of the LEA right of veto in 1983.

The Local Studies

Our local studies included urban, suburban and semi-rural catchment areas, mainly where the numbers of assisted places were substantial. It became clear that single LEAs were inappropriate units for a study involving non-local independent schools, and our initial intention was to focus on two clusters of LEAs — one in the South-east and one in the North-east. However, the refusal of independent schools to provide access to pupils in one of these areas, and of one LEA to cooperate in the other, led us (with the encouragement of our steering group) to add to the study a further cluster of LEAs in the North-west of England where the full cooperation of independent schools and LEAs had already been assured. Thus, while the choice of study areas was shaped by their share of assisted places and their accessibility to the research team, an equally significant factor proved to be the willingness of schools and LEAs to cooperate in research into a Scheme which had been defended and attacked with a ferocity apparently out of all proportion to its modest scope and which seemed vulnerable to early termination by an incoming Labour government. We therefore had to use a system of 'opportunity sampling', followed by 'snowball sampling', in order to achieve adequate coverage for the type of study envisaged. Given the nature of the local areas originally selected for study, our work in participating boarding schools in the final year of the project was not restricted to those areas.

The School Studies

Within each local study area, we interviewed (see table 3) heads of independent and state secondary schools, senior staff in independent schools who had particular responsibility for selecting assisted-place pupils and monitoring their progress, and heads of primary schools, some of whom were experiencing pressures to prepare children for the entrance examinations (sometimes despite an explicit local authority ban on any cooperation with the Scheme). The content of these interviews has been analyzed in relation to arguments and predictions identified in the debate surrounding the Scheme's inception.

Table 3: School interviews

Type of School	No.
Independent school	25
LEA secondary school	14
LEA primary school	14
Tertiary college	1

In the independent schools selected for detailed study (including boarding schools outside our local study areas), we tried to interview equal numbers of assisted-place and full fee-paying pupils from the same year groups, using semi-structured interviews which included questions about their home backgrounds, their reasons for coming to the school, their views of the school, their plans for higher education and for employment, and any contacts they continued to have with friends made at primary school. Within the local study areas, the same interviews were conducted with some of their contemporaries in selected state schools (see table 4). The data from the interviews with staff and pupils has been used to produce a series of case studies highlighting the character of the different schools and their pupils, copies of which have been sent to the headteachers for comment.

Table 4: Pupil interviews

	AP pupils		Full-fee		LEA pupils	
	M	F	M	F	M	F
Independent schools	90	67	83	62		
Comprehensive schools (upper band)					95	153
Maintained grammar schools					28	33
Secondary/comprehensive (other bands)					31	33
Tertiary college					8	6

The state schools we studied were among those which had been available to the assisted-place pupils, might have been attended by them if the Scheme had not existed, and were attended by their former friends from primary school. This component of the research has enabled us to make detailed comparisons between the characteristics and educational careers of assisted place holders, full fee payers in the same school, and state secondary pupils from the same local areas. Though there are major objections to comparing the actual careers of pupils with what they 'might have been' in some other school, it nevertheless proved possible to make comparisons of resources, curriculum, subject choice and academic orientations in schools from the two sectors. Indeed, it is difficult to see how such comparisons can be avoided, given the references in the Scheme's rhetoric of legitimation to rescuing able children from schools unable to provide genuine academic education.

It might be expected that the Scheme would be less needed, and have less appeal, where state schools were seen to be doing a relatively good job for academically-oriented pupils. In the final year of the project, we have given particular attention to the role of maintained grammar schools in areas where the Scheme is operating, while from our earlier studies we have also identified comprehensive schools which seemed to be both competent and confident in nurturing the talent of academically able pupils. In our case studies of these schools, we are seeking to explore the basis of their success in meeting the aspirations of pupils who, in other areas, might be tempted into the independent sector.

The Pupils and Their Families

We also sought interviews with a smaller sample of parents. Where parents agreed to be seen, the interviews were lengthy, extending from pre-coded items on their own (and their parents') education and occupations to open-ended questions about their choice of school, their objectives and strategies in making that choice, and their more general views about educational opportunities and the 'openness' of British society. Here, again, we interviewed parents (or pairs of parents) of assisted place holders and full fee-payers in the independent sector and parents whose children were in state schools (see table 5).

Table 5: Parent interviews

Status of pupil	No.
Assisted place holder	87
Full fee payer	82
State school pupil	154
Tertiary college student	5

The full data from these parental interviews are still being analyzed and some very recent data is currently being coded. We report here our preliminary analyses of pupil and parent interviews in relation to a number of issues that currently seem to be significant. Some of these have emerged or become more sharply defined as a result of our own research, while others derive their significance from the continuing national debate about the effects of the Scheme:

1 There have been frequent claims that some pupils are participating in the Scheme who could not be held to 'need' assistance in any accepted sense of need. Our evidence suggests, however, that only a small minority of parents abuse the Scheme financially. Some of these are able, by clever accountancy, to mislead school bursars much as they mislead the Inland Revenue system. Indeed, concern about such

abuses, and the damage they might cause to the Scheme's public image, was expressed in most of our interviews with senior staff in independent schools. The appropriateness of parental income as the criterion of eligibility can also be questioned when some parents qualify for full assistance even though cohabiting with affluent partners, and others would otherwise have received assistance with school fees from more wealthy members of the child's extended family (usually grandparents).

2 Much interest has also been shown, by proponents and critics of the Scheme, in the social backgrounds of those assisted place holders who do legitimately qualify for assistance. Our initial analysis of the family backgrounds of our sample of assisted-place pupils indicates that:

(a) Nearly 33 per cent can be identified from the pupil interviews as coming from single parent families, almost all of them headed by women. Analysis of the responses to more specific questions on this issue within the parental interviews points to a figure of 36 per cent.

(b) On the basis of information provided by the pupils, about 9 per cent of fathers and about 4 per cent of mothers had occupations which the Oxford Mobility Study classifies as working class.[7] However, initial analysis of the more explicit information provided by parents suggests that these figures exaggerate the proportion of parents who can properly be assigned to this category. On the other hand, over 30 per cent of the mothers were clearly in routine non-manual jobs, some of which recent critiques of the OMS suggest should be reclassified as working class occupations for women.

(c) About 50 per cent of fathers and over 20 per cent of mothers were in jobs that are classified by the Oxford Mobility Study as service class occupations, though these proportions were significantly lower than those for the parents not only of full fee payers in independent schools but also of children classified as academically able in maintained schools.

(d) About 7 per cent of fathers and 30 per cent of mothers were not in paid employment, though less than 2 per cent of the mothers were registered as unemployed.

(e) Nearly 58 per cent of mothers had attended academically selective secondary schools, while a further 10 per cent had attended independent fee paying schools. Of the fathers, 40 per cent had attended academically selective secondary schools, with a further 10 per cent having attended independent fee paying schools.

(f) Twenty-five per cent of the siblings of our sample were, or had recently been, at independent schools.

(g) Forty-four per cent of our sample qualified for full fee remission and a further 11 per cent paid less than £100 in fees per annum, figures which closely match the official national statistics produced by the DES.

While our figures affirm the claim made in defence of the Scheme that the majority of assisted places are going to children of families with low or modest 'relevant income', they also point to a low participation rate by manual working class families and especially by those where the fathers are in semi-skiled or unskilled occupations (see table 6). On the other hand, the children of such families are far from prevalent amongst our sample of pupils classified as academically able within comprehensive schools and they are virtually absent from our samples of pupils in maintained grammar schools and fee-paying pupils in independent schools. Compared with these other samples, the parents of assisted place holders are less likely to be in 'higher grade' professional and managerial positions and more likely to be in middle range occupations. Nevertheless, when taken together with our ethnographic evidence, these findings suggest that many assisted-place holders come from 'submerged' middle-class backgrounds already well-endowed with cultural capital. Indeed, in broad terms, the social character of our own sample of beneficiaries does not differ substantially from that found by Douse, who studied the Scheme's operation in different local areas from our own and concluded that relatively few assisted place holders came from 'unambiguously working class backrounds', that many came from single-parent families or from other families where a low income reflected 'unusual' circumstances, and that a large minority were already within what he called 'the independent school frame of reference'.[8]

Publicly, most supporters of the Scheme have not treated such findings as a problem, because the 1980 Education Act merely states that the Scheme is intended to help 'pupils who might not otherwise . . . be able to benefit from education at independent schools', while the high proportion of existing place holders receiving full remission of fees (a rather higher percentage than the government itself originally anticipated) is used to support the argument that the Scheme is proving conspicuously successful in directing aid to those who need it. According to Bob Dunn, the Junior Minister then responsible for administering the Scheme, by 1983–84 it had served to open up a third of places in participating schools to 'pupils from low-income families who are selected on merit alone' and thus to 'give children from disadvantaged and poor homes an education that they would not normally receive'[9]

In view of the evidence that was already emerging from the independent schools' own surveys by the time of those statements, it is clear that the terms 'disadvantaged' and 'poor' were being used here in a rather broader way than is usual within educational discourse. This obscured the fact that the sample contained very few examples of pupils who fitted the more usual definition of those categories. However, Douse claims that such findings do not 'constitute a criticism of the Scheme' because the legislation which created it was never couched explicitly in terms of reaching out to the 'working class', and that 'aiding bright youngsters from single-parent homes or from ones in which the main wage-earner is unemployed, even if the family might reasonably be characterized as "middle-class", is certainly not a self-evident misallocation of funds'.[10] In our own research, however, which seeks partly to explore the

Table 6: Occupational status of parents (percentages using a classification derived from the Oxford Mobility Study)

	Service class		**Intermediate class**			**Working class**		**Not in paid employment**
	I	*II*	*III*	*IV*	*V*	*VI*	*VII*	
Fathers								
Full feepayers	65.3	20.7	0	12.0	0	0	0	2.0
AP holders	11.9	38.1	10.2	15.3	8.5	6.8	2.5	6.8
Upper band comprehensive	24.5	34.0	7.5	11.2	6.6	6.6	6.2	3.3
LEA Grammar	54.3	34.7	0	6.5	0	0	2.2	2.2
Mothers								
Full feepayers	7.6	30.5	16.6	5.6	0	0	0	39.6
AP holders	0	22.2	36.8	2.8	1.4	1.4	2.8	32.6
Upper band comprehensive	1.2	29.0	32.8	2.3	1.5	0	6.2	27.0
LEA Grammar	2.0	46.0	28.0	4.0	0	0	0	20.0

Note: This table is derived from pupil reports of parental occupations. Final classification of data based on parental interviews is currently being completed.

operation of the scheme in terms of the claims made by its advocates and critics, it is certainly pertinent to ask whether funds are being allocated to the groups originally anticipated. The defence of the Scheme in terms of financial need alone minimizes the significance of a change in the representation of the typical assisted place pupil within the rhetorics of legitimation employed by ministers over the years. While there was certainly little reference to any concept of 'class' in the official justifications for the Scheme in 1979–81, Parliamentary references being mainly to (for example) 'children from inner urban areas' or to 'academically-minded children of poor parents' and 'children from deprived backgrounds', there can be little doubt that these phrases conjured up images of working class children for whom opportunities for upward mobility through educational success were being restored.

Certainly our analysis of Black Papers and associated writing, and of how support for an assisted places scheme was canvassed, indicates a pervasive and explicit concern for clever working-class children denied opportunity by neighbourhood comprehensive schools. Such images of working class children inadequately stretched by inner city comprehensives were particularly prominent in a televised interview with Junior Minister Rhodes Boyson in the week in which the Scheme got under way,[11] in our own interview with Mark Carlisle, Secretary of State responsible for the 1980 Education Act, and also in an interview we conducted with a leading advocate of the Scheme within the Headmasters' Conference, who characterized it as an attempt 'to pluck embers from the ashes'. Significantly, this same headteacher's interest in our own research stemmed from a desire to know whether the Scheme would, in fact, attract the sorts of pupils signified by such images. Despite the considerable optimism on this point expressed by many of the independent school heads we interviewed, there is little evidence in our own sample of assisted place holders that even those children from single parent families or from families where parents are unemployed come from the kinds of material and cultural backgrounds which are conveyed by these images.

This may well account for the fact that, although ministers have always been careful to point out that children from inner city areas were only one of the disadvantaged groups which the Scheme might benefit, there remains some unease among its promoters about their failure to appear in large numbers among its beneficiaries. This is indicated by the fact that, while the numbers eligible to have all, or most of, their fees remitted are cited as vindication of the Scheme, the annual publicity exercises mounted by the Independent Schools Information Service (ISIS) and by the DES place particular emphasis on those pupils who come from manual working class backgrounds.[12] To this extent, the celebration of the unanticipated consequences of the Scheme for the submerged middle classes may not be adequate compensation for its failure to reach its core target group, especially when these consequences were predicted by critics and denied by advocates at the time of its launch.

The evidence in respect of the claim that the Scheme is reaching a group that might otherwise not have received the same form of education is mixed.

It seems clear that a majority of assisted place holders in our sample would not have attended independent schools without this form of assistance and that the Scheme has introduced into some of these schools a small number of pupils from social groups not represented amongst their full feepayers. Yet, like Douse, we also found a significant minority of assisted pupils who claimed that they would have attended their own school or another independent school had the Scheme not existed. There has always been a degree of ambiguity about how far this is consistent with the intentions of the Scheme in that, although there was little suggestion in public advocacy of the Scheme that one of its prime purposes was to give assisted places to pupils who would have attended the same schools without them, the regulations actually permitted the award of a minority of places to pupils already in the independent sector. It is difficult to argue that the Scheme has significantly widened choice for such pupils, although it has certainly subsidized it.

The data on parental and sibling education provides a further indication that involvement with the independent sector was not new for many of the families of assisted place holders. However, even these families were less locked into the 'independent school frame of reference' than the traditional clientele of independent schools. Thus, the 25 per cent of siblings of assisted place holders in our sample who were or had recently been in independent schools, has to be compared with 67 per cent of the siblings of pupils paying full-fees in independent schools. More significantly, virtually all of those siblings of assisted place pupils were in independent secondary schools. Yet, whereas 56 per cent of younger siblings of fee-paying pupils were in private primary schools, the equivalent figure for those of assisted place holders was only 8 per cent.

This choice of the independent sector for children at the age of 11 provides an important clue to the attraction of the Scheme not only for those assisted place holding families whose prior commitment to the independent school frame of reference was limited but also for the majority for whom it was non-existent. Our interviews with parents of assisted place holders certainly revealed a general belief that their children were getting a better education than had been available to them in the public sector. They felt this as strongly as parents who were paying full fees. Not surprisingly, state school parents were significantly less likely to hold such a positive view of the private sector, though a minority did share it. Detailed case-studies are being produced of how and why some parents decided to seek a place in an independent school,[13] how far their decision was shaped or made possible by the Assisted Places Scheme, and why other parents with similar occupations and incomes decided to remain within the public sector. What is already apparent is the extent to which many parents of assisted-place pupils, especially in the North and in those schools which formerly had direct grant status, see those schools primarily, even entirely, as grammar schools. It is their academic selectiveness, not their independence or (at least directly) their social exlusiveness, which is most highly valued by these parents. As many as 75 per cent of the parents of our assisted place holders would have liked to see LEA grammar schools retained, compared with 61 per cent of the parents of full fee payers and only 39 per cent of those of state school pupils.

The Effects of the Scheme on the Educational system

The above figures suggest that the architects and advocates of the Scheme have had some degree of success in mobilizing a constituency of parents behind their belief in the distinctive academic education offered by good grammar schools, and around their doubts about the capacity of some comprehensive schools, or even of any comprehensive school, to extend very able children. In the absence of LEA grammar schools, these parents have come, often reluctantly, to regard independent schools as synonymous with selective schools and thus with high levels of academic achievement. Despite the fact that the presumed association between academically-selective schools and academic achievement is far from conclusively demonstrated by research,[14] our evidence suggests that the supporters of comprehensive education have yet to convince many parents, including some who are traditional Labour voters, of its potential.

Labour critics of the Scheme argue that there is no firm evidence that comprehensive schools cannot cater for the full range of ability, but that their chances of doing so are significantly diminished (especially at the sixth-form stage) by the 'pirating of scholastic talent' which the Assisted Places Scheme is said to have encouraged.[15] Nevertheless, some advocates of the Scheme suggest that it will actually contribute to the success of state schools by exerting an additional competitive pressure on them to improve their own standards. This view was not shared by the majority of heads in our sample of maintained grammar schools and academically successful comprehensive schools. How far such schools could be encouraged to do an even better job by the existence of the Scheme itself is doubtful, given that some assisted-place pupils would not have considered a state school anyway, and in view of the possibility that the Scheme may be increasing the academic selectiveness of independent schools and thus enhancing their 'results' beyond what would have been attainable through the operation of 'pure' market forces.

At the start of the Scheme, the journal of the Headmasters' Conference recognized that 'a Scheme designed to attract working-class children who would otherwise go to a poor neighbourhood comprehensive [might] simply attract middle-class children who would otherwise go to a good comprehensive'.[16] In so far as our own findings suggest that this is precisely what has occurred in many cases, it is likely that these good comprehensives will have lost at least some of those pupils whose future examination performance would contribute to continuing parental perceptions of those schools as 'good'. This, in turn, could actually have negative long term consequences even for their capacity to compete with the independent sector. In these circumstances, it seems somewhat naive to expect that those schools which are *not* currently perceived as 'good' will be spurred into improvement by the operation of this Scheme. As a leading Conservative critic of this and other possible government initiatives has recently pointed out:

> they do nothing to improve the quality of education in schools that the vast majority of young people are educated in. These schemes all help most those children with parents best able to play the system to escape from poor schools. They do nothing for the quality of education of the majority who remain behind.[17]

Furthermore, the symbolic consequences of the Assisted Places Scheme probably far outweigh its direct creaming effects on the maintained sector or the 'opportunity costs' of not spending the money devoted to the Scheme on the maintained sector, had it indeed been available for that purpose.[18] Even though the Scheme is currently available to less than 1 per cent of pupils entering secondary schools for the first time, its very existence reinforces a belief in the inability of state schools to match the quality of private provision or develop credible alternatives to the type of education which the Scheme has so powerfully sponsored. This is why, even though at present we are able to identify comprehensive schools that are capable of competing academically with schools in the Assisted Places Scheme, it is important to keep under review the potential systemic consequences of the Scheme and its relationship to other attempts to redefine the roles of the state and private sectors.

For the moment, the limited scope of the Scheme reflects the peculiar nature of private schooling in this country. Where private schools in other industrial countries are defended as expressions of religious, ethnic and cultural diversity, their predominant function here has been to provide appropriate training for high-status occupations within the cultural mainstream. They have been increasingly seen as complementing the public sector by offering a quality of provision no longer available within it and extending access to such schools has therefore been represented as making a real contribution to social mobility. Since it was in that context that the objectives of the Assisted Places Scheme were originally defined, arguably its scope was appropriate to them. Even in its own terms, there therefore seems to be little scope or justification for an extension of the Scheme, at least in its present form, beyond perhaps ironing out some of the anomalies to which we have referred earlier in the chapter.

It has, however, been suggested that the Scheme is only part of a planned large-scale intrusion of private provision into the state sector. Furthermore, proposals to extend the Scheme, to experiment with Crown Schools, to seek private funding for schools in inner city areas and even to find a feasible way of introducing vouchers remain potential items on the government's future agenda.[19] Seen in this context, a Scheme that has so far had only marginal effects on the education system as a whole can take on a new significance. Even some members of the government have urged more radical ventures in extending parental choice. Boyson, for example, has been quoted as saying:

> If choice is a good thing and variety a good thing, which I obviously

> believe it is, then it should be open not only to academically able children but to all children . . . That is why I moved towards the voucher system or contracting out or specialist schools in the long term, without denying the virtues of the assisted places scheme. But politically and philosophically I must move along those lines myself.[20]

In such pronouncements, it is possible to detect the preparation of the ground for a redefinition of the Assisted Places Scheme as the precursor of a radical new policy of privatization rather than a 'natural' extension of the traditional scholarship ladder. For the more extreme privatizers in and around the Conservative Party, the ultimate goal would be a largely privatized education service with the state providing only a 'safety-net' for those unable or unwilling to compete in the market.

Despite some diffidence in government circles (and indeed in the more prestigious reaches of the independent sector) about such a redefinition of the relations between state and private education, even speculation along these lines could have a powerful backwash effect on public attitudes towards state provision. This could make a full-blown policy of privatization more feasible should the balance of forces within the Conservative party shift further to the Right in the future. Prolonged uncertainty about the future role of state schools could lead to just that process of sponsored withdrawal from the state sector predicted by the Chief Officer of the ILEA as the Assisted Places Scheme was getting under way, when he claimed that, in the longer term, the Scheme could 'really create a fee-paying grammar school system and a secondary modern maintained sector'.[21] Such a development would be likely to have particularly dire consequences for those living in the inner cities for, not only would they be unable to attain access to educational and welfare services beyond a bare minimum provided by the state, they would increasingly become the only groups receiving this form of public provision. While, in those circumstances, a few children might 'escape' from the inner cities into the middle classes via assisted places or similar devices, they would be relatively few on present evidence and those remaining would, in turn, lack even present levels of middle class support in their efforts to improve the quality of state provision.

Even though such speculation gains some credence from our own observations of the limited effects of the Assisted Places Scheme to date, this scenario remains but one possible outcome for the future. While the political climate has certainly become much more favourable to independent schools, the Scheme itself remains a limited and imperfect expression of the educational policy 'preferences' of a government explicitly committed to reducing the share of national resources taken by the public sector, and the 'logical' next steps predicted at its inception have not yet materialized into legislation. Even the mechanism most favoured by market liberals, that of the educational voucher, has continued to be found 'intellectually attractive' but impractical by the ministers responsible, leaving its advocates dissatisfied with a Scheme in which a very limited extension of parental choice is itself confined to the parents of academically able children.[22] We cannot therefore be certain how a more fully privatized system with a greater degree of parental choice would actually operate. As soon as we try to interpret our data for this purpose, we are forced, in much the same way as Coleman *et al*[23] in the USA, to make informed guesses about the effects of possible future policies on the basis of evidence collected from a system in which those policies have hardly taken root.

Methodological Reflections

The very fact that the future relationship between state and private education remains a live political issue means that virtually any attempt to interpret findings from research in this field and to theorize about their significance is likely to be more than usually contentious. The intensely political nature of research in this field helps to explain the concern of others both to control the researchers' access to data and enquire into the use to be made of any findings. In many ways, this issue has been the sub-text of our research programme, and one which became at times a major pre-occupation. It is therefore fitting that we should conclude this chapter with some observations on the political and methodological difficulties of undertaking research on an issue of this nature.

Our original application to the Social Science Research Council (SSRC) came at a time when the Council was short of funds and was itself the object of close political scrutiny. These circumstances may have contributed to an unfortunate delay in funding which prevented us entering the schools at the same time as the first assisted places holders. The political sensitivity of the issue under consideration also led to the Council's insistence on a Project Steering Group Committee which would (among other tasks) assist us in avoiding any 'misinterpretation' of our findings. Once the project had got under way, the detailed negotiation of access, even in those schools and LEAs that had provisionally agreed to cooperate with the research, became the immediate preoccupation of the research team and one which produced some early slippage in the research timetable. A controversial policy innovation of this kind engenders such loyalty and hostility that its gatekeepers are unusually inclined to doubt whether any research can be impartial and unusually concerned to discover the views of the researchers themselves. There were times, of course, when to be viewed suspiciously from one side proved helpful in gaining access to the other. On the other hand, though it sometimes has proved difficult to maintain a non-partisan stance across a variety of contexts where the participants were keen to elicit our views and the research team never adopted the classic positivistic stance of refusing to discuss the project with informants, the political sensitivity of the research did not generally confront the researchers as an issue when actually undertaking the fieldwork.[24]

In some independent schools, however, the grounds for resisting or limiting their cooperation were not so much the politically sensitive nature of the Scheme but rather what was perceived as the impossibility of any systematic comparison of schools or types of schools in the opportunities they offer. The controversy surrounding attempts to compare the effectiveness of selective and non-selective schools might well seem to support this scepticism. Nevertheless, it seems to us a position difficult to justify in principle in the context of a publicly funded Scheme, the essential defence of which is that it offers opportunities to able pupils in schools with established academic reputations which they would be unlikely to find within a comprehensively reorganized public sector. Much more readily understandable was the unwillingness of some heads to allow any enquiry which might seem to make assisted place pupils an object of special attention and so hamper their equal treatment. In our fieldwork, we therefore constructed our samples in such a way as to minimize the possibility of assisted place holders becoming stigmatized.

In many ways, it was opponents of the Scheme who posed the more formidable barriers to the investigation. The fact that the Scheme was largely protected from LEA intervention, while most Labour-controlled authorities were totally opposed to it, made some of the negotiations extremely difficult. To some LEAs research into how the Scheme worked was seen as implying support for it or, at best, giving publicity to something which they would prefer to have seen ignored. In its refusal to cooperate with the project, one LEA made this explicit by stating that since it was opposed to the Assisted Places Scheme, it saw no good reason why it should devote time to research into the scheme. Nevertheless, we would question whether liking or disliking a policy is a good reason for either ignoring it or simply assuming its effects.

Some anxieties emerged more or less intensely at different stages of the research. Many advocates and critics of the Scheme were rightly concerned about the danger of drawing conclusions from short-term evidence. The Council's own fear, that our findings might be used prematurely or out of context for politically-motivated purposes, was an especially pertinent one during the early years of the Scheme, when the possibility of a Labour election victory put its immediate future in jeopardy. An important reason why independent schools themselves became increasingly willing to cooperate with our project as time went on was their renewed self confidence in the aftermath of the landslide victory by the Conservatives in the 1983 General Election. Conversely, heads of some maintained schools were unwilling to permit fieldwork in their schools during the teachers' industrial action of 1985, thus enforcing a reduction in the number of public sector schools included in that stage of the research. Nevertheless, the methodological consequences of such difficulties have been minimized in that the research has been conducted in both sectors over a number of years.

Meanwhile, as agreed with the ESRC, no findings were released during the course of the funded project, despite pressure from politicians and the media for access to our data and despite the fact that other researchers in the same field released their own findings during this period. Furthermore, the co-directors of the project have undertaken to monitor the progress of the Scheme, and of the pupils involved in it, beyond the four years of ESRC funding, as well as continuing with their broader study of the changing relations between state and private education. This commitment to continue both to analyze and collect data means that, although the research has already generated a detailed account of the origins of the Assisted Places Scheme and of its operation during the first five years of its existence, our evaluation of the potential effects of the Scheme must clearly be understood to be an interim one.

Acknowledgements

This paper was first presented to the annual conference of the British Educational Research Association at the University of Bristol on 4th September 1985. The authors are grateful to SSRC/ESRC for their support of this project from 1982–86 (Award no. C00230036). They also wish to acknowledge the assistance given by Bristol Polytechnic and the University of Newcastle, and by King's College, London, where the project was based from 1982–85. They are also indebted to Dr Mary Fulbrook, research associate on the project from 1982–83, and Geoffrey Cockerill, honorary consultant to the project from 1982–85.

Notes

1 These counter arguments are reviewed in WHITTY G. and EDWARDS A. (1984) 'Evaluating policy change: The Assisted Places Scheme' in WALFORD G. (Ed) *British Public Schools: Policy and Practice*, Lewes, Falmer Press.

2 The early stages of this analysis are reported in EDWARDS, A., FULBROOK, M. and WHITTY, G., 'The state and the independent sector: Politics, ideologies and theories' IN BARTON, L. AND WALKER, S. (Eds) *Social Crisis and Educational Research*, London, Croom Helm.

3 The first prediction was made by Rhodes Boyson, the Junior Education minister, writing in the *Daily Mail*, 25 June 1981; the second view was cited in an editorial in *The Guardian*, 2 February 1980.

4 The first claim is made explicitly in *The Case for Collaboration*, London, Independent Schools Information Service 1981; there is a forceful statement of the counter-argument in RAE, J. (1981) *The Public School Revolution*, London, Faber, pp. 178–83.

5 In doing so, we follow the example set in CONNELL, R. *et al* (1983) *Making the Difference: Families and Social Division*, Sydney, Allen and Unwin.

6 It is seen in that light in (for example) DALE,R. (1983) 'Thatcherism and education' in AHIER, J. and FLUDE, M. (EDS) *Contemporary Education Policy* London, Croom Helm.

7 See GOLDTHORPE, J. and HOPE, K. (1974) *The Social Grading of Occupations*, Oxford, Clarendon Press.

8 DOUSE, M. (1985) 'The background of assisted places scheme students' *Educational Studies*, 11, 3, pp. 211–7.

9 See *Hansard*, 6 December 1983 and 15 May 1984.

10 DOUSE, M. (1985) *op. cit.* p. 217.
11 Interview with Rhodes Boyson during a London Weekend Television Programme 'Starting Out', 11 September 1981.
12 Such exercises are arranged annually by the Independent Schools Information Service on the publication of the findings of a survey of schools participating in the Scheme carried out for the Independent Schools Joint Committee.
13 We are comparing our own findings with those reported by FOX, I. (1985) *Private Schools and Public Issues*, London, Macmillan, and in her chapter on 'The demand for a public school education' in WALFORD, G. (Ed) (1984) *op. cit.*
14 The best known British conflict over the 'facts' is between MARKS, J. *et al*, (1983) *Standards in English Schools*, London, National Council for Educational Standards; and STEEDMAN, J. (1983) *Examination Results in Selective and Non-Selective Schools*, London, National Children's Bureau.
15 For example, Neil Kinnock, then shadow spokesman on education, at a Labour Party press conference on 11 December 1979.
16 See an editorial in *Conference*, February 1980.
17 See ARGYROPULO, D. (1986) 'Inner city quality', *Times Educational Supplement*, 1 August, p. 4.
18 Mark Carlisle always claimed that the money for the Assisted Places Scheme was 'new' money, not otherwise available to the education service. See, for example, the *Times Educational Supplement*, 15 February 1980.
19 See, for example, the reports about future policy initiatives in the *Times Educational Supplement*, 28 February, 7 March and 4 April 1986 and *The Financial Times*, 3 March 1986. Later, the government announced the proposed establishment of about twenty city technology colleges. These would be central government funded 'independent' schools for 11–18-year-olds mainly in inner city areas and would seek to attract private sponsorship. Much of the rhetoric surrounding this proposal was reminiscent of the claims which had accompanied the announcement of the Assisted Places Scheme. See the *Times Educational Supplement*, 10 October and 17 October 1986.
20 Rhodes Boyson quoted in ALBERT, T. (1982) 'The cheapest way to help the brightest and the best', *The Guardian*, 23 November.
21 Peter Newsam made this prediction during the London Weekend Television programme 'Starting Out', 11 September 1981.
22 Arthur Seldon's *The Riddle of the Voucher*, London, Institute of Economic Affairs (1986) gives a very minor place to the Assisted Places Scheme in its advocacy of a thorough-going introduction of consumer sovereignty into the education system.
23 COLEMAN, J. HOFFER, T. and KILGORE, S. (1982) *High School Achievement: Public Catholic and other Private Schools Compared*, New York, Basic Books. Our own work has taken us increasingly into the comparative analysis of private schooling, a field of analysis which is developing rapidly. See, for example, MASON, P. (1985) *Private Education in the EEC*, London, ISIS, 1983, and *Private Education in the USA and Canada*, London, ISIS; EDWARDS, A., FITZ, J. and WHITTY, G. (1985) 'Private schools and public funding: A comparison of recent policies in England and Australia', *Comparative Education* 21, 1, pp. 29–45; WEISS, M. (1986) 'The financing of private schools in the Federal Republic of Germany', paper given at the Comparative and International Education Society conference at Toronto, 13–16 March; and JAMES, E. (1986) 'The public/private division of responsibility

for education: An international comparison', paper presented at the annual meeting of the American Educational Research Association, San Francisco, 16–20 April.

24 In practice, we encountered more ethical problems with the archive research than we did in the course of the fieldwork.

Chapter 8

HMI and Aspects of Public Policy for the Primary School Curriculum

R J Campbell

This chapter attempts to describe and analyze three aspects of public policy designed to enhance the quality of the curriculum in primary schools. The three aspects are concerned with 'subject specialization', 'differentiation', and 'breadth', which were all floated in HMI *Primary Education in England* (1978), have bobbed about in several DES documents since then, and surfaced most visibly in Sir Keith Joseph's Sheffield speech to the North of England conference (1984) and the White Paper *Better Schools* (DES,1985d). The first of these — the pressure for 'subject specialization' — is given more attention than the others, partly because the significance currently being attached to it, and partly because of the research evidence on it is rather less insubstantial. The definition of primary being used is the age range 5–12, partly to take account of those middle schools deemed primary, where some of the experimentation with subject specialization has been occurring, but also to exclude from consideration issues associated with pre-schooling, nursery education, rising 5s etc., where it is even more difficult than elsewhere to discern any coherent national policy. The period in focus is from 1977 to the present; that is from the publication of the Green Paper *Education in Schools* (DES,1977b) and the 1978 survey by HMI of curriculum practice in a representative sample of classrooms, *Primary Education in England* (the Primary Survey).

The chapter is presented in three stages. Firstly, there are some introductory points about policy making and the primary curriculum generally. Secondly, the three aspects of policy are described and appraised for their impact upon practice. Finally, some conclusions are drawn about curriculum policy and expenditure policies.

Educational Policy Making and the Primary School Curriculum

Models of Policy Making in the System

The traditional model of policy making is represented in the 1977 Green Paper (DES,1976) which shows three levels of reponsibility - the DES identifying national needs and promoting policies to meet them; the LEAs providing education, allocating resources, appointing staff and the education committee; and the schools, given devolved reponsibility for the implementation of the curriculum. Briault's version of this model, in Kogan (1975), is a 'triangle of tension', with the three partners mutually attracted, as though through some perverse magnetic force, by their focus on the educational process in schools, but simultaneously mutually repulsed by their differing priorities and corporate interests. Briault's metaphor has incorporated more of the political conflict than the Green Paper's rational decision-making model, but it still fails to capture the realities of the policy making processes. The most obvious problem is that LEAs make policy, they do not simply make provision for it. Support for this view has been provided by my colleagues at the University of Warwick, in the case of middle schools in the old West Riding of Yorkshire, documented by Hargreaves (1983 and 1986), and more generally by Tomlinson (1986), who argues that in the post-war period most educationally worthwhile policies have been created at the local rather than the national level. Shipman's (1985) evidence about Coventry and the ILEA makes the same point, whilst suggesting that LEAs could be broadly distinguished by their tendency to be initiatory (proactive) or responsive (reactive).

Shipman (1984) makes a further point, that the realities of policy making are messy, subject to pressure groups and entrenched corporately determined interest groups, and to conflict between the key partners:

> The inadequacies of the image (of partnership) arise partly out of differences within and between partners. Unions rarely agree. The shire county LEAs oppose the metropolitan authorities. HMI can adopt an independent line when detailing the harm done by sustained cuts in the education budget.

Shipman, at one time Research Director at the ILEA, suggests that 'horse trading' rather than 'partnership' reflects the realities of policy making especially at local authority level. And a similar view of policy making at national level has been provided by Ponting (1986) an ex-Whitehall insider, who characterized it as created mainly out of inter-departmental bargain striking, pursuit of personal ambition, concern for votes, and sometimes a large element of the fortuitous.

Thus Ponting argues:

> The real Whitehall problem is that there is nobody whose role it is to define and implement a government policy — it is either tragic or

> farcical depending upon your viewpoint. Policy emerges ad hoc through a series of compromises between departments headed by powerful ministers with their own ambitions.

These problems create difficulties for anyone attempting to investigate policy on the curriculum. Firstly, since the processes themselves are not open to inspection, what counts as evidence for a policy is problematic. Secondly, the horse trading characteristic makes public documents unreliable sources on their own, since they often disguise variations in the degree of support for, and the funding of, different parts of them. And thirdly there is the quite serious problem of the influence of policy statements upon practice. A policy that influences practice hardly at all, especially in terms of the curriculum, is only a policy in rhetoric. It may serve its makers more effectively at vote-catching times, than it does the education system. The empirical problems posed in identifying the impact of policy upon practice are very great, and have not, to my knowledge, been addressed in relation to primary schools. Thus the overall problem of what counts as a policy, what meanings can legitimately be attached to public documents, and what impact they have, all raise the need to be extremely cautious and tentative in the way we treat policy issues. Despite all this caution, we need to describe and analyze public policy on the primary school curriculum, because of the importance of the primary phase itself, and because of the relative vulnerability of primary school pupils.

The Neglect of the Primary Curriculum

I do not fully share the widespread anxieties about the tendency towards more centralized direction and control over the school curriculum, if by that is meant the negotiation by central government of a broad agreement over the general aims and purposes of the curriculum — the creation, so to speak, of a national curricular framework. The reason for this is partly that I consider the development of such a framework long overdue and likely to be welcomed by primary teachers, as Wicksteed and Hill's (1979) study showed, and by parents. More importantly however, such a framework could become the basis for an 'entitlement curriculum' for primary school pupils, who under present arrangements may experience a curriculum too arbitrarily dependent upon the accident of their teachers' expertise, their headteacher's preferences, their governors' prejudices, and their local authority's funding practices and ideologies.

An extension of this point is necessary. Accept for the moment a crude re-drawing of Lawton's (1983) analysis of the internal ideological divisions within the DES, that is the 'bureaucrats and politicos', (the permanent civil servants and the political appointments) — on the one hand, and the 'professionals', (the Inspectorate) — on the other. From the former grouping, the government officials directly charged with policy making, there has been an absence of coherent policy towards the primary school curriculum bordering on neglect. Compared to the range of initiatives at secondary level — the Certificate of Prevocational Education (CPVE), Technical and Vocational Education Initiative (TVEI), Low Achieving Pupils Project (LAPP) and the General Certificate of Secondary Education (GCSE), and new patterns of assessment, and their associated funding, government policy towards primary education has been nugatory and confused — a bizarre combination of kite-flying leaks about company schools, crown schools, assisted places and vouchers, together with some serious initiatives on governing bodies, inter-school liaison, and specific grants (ESG and others) which are not distinctively primary phase matters. This apparent policy gap is probably explained not merely by the low status routinely accorded to primary education, but mainly by the fact that disaffected and underachieving primary school pupils do not pose the same threat to social stability, and can not plausibly be used as the same scapegoats for industrial decline and football hooliganism as can their secondary counterparts. In education as elsewhere policy initiatives and funding, are drawn in *ad hoc* to prevent system collapse rather than to strengthen foundations.

The Role of Her Majesty's Inspectorate

This has not meant, however, that there has been no policy, for the policy gap at primary level has been plugged, over the decade under consideration, by the intervention of HMI (as distinct from other DES officials) in whose publications — usually publications expressly eschewing the notion that they represent 'policy' — it is possible to see a coherent and incrementally developing policy for improving the primary school curriculum.

There are some problems with this claim — for example what would count as evidence in its support or refutation — and I shall face one of them at this stage. According to the Raynor Report (HMI 1982), HMI constitutionally speaking does not make policy; it provides information on policy outcomes, and makes recommendations for change. In practice however, whatever the constitutional position, it is naive to consider that HMI has not been creating much of the *de facto* policy on primary education, and almost all of what there has been on the primary curriculum over the past decade.

This has been happening in at least two ways. Firstly, as Salter and Tapper (1981) point out, the role of the Inspectorate is changing in that it is being used to some extent to replace the work of the old Consultative Committees such as Crowther, Plowden and Newsom, which *were* consultative and therefore had to negotiate consensual policies, or at least record dissensus. According to Salter and Tapper's analysis, HMI has been acting more and more as a substitute for such committees by providing what they refer to as an 'in-house information service', upon which policy is based. ... om this point of view, HMI has moved into a very close relationship ... ier parts of the DES, a move which may help to explain anxieties about HMI autonomy and independence. It also serves to underline Lawton's point that the distinctions he makes about the internal groupings in the DES are ideological and not necessarily positional.

Secondly, HMI has gone into a very high profile publishing enterprise since the mid-1970s, concentrating almost exclusively upon the school curriculum. Most of the documents are not presented as policy statements but as 'for discussion', or as surveys and reports of practice in schools, though these latter are a liberal mix of description and prescription. Nonetheless, the documents have as an explicit aim the creation of 'broad agreement about the objectives of the curriculum', and presumably at some stage soon it will be claimed that such agreement has been secured. In 1985, the first document from the DES describing itself as a statement of policy was published, predictably enough on science (DES,1985c).

Very recently, Richards (1986), himself an HMI, has published a lucid analysis of this publishing output, showing how it might be seen as creating an overall conception of the primary curriculum, and the priorities such a conception implies for practice. Interestingly, Richards introduces his analysis by linking it to the policy making enterprise in a specific way:

> Those professionally engaged in the education service . . . attest to the importance of the curriculum. But such general assent is not sufficient to give direction to the formulation of policy or the improvement of practice. To do this closer agreement is required as to the purpose informing the curriculum and to the way in which such purposes might be realized in schools and classrooms

Thus on my reading of the situation, HM Inspectors have taken a directly interventionist role in policy formulation, despite their constitutional position, and regardless of the cautiously laundered language in which they write. Furthermore, as I shall argue later in this chapter, their intervention, although an integral part of the centralizing tendency, has been substantially beneficial, and protectionist towards liberal traditions of the curriculum, in the face of what must have been some hostile and unenlightened attitudes in the back reaches of the DES in recent years.

Even so, HMI has not been operating without political constraints, two of which need comment from a primary school perspective. During the period in question any policy for the primary curriculum has had to show consistency with two more general initiatives. One is the so-called *Better Schools* movement, traceable to the 1977 Green Paper, and including not only the curriculum but also teacher quality, assessment and standards and education's relationship to the world of work. Only policies that harmonised with and appeared to address the issues raised by this movement stood a chance of surviving intact. Secondly there has been the *Curriculum 5–16* initiative, compelling consideration of the school curriculum in the statutory years as a coherent whole, and launched in a depressingly perfunctory document, rather oddly subtitled a 'Note from the DES' (1984), *The Organisation and Content of the 5–16 Curriculum* and elaborated by HMI in the *Curriculum Matters* series.

This initiative, whatever its virtues for inter-phase continuity, has made consideration of distinctively primary approaches extremely difficult to maintain, since by definition almost, they are ruled out of court. This may help to explain the absence of any sustained treatment of the curriculum by HMI in the most distinctively primary phase, the infant years, and its low visibility in the *Curriculum Matters* series generally.

Three Aspects Of Public Policy

Subject Specialization

The fundamental plank in this platform of curriculum policy is that the primary curriculum should be planned and implemented mainly by reference to 'subject' expertise, and that 'more often than now', as the White Paper put it, older children in particular should be taught by specialist teachers. The sources for this are *The Primary Survey*, (DES, 1978, para. 8.42) *Education 8–12*, (DES, 1985b, paragraphs 6.8–6.15), even *Education 5–9*, (DES, 1982a paragraphs 3.19–3.21), *Curriculum Matters 2*, paragraph 16, and most explicitly the White Paper *Better Schools*, (DES, 1985d) para. 62:

> Older primary pupils need to benefit from more expertise than a single teacher can reasonably be expected to possess: this has consequences for staffing and the deployment of staff within a school, including the use of teachers as consultants. (paragraph 62)

Education 8–12 identified this as a major issue for discussion in paragraph 8.13, arguing that schools,

> could usefully re-examine their teaching arrangements to see if the learning needs of more of their older pupils might be better met by more effective use of consultants, or by some exchange of classes to allow teachers to share their particular skills and interests, thus introducing these older pupils to a combination of class and specialist teaching

This pressure for subject specialism has, of course, been strengthened through two powerful central initiatives. Firstly, undergraduate students training to be primary teachers now have to demonstrate a subject specialism by following courses with half the time in a 'subject' of relevance to the primary curriculum. Secondly, most of the specific grants are for subjects, even at the primary phase. There are no specific grants to improve topic work, to develop learning through play in the infant years, or in any of the primary practices that stubbornly refuse to acknowledge 'subjects' as the only way of defining curriculum knowledge.

At the level of schools and local authority the impact of this policy seems to have been fairly direct and swift, with enormously increased significance to the role of those teachers holding posts of responsibility for curriculum subjects, variously called curriculum consultants, subject advisers, curriculum coordinators or curriculum postholders. The importance of this role was first put on the agenda in the *Primary Survey*, which reported that work was better matched to pupils' capacities where postholders had a strong influence throughout the school, and recommended that postholders should take a leading part in in-school curriculum development, planning programmes of work with other staff, advising colleagues, occasionally teaching alongside their colleagues, and becoming involved in monitoring the work in their subject throughout the school. *The Primary Survey* further recommended that the status of postholders needed to be improved, and suggested that they should be given time in school for carrying out all these subject consultancy duties. The idea of injecting a shot of subject strength into primary schools through curriculum coordinators has remained a dominant theme in every document from 1978 onwards. It was powerfully pushed in the Cockcroft Report, *Mathematics Counts* (DES, 1982b) which identified a clear specification of the expectations of mathematics coordinators in primary schools in paragraph 354:

1. prepare scheme of work in consultation with other staff and feeder schools;
2. provide guidance and support to other members of staff in implementing the scheme through meetings and teaching alongside them;
3. organize resources, materials etc., and make them accessible to the staff;
4. monitor work in mathematics throughout the school and organize record keeping;
5. assist with the diagnosis of children's learning difficulties and their remediation;
6. arrange school-based in-service;
7. maintain liaison with linked schools and with the advisory service;
8. keep up to date in mathematical education;
9. help probationers;
10. advise colleagues lacking confidence in mathematics.

It has been easy, in my view too easy, for critics to construct this pressure for subject specialization as an attempt by the neo-Black Paper people of the Conservative party to impose the subject-based curriculum of the preparatory school upon state primary schools, with the consequent devaluing of the generalist model operating through the class teacher system. Equally, the sceptical might see it as a bid to pre-empt the Audit Commission, by getting value for money from those teachers being paid above scale 1. Although there may be something in the latter, the former criticism seems willfully to distort the careful expressions of support in most of the documents for the class teacher system. Richards (1986) again makes the point explicitly:

> the long standing and valued primary tradition that one teacher should be responsible for ensuring that his/her class receives a curriculum adequate in range and depth is not in dispute, but the way this responsibility is to be properly exercised and supported is open to reinterpretation . . . what is being discussed is not the dismantling of the class teacher system but its strengthening through sensitive deployment and development of expertise.

This more constructive interpretation has been provided in analyses in which the idea of collegiality has been promoted as a way of conceptualizing the new relationships of class teaching and subject consultancy implied for primary school teachers in HMI policy. This idea involves a collaborative approach to curriculum development in schools through staff planning groups led by curriculum coordinators strong in their subject base. These groups, with decision-making devolved to them by headteachers, are expected to create whole school curriculum policies, implemented predominantly through the class teachers, advised where necessary and informally by the coordinators. The coordinators themselves of course are also class-teachers. This approach has recently found prestigious support in the ILEA report (1985) produced by a committee chaired by Thomas, himself a former Chief Inspector for Primary Education. This identified what was referred to as a 'dual role' for primary teachers, irrespective of their salary position — the role combining class teaching with advising the school staff on a curriculum subject. Thomas's Committee recommended that school policies developed in this way should be viewed as contractual. And acknowledgement of the formal significance attached to this policy for raising standards has been given in the White Paper *Better Schools*, (DES, 1985d) which accepts (paragraph 152) that primary schools have first claim upon resources for extra staffing to free teachers from teaching for in-school development. Although the new contractual arrangements and career structures are still unclear, it looks as though the role defined for what were previously called postholders will now be an expectation laid upon all teachers in the career grades.

There have been time and interest enough for a number of empirical studies, of what the adoption of such a policy might mean in practice (Rodger, 1983; PSRDG, 1983; Goodacre and Donoughue, 1983, Campbell, 1985) while cognate research on staff relationships is currently being conducted at Cambridge by Nias and her colleagues. There have also been two conceptual appraisals, by Alexander (1984) and by Taylor (1986). Although there were some methodological differences in the empirical studies, important similarities in their findings emerged, which enable some conclusions to be drawn as to the likely effectiveness of the policy. They concern three areas of the primary school culture.

First, there are difficulties in the *occupational culture* of primary school teachers, whose basic ideologies include high commitment to classroom autonomy, and who view with suspicion the whole idea that their colleagues can be viewed as 'subject experts' (except perhaps in the field of music), able to roam throughout the school monitoring work in everyone else's classes, advising other teachers, and exercising curriculum leadership generally. Thus the policy has underestimated the actual and potential conflict that may be generated by its implementation.

Secondly, there is *the complexity of contemporary primary school teaching*. The job expectations and demands being made on class teachers, throughout the time the policy has been promoted, have been expanding substantially, with changing compositions of classes, in terms of mixed age groupings, mainstreaming of some children with special educational needs, the introduction of new technology, as well as the more openly political issues of accountability to parents and governors, reduced career opportunities, and perceived expenditure cuts. To add a new dimension to an already demanding role spread, is seriously to underestimate the complexity of primary school teaching today. Thus the policy is creating an unrealistic set of expectations for teachers. The studies show coordinators able to fulfil the curriculum leadership role only at the expense of other more routine, but equally important, concerns.

Thirdly, and in my view most importantly, the *working conditions* of primary schools are not conducive to the effective adoption of a curriculum leadership role. One aspect of these conditions is the lack of access to facilities and ideas — the cosy insulation of the conventional primary school staff-room — but by far the most significant is the amount and nature of the time free of teaching normally enjoyed by primary school teachers. The new subject co-ordination role has to assume that teachers will be free to work alongside their colleagues, that time will be available in the day for working groups to meet in a relatively unhurried atmosphere to review schemes of work, for coordinators to visit other schools to observe good practice in their subject, and to implement some ways of assessing the quality of work in the school as a whole. Every study, and every HMI survey, has identified lack of time as a major problem. Even where coordinators have some time allocated, it is conceived of in inappropriate and inflexible ways, with a fixed amount at the same time each week.

My study (Campbell, 1985) went some way towards identifying the conditions in which effective subject specialization in its collegial form might be established, assuming that the problem of time could be resolved. Amongst these were the following four:

(i) high level of respect for the curriculum postholder as a generalist class teacher first and foremost, rather than a subject expert;

(ii) a good match between the initial training (main subject), or in-service training of the postholder and the subject area for which she had responsibility:

(iii) a school climate stressing mutual accountability, devolution of responsibility by the head, and supportive colleague relationships:

(iv) a high level of personal charm and sensitivity, together with considerable social skills, on the part of the postholder.

I concluded then, and I see little reason for altering my view as yet, that as a policy for an individual school, where these pre-conditions were met, planning the curriculum through greater exploitation of subject expertise had proved effective, and was perceived by the teachers involved as such. But I judged the pre-conditions to exist in relatively few schools, and the expertise to reside in relatively few curriculum coordinators. For that reason, as a *national* policy to renew the quality of the curriculum offered to children, and to raise the standards they achieved, I believe 'subject specialization', even it in its collegiality version, is a policy likely to lead to even greater disparity between schools, and thus basically flawed, unless the occupational culture, the role demands and the working conditions of the primary school teachers as a whole are significantly modified. I think there is some evidence that aspects of the culture of primary schools are being so modified, but its extent and spread is uncertain. In this respect the new conditions of service may prove crucial to the success of the policy long term.

Differentiation

The second plank in the platform for curriculum improvement is what was called in the *Primary Survey*, 'match', and in later documents, including the White Paper, 'differentiation'. What is involved here is that work set for pupils in primary classrooms should reflect more closely their perceived capacities and previous attainments. The picture of practice presented in HMI surveys, is of teachers pitching their work at the middle range of ability, and thus not catering very effectively either for the pupils regarded as less able or more able.

The annexes to the *Primary Survey* in particular show a picture across all age groups surveyed, and across subjects, of pupils considered as more able consistently being set work judged by HMI to be below their capacities. The picture of poor matching for able children was repainted in the middle and first school surveys, where recommendations about setting, and other forms of grouping to encourage better matching were made.

In *The Curriculum from 5–16* (DES, 1985a) a section (paragraph 21 ff) on the grouping of pupils included the statement:

> Grouping according to ability attainment and experience is one (sic) means by which teachers provide for differentiated work to cater for differences among children. Group work makes a possible contribution to children' learning because it recognizes similarities among them as well as differences . . .

And in the White Paper *Better Schools* (DES, 1985d) (para 138) the recommendation is firmed up even more clearly:

> Classes spanning a wide range of ability or age call for careful adaptation of teaching style . . . Organizing classes in bands or sets so

> that they contain pupils of broadly similar ability or aptitudes is often a helpful way of alleviating the learning and teaching problems posed by a wide range of pupils . . .

There seems little doubt that the professional problem identified by HMI is an authentic one, as the much more detailed and grounded evidence from Bennett and Desforges *et al* (1984) and Bennett *et al* (1987) demonstrates, where the mismatch of task to capacity in infant and junior classes respectively is sharply delineated. I do not dispute the problem, But I would want to make three points about the policy of differentiation, as promising a solution to it.

Firstly there has been a worrying slippage in the policy and the language used to describe it, from 'match' to 'differentiation'. In the *Primary Survey*, match was seen as predominantly a state of classroom task setting for the teaching to achieve. The problem was defined as needing a more precisely focused pedagogy on the part of the class teacher, who needed to raise her expectations of able pupils, to set more appropriate assignments, possibly after consultation with the relevant curriculum postholder, and to diagnose more effectively the next steps needed for pupil progress. In later documents, however, the problem has been reconstructed as in the main an organizational and management issue, in which the solution is tracking, setting and other forms of differentiated pupil groupings, including groups taught by teachers as specialists. This is despite the evidence offered in the 8–12 survey, (paragraph 7.3) that the Inspectors could find no association between setting in English and Mathematics and the quality of pupils' work in these areas. It is easy to see this slippage as a shift from the practice of children pursuing the same curricular aims at their own level within a stable class group, to the position where children follow differentiated curricula in groupings, other than their normal class, determined largely by reference to ability.

The second point is an obvious one. The policy of differentiation interpreted as setting children by ability flies in the face of all the evidence gathered in the 1950s, 1960s and 1970s about the unreliability of the criteria for such grouping, its social, ethnic and gender bias, and the damaging and depressing impact upon pupils put into the lower groupings. Given the long research background, how has 'ability' or its euphemistic alternative 'capacity' become such an unproblematic term in the Inspectorate's language?

Thirdly, the primary teaching profession, faced with increasing demands upon it for better performance, and for accountability to the most vocal parents, may already be shifting back to earlier patterns of organization, especially of grouping by ability, as Barker Lunn's (1982) research has shown. For government policy to be appearing to encourage such a shift, with the consequences it implies for all but the pupils defined as able by their teachers, seems verging on the irresponsible. The much more difficult professional practice of enabling teachers more effectively to diagnose children's learning needs, to observe and interpret their learning strategies as a basis for curriculum planning, has been illustrated in the work of Harlen and her associates (1977 and 1982) and in the work of such teachers as Armstrong (1977) and Rowland (1984). But the potential of such approaches seems to be being largely ignored.

Thus the policy of differentiation plays for the safe political option, and the dangerous educational one, giving priority to the perceived needs of the allegedly able pupils at the expense of those of other pupils. Simultaneously, it offers a rhetoric about the need to raise the achievement of all pupils. In its worst form, it is a recipe for pupils to experience at an earlier stage than at present, a polarised school culture, anticipating the divided society they will inherit as adults.

Breadth

There has been a systematic and consistent policy for primary schools to broaden the base of their normal curriculum provision. The picture emerging from HMI surveys, and especially the *Primary Survey*, is of a rather narrow curriculum delivered in restricted form, with a heavy emphasis on formal work in mathematics and language, with pupils given large amounts of practice in computational and comprehension skills they already possess, focused upon exercises as isolated from the rest of the curriculum as they are from the life situations of the pupils. The picture, however depressing, is consistent with that provided by most researchers over the decade, including Bennett, (1976); Bealing, (1972); Galton and Simon, (1980); and Barker Lunn, (1982 and 1984) all of whom found broadly focused 'child centred' teaching, however defined, a minority pursuit.

Attempts to quantify the curriculum provided in primary schools have been bedevilled by definitional problems, but the quantitative picture provided by the 8–12 survey (DES, 1985b) is not dramatically different from other studies. This showed some 40–45 per cent of time per week given over to language and mathematics, about 10 per cent each for history/geography/topic, PE and art/craft, leaving about 25 per cent of the week for all science, CDT, home studies/health education, music, RE and other subjects.

CDT, science and music were singled out by the Inspectors as being particularly badly catered for in the simple terms of how much time was given over to them — or whether any time at all was provided for them. We should bear in mind that middle schools offer a best case analysis, given their favourable staffing formulas, and the tendency for their staffing to be curriculum-led. The picture in junior and infant schools is not only likely to be worse, but is also likely to show more variation. Bennett and his colleagues (1980), for example in their study of open plan schools, reported that time provided for mathematics varied between two and seven hours, and for English, between four and twelve hours weekly.

The documents from HMI see this situation as unsatisfactory either from the point of view of pupil entitlement, or of consistency nationally, and all make out a case for a common curriculum, in terms of the kinds of knowledge that pupils should be initiated into, in primary schools. The conception of the curriculum that should be provided for all pupils is outlined in *The Curriculum from 5–16* (DES, 1985a) and is a broadly conceived one in the liberal tradition. The curriculum should introduce pupils to the 'nine areas of learning and experience', listed as: aesthetic and creative, human and social, linguistic and literary, mathematical, moral, physical, scientific, spiritual, technological.

Curiously, the White Paper has a somewhat more arbitrary list, but nonetheless a similarly broad coverage is implied by the range of categories. There may be problems for the epistemological purists in these lists, but neither document could be used to invoke a back-to-basics movement, especially in the light of the *Primary Survey's* open claim that where a broad curricular approach had been adopted, as opposed to a narrow concentration on basic skills in language and maths, higher standards of achievement had been reached.

It is difficult to read these documents as anything else than a deliberate attempt by the Inspectorate to redefine the basics of primary education, to provide teachers, parents, governors and LEA officers with the grounds for claiming in political debate that a curriculum that does not adequately enable primary children to experience the full range of ideas, skills and values involved in all nine areas, is an indefensible one. It follows from this that a school staffed and resourced in ways that prevent such a broad curriculum being offered can not be publicly justified. Pupils entitled to broad curriculum are entitled to the resources needed to provide it.

This has, of course, been bought at a cost. In the first place the provision of such a broad curriculum is realistic only in medium and large-sized schools, or in clusters of small schools sharing staff. The establishment of children's entitlement to a broad curriculum has simultaneously strengthened the argument for closing schools too small to provide expertise in all nine areas.

A second cost is that the overall conception of the curriculum in the statutory years is still very much a secondary-oriented one. The 'areas of experience' approach fits more easily conceptions of the curriculum in the secondary school than in the early years of primary schooling, not surprisingly given that the model is derived from three documents concerned exclusively with secondary schools (*Curriculum 11–16*, 1977; *Curriculum 11–16: A Review of Progress*, 1981; and *Curriculum 11–16: Towards a Statement of Entitlement*, 1983a). One consequence of the basic model adopted is thus that the policy addresses few of the normal curricular and organizational issues of concern to those working in early childhood settings.

It is too early to seek clear evidence about how far such a policy is affecting curriculum practice in schools, although HMI claims to have evidence, as yet unavailable, that the provision for science has dramatically increased since the publication of the 1978 survey.

My value position is that if the policy can be made to stick in the local authorities and schools, the cost will be worth it. Future historians of education may look at this decade as the period in which the primary schools grew out of the elementary tradition at last, offering as a right to primary school children an entitlement to a modern liberal curriculum, which populist Black Paper ideologies and small minded civil servants alike would no longer be able credibly to resist.

We should not hold our breath until it happens in reality, but the first steps have occurred; all the LEA curriculum statements that I have seen follow the broad-based approach. These include not only Coventry, Warwickshire and Northamptonshire, but also authorities such as Solihull and Croydon, where the elected representatives might have been expected to go back to narrow basics. There is some indirect evidence that centrally defined curricular initiatives may influence schools in ways that broaden rather than restrict the curriculum, from Gipps' (1985) analysis of the impact of the APU upon teachers' conceptions of the curriculum, although the evidence strictly speaking refers to broadening coverage within subjects, rather than across the curriculum as a whole.

Conclusion

Educational Policy and Public Expenditure

In conclusion I shall briefly comment on the relationship of the policy dimensions raised in this chapter to aspects of the financing of education. Two of the policies will cost money in that their implementation will require substantial increases over and above current and planned expenditure. The subject specialization policy will require additional teaching staff in order to free primary teachers from the constraints of their absurdly high contact ratios — above 90 per cent according to the figures in the White Paper. The ILEA report arrived at a figure of about 10 per cent extra teachers designed to enable teachers to take on the dual role, and to allow for legitimate absences from school.

In respect of making provision for a broad curriculum, the improved provision is mainly in the high cost curriculum areas: science, CDT, computer applications, and music. These are high cost in terms of equipment, facilities, maintenance and consumables, relative to other parts of the primary school curricula. But in addition, they are areas where there are current and predicted shortages of subject expertise in teacher supply. In primary schools this shortage is already chronic, with HMI surveys revealing a massive bias towards the arts/humanities in the qualification of staff — a shortage currently disguised by the generalist model of staffing. Primary schools will have to grow their own expertise in these areas for the most part, through relatively expensive forms of in-service training — a position that seems to have been recognized, except for music, in the new (1986) specific priorities.

By contrast and in pessimistic vein, it is worth pointing out that the policy for differentiation, likely to damage primary practice rather than improve it on my construction of it, will cost nothing to implement.

Thus at the heart of government policy there is a fundamental contradiction. It is a contradiction created out of educational policies generated within the DES by the Inspectorate, and requiring for their implementation, substantial increases in expenditure if standards and quality in primary schools are to be sustained and raised: and financial policies generated from within the Treasury and requiring reduced public expenditure. The contradiction cannot be resolved within existing government policies. Whatever anxieties are felt about centrally-derived definitions controlling what is to count as curriculum in state schools, the Inspectorate has provided a clear framework which offers the possibility of improvement. Such improvement is to the routine experience of children in their everyday life in classrooms. It lacks the drama and voter appeal of grander initiatives at secondary level. The extent to which low profile policy proposals are met with real increases of expenditure will be a good test for discovering whether a government's commitment is to the public education system or to political rhetoric.

Author's Note

Since this chapter was originally presented, the Select Committee on Achievement in Primary Schools (House of Commons, 1986) has reported. It has provided the basis for a set of policies very much in line with what I have argued HMI has been promoting (with the notable exception of a lack of concern for differentiation). In particular, it has pointed up the resource and staffing implications of its proposals for 'curriculum coordinators' (roughly equivalent to postholders in this chapter) arriving at a figure of 15,000 extra primary teachers, and articulated more effectively the argument about an entitlement curriculum, outlined on page 26. The DES has yet to respond but the Select Committee report could become the basis for the most comprehensive policy on primary education in England since Plowden. It could also face the policymakers with the task of resolving the contradiction between their educational and financial policies, identified above.

References

ALEXANDER, R. (1984) *Primary Teaching*, London, Holt, Rinehart & Winston.

ARMSTRONG, M. (1977) *Closely Observed Children*, London, Penguin.

BARKER-LUNN, J. (1982) 'Junior schools and their organisational policies', *Educational Research*, 24, 4.

BARKER LUNN, J. (1984) 'Junior school teachers: Their methods and practices', *Educational Research*, 26, 3, November.

BEALING, D. (1972) 'The organisation of junior school classrooms', *Educational Research*, 14, pp 231–5.

BENNETT, S. N. (1976) *Teaching Styles and Pupil Progress*, London, Open Books.

BENNETT, S. N. *et al* (1980) *Open Plan Schools: Teaching Curriculum and Design*, Slough, NFER.

BENNETT, S. N. *et al*, (1987) 'Task Processes in Junior Classrooms', *Education 3–13*, 15, 1.

BENNETT, S. N., DESFORGES, C. *et al* (1984) *The Quality of Pupil-Learning Experiences*, London, Lawrence Erlbaum Associates.

CAMPBELL, R. J. (1985) *Developing the Primary Curriculum*, London, Holt, Rinehart & Winston.

DEPARTMENT OF EDUCATION AND SCIENCE (1977a) *Curriculum 11–16*, London, HMSO.

DEPARTMENT OF EDUCATION AND SCIENCE (1977b) *Education in Schools*, London, HMSO.

DEPARTMENT OF EDUCATION AND SCIENCE (1978) *Primary Education in England* (The Primary Survey), London, HMSO.

DEPARTMENT OF EDUCATION AND SCIENCE (1981) *Curriculum 11–16: A Review of Progress*, London, HMSO.

DEPARTMENT OF EDUCATION AND SCIENCE (1982a) *Education 5–9: An Illustrative Survey*, London, HMSO.

DEPARTMENT OF EDUCATION AND SCIENCE (1982b) *Mathematics Counts* (The Cockcroft Report), London, HMSO.

DEPARTMENT OF EDUCATION AND SCIENCE (1983a) *Curriculum 11–16: Towards a Statement of Entitlement*, London, HMSO.

DEPARTMENT OF EDUCATION AND SCIENCE (1983b) *9–13 Middle Schools: An Illustrative Survey by HMI*, London, HMSO.

DEPARTMENT OF EDUCATION AND SCIENCE (1984) *The Organisation and Content of the 5–16 Curriculum*, London, HMSO.

DEPARTMENT OF EDUCATION AND SCIENCE (1985a) *The Curriculum from 5–16*, London, HMSO.

DEPARTMENT OF EDUCATION AND SCIENCE (1985b) *Education 8–12 in Middle and Combined Schools*, London, HMSO.

DEPARTMENT OF EDUCATION AND SCIENCE (1985c) *Science from 5–16: A Statement of Policy*, London, HMSO.

DEPARTMENT OF EDUCATION AND SCIENCE (1985d) *Better Schools* (Cmnd 946g), London, HMSO.

GALTON, M. and SIMON, B. (1980) *Inside the Primary Classroom*, London, Routledge & Kegan Paul.

GIPPS, C. (1985) 'A critique of the APU' in RAGGATT, and WEINER, G. (Eds) *Curriculum and Assessment*, Oxford, Pergamon/Open University.

GOODACRE, E. and DONOUGHUE, C. (1983) *LEA Support for Language Postholders*, School of Education, Hayes, Middlesex Polytechnic.

HARGREAVES, A. (1983) 'The politics of administrative convenience: The case of middle schools' in FLUDE M. R. and AHIER, J. (Eds) *Contemporary Education Policy*, London, Croom Helm.

HARGREAVES, A. (1986) *Two Cultures of Schooling: The Case of Middle Schools*, Lewes, Falmer Press.

HARLEN, W. *et al* (1977) *Match and Mismatch*, London, Schools Council/Oliver and Boyd.

HARLEN, W. (1982) 'The role of assessment in matching', *Primary Education Review*.

HER MAJESTY'S INSPECTORATE (1982) *The Study of HMI in England and Wales* (The Raynor Report), London, HMSO.

House of Commons (1986) *Achievement in Primary Schools* (Third Report of the Education, Science and Arts Committee), London, HMSO.

Inner London Education Authority (1985) *Improving Primary Schools* (The Thomas Report), London, Learning Resources Centre, ILEA.

Joseph, Sir K. (1984) speech to the North of England Conference, Sheffield.

Kogan, M. (1975) *Educational Policy Making: A Study of Interest Groups and Parliament*, London, George Allen & Unwin.

Lawton, D. (1983) William Walker lecture, quoted in the *Times Educational Supplement*, 4 November.

Primary School Research and Development Group (1983) *Curriculum Responsibility and the Use of Teacher Experience in the Primary School*, Birmingham, Department of Curriculum Studies, University of Birmingham.

Ponting, C. (1986) *Whitehall: Tragedy or Farce?*, London, Hamish Hamilton.

Richards, C. (1986) 'The curriculum from 5–16', *Education 3–13*, 14, 1.

Rodger, I. *et al* (1983) *Teachers with Posts of Responsibility in Primary Schools*, Durham, School of Education, University of Durham.

Rowland, S. (1984) *The Enquiring Classroom*, Lewes, Falmer Press.

Salter, B. and Tapper, T. (1981) *Education, Politics and the State*, London, Grant McIntyre.

Shipman, M. (1984) *Education as Public Welfare*, London, Methuen.

Shipman, M. (1985) 'Local education authorities and the curriculum' in Raggatt, P. and Weiner, G. (Eds) *Curriculum and Assessment: Some Policy Issues* Oxford, Pergamon/Open University.

Taylor, P. (1986) *Expertise and the Primary Teacher*, Slough, NFER.

Tomlinson, J. (1986) 'Public education, public good', inaugural lecture, University of Warwick.

Wicksteed, D. and Hill, M. (1979) 'Is this you? A survey of primary teachers attitudes to issues raised in the Great Debate', *Education 3–13*, 7, 1.

Chapter 9

Accrediting Teacher Education Courses: The New Criteria

Jean Rudduck

In 1983/84 the Secretary of State for Education and Science announced plans for, and established, a Council for the Accreditation of Teacher Education (CATE). In January 1985 it began its work. In September 1986 the Select Committee on Education recommended that the CATE remit should not be renewed when it expired in 1986: it maintained that CATE's 'methods of operation have aroused much anxiety and confusion in teacher education institutions' (*Times Educational Supplement*, 26 September 1986).

CATE's task is to advise the Secretary of State on the accreditation of initial teacher training courses. It is required to undertake a review of all existing approved courses and to consider proposals for new courses. Accreditation, a process distinguishable from validation, includes administrative approval for the running of particular courses in the light of nationally planned target numbers, and an assessment of the suitability of courses for the professional preparation of teachers. It is the latter responsibility that CATE's work is particularly designed to assist with.

In arriving at a recommendation about a particular course, which has then to be passed on to the Secretary of State, CATE normally considers a variety of evidence:

— written information about the content and structure of the course and the qualifications and experience of the staff involved. This information is compiled by the staff of the institution whose course is under scrutiny;
— additional information supplied in a face to face interrogation when a sub-group of CATE meets a small team of staff from that institution;
— an account of the deliberations of a local committee, set up as a necessary part of the new accreditation process with the task of scrutinizing and reporting on all aspects of the course;
— a report on the course prepared by a team of HMI and made available to CATE together with a copy of any statements of contested

interpretation that the institution concerned thought it prudent to offer.

The criteria that were laid down to guide CATE's work (see Department of Education & Science (1984) Circular 3/84) can be summarized as follows:

(i) that postgraduate certificate in education courses should be at least thirty-six weeks long;
(ii) that institutions should develop and run their initial teacher training courses in close partnership with experienced practising school-teachers;
(iii) that teacher trainers should maintain regular and frequent experience of classroom teaching and be released for this purpose;
(iv) that teaching practice and school experience together should amount to no less than fifteen weeks in postgraduate courses, and not less than twenty weeks in BEd (Bachelor of Education) or concurrent courses;
(v) that, taken overall, the higher education and initial training of all intending teachers should include at least two full years' course time devoted to subject studies at higher education level, and that courses should include the methodology of teaching the chosen subject specialism or curricular area;
(vi) that entrants to courses should have at least grade C in 'O' level maths and English; students going in for secondary teaching should hold an 'A' level appropriate to their intended main subject;
(vii) that students should be prepared to teach the full range of pupils they might encounter in an ordinary school, with their diversity of ability, behaviour, social background and ethnic and cultural origins;
(viii) that institutions should carefully assess the personal and intellectual qualities of candidates and should involve practising teachers in the selection of students.

Public challenge and criticism has focused on the following three points: the coherence and educational integrity of the criteria and the view of teaching and teacher education that they are seen as projecting; the failure of the Secretary of State to provide an adequate resource base for the implementation of the criteria; and the implicit assumptions about power and control which CATE embodies.

Issues of Power and Control

Early criticism was directed towards the membership of the Council and the mode of appointment of its members. A colleague's irreverent caricature of the CATE membership captures the unease felt by many teacher trainers. He is on record as saying — while acknowledging the inaccuracy of his report —

that appointments included the person who designs wire trolleys for supermarkets and the racing correspondent of a national newspaper! Bill Taylor, Chairperson of CATE, has however 'refuted any suggestion that the members of the Council are not representative of teacher education or the profession as a whole or that few possess recent and direct experience of teacher training' (*Times Higher Education Supplement*, 28 September 1984.) Of the eighteen members — all ministerial appointees — only two were in fact recruited from institutions with responsibility for teacher training, and these two, a college principal and the head of a university department of education (UDE), might be thought to offer an administrative perspective rather than one based on first-hand involvement in the day to day practice of teacher education. The Universities Council for the Education of Teachers (UCET) expressed its concern (1984) with courteous restraint:

> The membership of CATE was of some surprise to everyone, not least in its omissions.

The issue of CATE membership is important because it highlights the question of who has the right and the competence to make professional judgments about teacher education courses. If accreditation is more than a simple technical process of ordering and quantifying clear-cut factual information and involves instead some interpretation and imaginative reconstruction, then the experience and shared understanding of those who judge is of crucial importance.

Judgments are also made by Her Majesty's Inspectorate (HMI), and HMI's role in the accreditation process, at least as far as universities are concerned, has raised the issue of academic freedom. A thin veneer of respect for academic freedom has been maintained in the rhetoric surrounding the conditions under which HMI may visit UDEs. HMI are only permitted to visit in response to 'an invitation' from the university — but it has become clear that UDEs which fail to 'invite' HMI to visit will not have their course accredited since the receipt by CATE of an HMI report is an integral part of the process of accreditation.

Then there is the issue of publication of HMI reports. Reports on the teacher training programmes offered by public sector institutions are publicly available and there has been pressure on universities to conform to this convention. Why, it is asked, should universities maintain any right — albeit in name only — to determine whether or not HMI should visit, and why should universities cling to an elitist and self-protecting right, which is in opposition to the spirit of public accountability, to determine whether or not their HMI report should be published? Comparisons across the binary line tend, I think, to cloud the real issues of academic freedom. The most important issue, in my view, is that of the preservation in higher education of a capacity for the independent critique of central policy. Sadly, in the context of financial constraints and the consequent threat of loss of jobs and closure of departments and institutions, higher education has become conformist rather than critical, and has offered little concerted resistance to those aspects of the CATE operation which are proper cause for concern. Departments have individually been quick to accept the bald prerequisites of accreditation, such as a thirty-six week course, even though the case for such a move is insubstantial and the resources inadequate. Indeed the knock-on effects of implementing such a criterion could be profoundly damaging to departments which wish to sustain or develop a good research profile, and research is a crucial factor in the restructuring being carried out in a number of universities in the wake of the University Grants Committee's (UGC) recent selectivity exercise. We have run like sheep towards the short-term security of conformity, but only at considerable cost to the longer term image and status of teacher education. CATE offers in effect a classic example of a power-coercive change strategy in action (see Bennis *et al*, 1969). The James Report (DES, 1972), in outlining a professional model for in-service work, emphasized 'the status and independence of the teaching profession and of the institutions in which many teachers are educated and trained'. CATE is part of a fundamental break with such a view of higher education and seems to represent further evidence of what Salter and Tapper (1981) call the 'creeping centralism' of the education system.

Resources

Here, criticism has been mainly directed at the Secretary of State's cavalier attitude to resources and in particular the absence of guaranteed funding to cover the additional professional and administrative costs of:

- extending the one-year PGCE (Postgraduate Certificate in Education) course to thirty-six weeks (an increase on average of four-six weeks, or one-fifth);
- allowing teacher educators to be released from normal duties to gain recent and relevant experience in classrooms;
- establishing or extending structures for involving practising teachers in the selection of applicants;
- building closer and more effective partnerships with schools;
- establishing and servicing local committees to scrutinize all aspects of teacher education courses.

Initially it was left to departments to fight their own battles for resources within their own institutions. Staff in departments which have no financial slack and which have not voluntarily been offered additional resources by their institutions can become desperately overworked if they attempt to maintain a proper research base for their teaching while moving towards the relationships and structures that CATE requires. UDEs seem to have been particularly hard hit. Many universities have traditionally held ambivalent attitudes towards education departments, and in the Gentlemen versus Players encounters of political gamesmanship, such departments tend not to command great support. The Association of University Teachers (AUT) produced a review (1986) too late and too thin to influence the battle for resources: all one can say is that it recognized the problems. The Universities Council for the Education of Teachers (UCET) did better by putting pressure on the UGC to make an allowance in the recurrent block grant of .2 unit of resource per student on teacher education programmes, expressly to assist with the cost of the thirty-six week course. But there appear to be no sanctions for universities who fail to pass on the bonus in ways that are genuinely supportive of new practices.

The dilemmas of resourcing extend beyond the departments of education themselves. A recent Select Committee Report pointed out — wise after the event — that 'there should be immediate and extensive consultation and discussion of the principles behind the criteria and of the various ways these might be implemented both at national and regional level between CATE, HMI, validating bodies, local authority associations and trainers' (*Times Higher Education Supplement*, 26 September 1986). To be effective CATE required such discussions at an early stage in its development. In particular it needed a careful orchestration of local education authority (LEA) resources to support the spirit and principle of partnership. This did not happen. A structure was built on sand rather than on the bed rock of shared professional understanding and commitment. In an address to a Society for Research into Higher Education (SRHE) conference, and voicing, according to the *Times Educational Supplement*, 'the suspicions and hostility of most of his audience', Ivan Reid said this:

> If we're serious about involving classroom teachers in the education of teachers . . . that assumes a willingness of the classroom teacher to cooperate. It also assumes their efforts will be diverted from the classroom into teacher education.

Money is needed to allow teachers to contribute to teaching sessions planned by higher education tutors and to assist with the selection of applicants. Money is needed to allow teachers in charge of students on teaching practice to give proper attention to their role and responsibilities, and in particular to spend time with each other and with tutors, at departmental level, on the collaborative assessment of practical teaching. Few teachers seem to have thought seriously, outside the conventional demands of teaching practice supervision, what partnership in teacher education might mean. Moreover, any plans that higher education departments might have had to use in-service activities to help teachers rethink their role in the induction of new entrants to the profession has been effectively demolished by the new arrangements for in-service funding: teacher education is not yet so high on most LEAs' lists of in-service priorities that they will set aside part of their limited budget for such programmes.

In short, the Secretary of State has insisted on partnership between tutors and teachers but failed to build into his scheme of things any incentives or directives to bring schools and LEAs into that partnership.

Coherence and Educational Values

Higher education has been giving so much busy attention to the logistics of implementing the CATE criteria — extra resources, staff conditions of service, study leave versus CATE leave, payments to teachers, balance of representation on local committees — that it has failed to examine the logic of the criteria, both individually and as a set. A slavish and conformist adherence to their surface demands could fracture the existing professional coherence of many teacher education courses. What I would like CATE to do — and perhaps it is, as a result of criticism, now moving in this direction — is to stop requiring departments of education to make discrete responses to individual criteria (as CATE does in its letter seeking preliminary information about particular courses) and invite them instead to describe the principles that give structure and meaning to their teacher education courses. If CATE were to request a course philosophy, it might then ask a team of tutors to show how the criteria can take their place within that unifying framework. In this way we would have responsibility as professionals to make a reasoned and coherent interpretation of the criteria and as a consequence we might then recognize that they have some value in making us think about important aspects of our work.

The CATE criteria are, as a 'list', a pretty crude assortment. Individual criteria do not seem to have been arrived at via research evidence or thoughtful analysis, and the lack of convincing justification is irritating. For instance, there is an insistence on a thirty-six week PGCE course. Was this a political move — a way of achieving greater parity between the courses offered in public and private sector institutions, or was it assumed that extending courses by four to six weeks would automatically improve their quality, irrespective of the difficulties created and the resentment generated by the lack of resources? The important question for CATE in scrutinizing PGCE programmes ought not to be '*Are* you moving to a thirty-six week course?' but 'How do you propose to use the extra four to six weeks?' In our own PGCE course we are using the extra weeks to allow students to undertake group tasks in schools working on topics identified by teachers. This new element strengthens the commitment of the course to principles that we happen to believe in: the principles of collaborative enquiry and reflection on action as a basis for professional learning. That is the unifying thread of our course, and the extra time may well strengthen its impact.

Another controversial criterion is that teachers be involved in the selection of students for teacher education courses. Again, no systematic research evidence has been offered to justify such an investment of time and energy on both sides. It is not clear that the involvement of practising teachers does significantly modify the judgments of higher education tutors. Indeed, it seems that the agreement between teacher and tutor is generally so close that busy teachers could well argue that this is one part of the process of teacher education that higher education tutors should manage on their own! If we were seriously worried about the judgments made during selection, and if we were agreed about the need for more rigorous procedures, then we would probably move experimentally to school-based and pupil-involved interviewing. By observing applicants interacting with pupils in a classroom or other setting we are able directly to monitor students' capacity to relate to young people, assess their skill in analyzing situations, and so on. These are the qualities that it is difficult to get at in the traditional interview. So, if CATE is concerned about improving the screening of applicants, then we might need to do something more challenging and compelling than merely ensuring that practising teachers are present at conventional interviews.

Then there is the emphasis on the personal qualities of applicants for places on teacher education courses. Hargreaves (forthcoming) offers a wry comment:

> In the main, exactly which personal qualities are likely to make a good teacher are not discussed; nor is there any discussion of whether those qualities might vary according to the age group being taught, the special requirements of a teacher's subject, or the ethos of the school, for instance. And no advice is forthcoming on *how* these (largely unstated) qualities might be identified through the selection process either. HMI certainly give no indication of the measures they themselves used for identifying the relevant qualities. All that is recommended is that experienced, practising teachers be increasingly involved in the selection process. It seems, then, that in the absence of more objective procedures and criteria, Government is here prepared to place its trust in the process described in a well-known British idiom: 'it takes one to know one'.

McNamara (1986) has also written a provocative critique of reliance on such an elusive concept as 'personal qualities' in making judgments about present or potential teacher effectiveness. In *The New Teacher in School* (DES, 1982) HMI suggest that 'personal qualities of the teacher were in many cases the decisive factor in their effectiveness'. There is no convincing exploration, however, of the basis of such a judgment. According to McNamara, researchers who scrutinized 800 relevant studies arrived at no definitive understanding of the qualities that made a good teacher: all that they could say with confidence was that good teachers were unlikely to be unsympathetic, depressed, and given to moral depravity. Other research shows how complex the issue of personal qualities is. Teachers who are likeable by other teachers may not necessarily produce the most sound learning in pupils, and teachers whom children appreciate, whom they get on with, and who help them to learn with enthusiasm, may have traits that fellow teachers find unattractive. To highlight the complexity, McNamara quotes Slater and Crompton's summary (1980) of teachers' and tutor's views of a particular student teacher:

> In the classroom he was more than competent by any commonly applied criteria: he had control, he dealt with all events successfully, he presented interesting material in a lively way and he was rewarded

> with the most lengthy, carefully done and lively writing to be found in the children's exercise books. The school, however, insisted on failing him for practical teaching on the grounds that (a) his behaviour in the staff room was unacceptable; (b) his appearance was repellent; and (c) his materials, aims and methods in the classroom were not what was desired in the school . . . He had long, lank hair to the shoulders, filthy clothing (his trouser flies were bound up with electric flex) and a disposition not to bathe very often . . . He had too a disposition to fear and detest authority figures . . . He also had a disposition to lick the teaspoons with which the coffee was made after stirring his own cup . . . (The tutor) insisted on passing him on the grounds that the children didn't find him repellent and did not remark on his appearance and that they did enjoy and find his lessons interesting. His basic disposition . . . was towards inspiring children with his love of poetry, in reading it and writing it.

Moving away from this particular example McNamara poses two important general questions that relate to the dilemmas of judgment in selection:

(i) If it is claimed that personal qualities are related to teacher effectiveness, is it sensible to make judgments about those qualities when they are manifested in non-teaching contexts such as staff rooms or selection interviews?
(ii) If, say, established teachers, the lay public or politicians are given more influence in deciding what sorts of people become teachers, will this not dispose the school system to greater conservatism and conformity?

He goes on to ask why it is that we are urged by the DES to look out for 'a robust but balanced outlook' in applicants when, given the well-documented conservatism of classroom practice, we perhaps might instead be looking out for teachers who have 'a critical and reformist attitude'. The issue of personal qualities, it seems, is more complex than both CATE and the DES appear to think it is.

But most contentious of all are two other criteria: one relates to the requirement of 'recent and relevant experience' among tutors on teacher education courses, and the other to the requirement that at least half a student teacher's programme of study on a non-PGCE course should comprise a subject or subjects studied at a level appropriate to higher education. A public statement issued on behalf of the Joint Professional Committee of Manchester Polytechnic and Manchester University (1986) argues the weakness of the latter proposal for would-be primary teachers. It does not, the Committee claims, 'hold its views in isolation. Rather it echoes voices raised in protest up and down the country':

> In the last decade the content of these (BEd) courses, for those students who want to teach in primary schools, has moved further and further away from subject specialization. Instead intending

> teachers have been required to study across a broad curriculum, comparable to (that of) primary schools themselves, and to concentrate far more on basic class management and classroom organizational skills . . . Similarly, more and more time during the training period (four years) has been spent in schools, observing and practising.

Sockett (1985) takes up the same argument: 'The Circular (3/84) reads', he says, 'as though there has been no history of development in teaching and teacher education in the last decade' (p.118). Reid (1985) attacks the subject studies criterion from a different angle. The requirement clearly emanates, he says, from the White Paper, *Teaching Quality* (DES, 1983), which in turn drew on another HMI document which reported that nearly a quarter of primary teachers and one in ten secondary teachers appeared to show some insecurity about the subject they were teaching when observed. It is not clear, Reid argues, whether this uncertainty was the result of a poor grasp of the subject, or inexperience in applying the knowledge at classroom level. He goes on to ask whether this is a serious cause for alarm — sufficient for example to divert the current trend of BEd courses. Hargreaves (1986 p.15) quotes the response of the National Union of Teachers (NUT) (1984) who see the CATE requirement, much as Sockett does, as a backward step:

> To reshape teacher education to produce teachers who can only work within a subject based curriculum, who regard themselves principally as transmitters of a certain body of knowledge, is to turn the clock back and ignore recent developments. (p.19)

And finally, the criterion of 'recent and relevant experience' of schools and classrooms. The proposal itself is not one that teacher educators would question, but what we have been wary of is the way CATE seemed initially to be interpreting it — although there is evidence now that CATE's view is changing. My straightforward reading of the early CATE documents yielded this argument:

1. Higher education tutors have a problem of credibility among both teachers and student teachers.
2. Credibility can be achieved by ensuring that higher education tutors become more like teachers (ie they must demonstrate their competence in the school classroom).
3. Partnership, looked at one way, is a strategy for blurring identities in the interest of making higher education tutors more like teachers. Hence CATE's interest in shared appointments and in short term job exchange opportunities.

I would challenge such propositions. The first, that higher education tutors lack credibility is, in my view, rooted in the pervasive theory/practice and ivory tower/chalk face dichotomies that continue to cloud our thinking about the relationship between higher education tutors and school teachers.

Yes, of course some of our colleagues have *not* taught full time in schools for five, seven or in some cases ten years. But if credibility as teachers is what it is about, then a statutory thirty days teaching in a comprehensive school will not, should not, make such colleagues credible as classroom teachers. To think that credibility can be won so easily is an insult to the teaching profession.

Recent and relevant experience we must have, but not as a means of proclaiming our credibility as school teachers. Teaching in the schools of the 80s, in the shadow of unemployment and with inadequate resources, is a complex and demanding task. Teaching in higher education is also a complex and demanding task. If we accept the DES's concern that training should be age-specific (ie, primary trained students should not teach secondary pupils), then we should not expect higher education tutors to be successful teachers in both schools and in higher education. *Our* credibility as 'teachers' must be based on the quality of our work with our higher education students.

Another CATE criterion, partnership with schools, must be interpreted in relation to the criterion of recent and relevant experience. Partnership as a principle in a working relationship is essentially about understanding and respecting what each partner can distinctively contribute. What teachers as partners in the enterprize of training can offer is practice-based knowledge rooted in sustained experience of a particular setting. What higher education tutors offer is an analytic perspective that is fed by observation in a range of classrooms and sharpened by the evidence of research. These two perspectives are the ingredients of a good dialogue and should be the basis of a good partnership in teacher education. Once it is accepted that our contribution is different from, and complementary to, that of the practising teacher, then we can begin to think what recent and relevant experience should really be about.

To fulfil our part of the contract, tutors in higher education need:

(a) to understand the problems and achievements of teachers and learners, in different contexts, taking into account social, historical and ideological perspectives;
(b) to be well-informed about changing structures and practices in the school system;
(c) to understand, and to accept responsibility for helping others to understand, the pressure and values that influence such structures and practices.

It follows that recent and relevant experience could be made up of a variety of activities. It could include periods of teaching in classrooms — but as a source of insight rather than as the basis of credibility as school teachers; periods of observation in schools and classrooms; opportunities for participation in school-focused in-service activities; opportunities to conduct research in pursuit of issues that teachers regard as important; opportunities to explore the pupils' perspective on the events and interactions of the classroom. 'Teaching' is thus only one way of understanding what classrooms are like.

Higher education tutors need to preserve their right to use the time they have in different ways. As Head of a PGCE course, I want to hold on to the variety of experiences with different teachers in different classrooms that my colleagues have enjoyed. I do not want to narrow that experience by urging them to rearrange their patterns of work in order to have a block of thirty days teaching experience in one school. At certain points in a career, such a sustained and focused experience may be very valuable, but we must be the judges of when and why that would be the best way of learning for a particular colleague.

It is, in my view, crucial for education departments to construe their contribution to training in terms of a broad, analytic and preferably research-based perspective. And it is crucially important for teachers to be exposed to such a perspective. As Schon (1983) points out, in teaching as in other professions we encounter certain types of situation again and again: 'Many practitioners, locked into a view of themselves as technical experts, find little in the world of practice to occasion reflection'. The habit of self-critical enquiry is both a defence against teaching becoming consigned to routine and a basis for the continuing improvement of practice. The distinctive contribution of higher education tutors is to help both new and experienced teachers develop ways of seeing that will help them to keep professional curiosity and learning alive. Most importantly they have to ensure that student teachers experience the excitement of learning through critical reflection on practice. As Stake (1987) says; 'A student teacher's literacy is a life long reaching . . . A teacher never learns the ending of the task of teaching'. The commitment must always be to the improvement of some aspect of practice.

Hugh Sockett, in his inaugural lecture (1985), denounced the CATE criteria as a 'second rate, second hand list of banalities' (p. 118). He went on: 'There is no identifiable underlying view of what a professional education in teaching is' and he commented that the word 'reflection', 'as a term appropriate to degree level work', appears only once in Circular 3/84. UCET makes a similar point in its discussion paper for CATE: it warns against overemphasizing the 'survival skills' aspect of training, arguing that:

> 'Students must also acquire an analytical, reflective and critical framework within which to examine such skills . . . It would seem to be the mark of a good teacher training programme that while giving proper weight to essential classroom techniques, it develops a broader capacity for professional judgment, recognizing the importance of independent thought and appropriate innovative action.

Surely it is, as Sockett suggests, the role of a department of education to ensure, through research, that assumptions about learning and teaching continue to be tested. But Circular 3/84, he says, is written as though research had little significance for knowledge about teaching and learning and as though the teacher-as-researcher movement does not exist.

If there is any unifying perspective in the CATE criteria it is that of teaching as a craft which can best be picked up through attachment to practitioners. Such a view may contain some powerful messages about the future location of training. Suspicion was renewed when I read a front page article in the *Times Higher Education Supplement* (2 January 1987) headed *PGCE is Worthless Says New Manifesto*. The authors, a group of right-wingers including Baroness Cox and Professor Roger Scruton, argue that schools should be free to employ graduates straight from universities and that the PGCE should be replaced by a system of working apprenticeships during which a teacher would receive a salary and so learn the skill of 'communicating with children in the circumstances most likely to engender it'. Is Circular 3/84, which appears to be promoting ways of making higher education tutors more like teachers, a covert first step towards the phasing out of higher education's role in the education of teachers? Let us hope that any General Teaching Council which is set up — and dissatisfaction with CATE has accelerated its planning — will embody an enlightened and coherent view of teacher education rather than the outdated and narrow concept of training which both CATE and the so-called 'new' manifesto seem to favour.

Note

This chapter is based in part on a talk given by the author at a one-day conference held in London on 17 May 1986 on 'Recent and relevant — The issue of professional updating'. The conference was organized by the Teacher Education Group of the Society for Research into Higher Education (SRHE). A revised edition of the talk was later published as 'Ingredients of a good relationship', *Times Educational Supplement*. 18 May 1986.

References

ASSOCIATION OF UNIVERSITY TEACHERS (1986) 'Effects of DES Circular No 3/84 on university schools and departments of education: Report of survey results', mimeo, London, AUT, November.

BENNIS, E. G., BINNE, K.D. and CHIN, R. (1969) *The Planning of Change*, London, HOLT, RINEHART & WINSTON.

DEPARTMENT OF EDUCATION AND SCIENCE (1972) *Teacher Education and Training* (The James Report), London, HMSO.

DEPARTMENT OF EDUCATION AND SCIENCE (1982) *The New Teacher in School: A Report by Her Majesty's Inspectors*, HMI series: Matters for Discussion 15, London, HMSO.

DEPARTMENT OF EDUCATION AND SCIENCE (1983) *Teaching Quality* (Cmnd 8836), London, HMSO.

DEPARTMENT OF EDUCATION AND SCIENCE (1984) *Initial Teacher Training: Approval of Courses*, (Circular 3/84), London, HMSO.

DEPARTMENT OF EDUCATION AND SCIENCE (1985) *Better Schools* (Cmnd 9469), London, HMSO.

HARGREAVES, A. (1986) 'Teaching quality and teacher thinking: An interpretive view', paper presented to the third conference on teacher thinking and professional action. University of Leuven, Belgium, 14–17 October.

HARGREAVES, A. (1988) 'Teaching quality: A sociological analysis', *Journal of Curriculum Studies* 20, 3, pp 211–31.

JOINT PROFESSIONAL COMMITTEE OF MANCHESTER POLYTECHNIC AND THE UNIVERSITY OF MANCHESTER (1986) 'CATE's criteria questioned' issued by the Communications Office, University of Manchester, June.

LODGE, B. (1985) 'Is there life after CATE?', *Times Educational Supplement*, November.

MCNAMARA, D. (1986) 'The personal qualities of the teacher and educational policy: A critique. *Journal of Curriculum Studies*. 12, 1, pp 29–36.

NATIONAL UNION OF TEACHERS (1984) *Teaching Quality*, London, NUT.

REID, I. (1985) 'Hoops, swings and roundabouts in teacher education: A critical review of the CATE criteria' in *The Impact of CATE*, report of a one-day conference, London, 26 October.

SALTER, B. and TAPPER, T. (1981) *Education, Politics and the State*, London, GRANT MCINTYRE.

SANTINELLI, P. (1984) 'Taking some of the credit', *Times Higher Education Supplement*, 28 September.

SANTINELLI, P. (1986) 'Select committee suggests phasing out of CATE', *Times Higher Education Supplement*, 26 September.

SANTINELLI, P. (1987) 'PGCE is worthless, says new manifesto', *Times Higher Education Supplement*, 2 January.

SCHON, D. A. (1983) *The Reflective Practitioner*, London, Temple Smith.

SLATER, K. S. T. and CROMPTON, J. (1980) 'Disposing of the dispositions, Professor HIRST and the PGCE', *British Journal of Teacher Education*, 6, 3, pp 253–61.

SOCKETT, H. (1985) 'What is a school of education?', *Cambridge Journal of Education*, 15, 3, Michaelmas, pp 115–22.

STAKE, R. (1987) 'An evolutionary view of programming staff development' in ANDREWS, I. and WIDEEN, M. (Eds) *Staff Development for School Improvement*, Lewes, Falmer Press.

UNIVERSITY COUNCIL FOR THE EDUCATION OF TEACHERS (1984) *Bulletin No 16*, London, UCET, autumn.

UNIVERSITY COUNCIL FOR THE EDUCATION OF TEACHERS (1985) 'Recent, substantial and relevant experience: A discussion paper for CATE from UCET', mimeo, pp 1–5.

Chapter 10

Better Schools? Present and Potential Policies about the Goals, Organization, and Management of Secondary Schools

David Reynolds

> The trouble with you damn liberals is that you don't know what you believe in
>
> (The newspaper editor in *Pravda*)

To describe and to analyze contemporary governmental policy in secondary education is a daunting task. The largest volume of policy changes from 1979 to date have been in this sector, making the simple descriptive task very large-scale. The sheer volume of governmental pronouncements that are overt explanations for why policy changes are being made has also been bewilderingly large and sometimes contradictory, as in the varied pronouncements on the reasons behind the perceived need for teacher appraisal (Wilby, 1986). The era of policy making by press release, by speech or by informal 'leak' (as in the first introduction of the phrase 'schools of proven worth' which later became enshrined in formal policy) makes description of policies and stated reasons for policies an even more complex task.

It is also important to note that attempted explanations of policy changes and their location in terms of their possible structural causes are also difficult to undertake. Within the sociology of education, there has recently been little of the close concern with policy and practice that characterises the discipline in other countries such as the United States, a point made repeatedly and forcefully by David Hargreaves (1981). When the sociology of education has looked at practice, it has usually looked at classrooms, not at the schools, the LEAs or the other educational sectors that are most involved in framing current policy changes. Studies of educational policy making, of educational policies and of administrative/organizational arrangments have been far more prevalent within the discipline of politics than within the discipline of education in Britain. Also, in conventional empirical British educational research, attention has usually been focused upon uncontextualized, unstructured and context-free educational settings — the educational policies (and their causes) that generated the phenomena under study were taken as a given in most studies of this kind.

For a variety of reasons, then, the attempt in this chapter to describe and explain governmental policy on secondary education starts with the odds stacked heavily against it! Readers are therefore referred to other authors that have attempted the same task for some alternative competing persepectives (Dale, 1987; Ball, 1987; Green and Ball, 1988; Simon, 1986)

The Goals of Govermental Policy 1979–87

Overall, these goals would seem to be as follows:

(i) Whereas past governmental attempts have involved the use of the system of education to be *transformative* of the wider economic and social structure (as in past Labour governments' concern for policies on equal opportunities or multicultural education for example), governmental policy is now to use the system to be *reproductive* of the existing economic structure and of existing social, ethnic and gender divisions.

(ii) Whereas past governmental attempts have concentrated upon improving the attainments of the bottom two-thirds of the ability range and on improving equality of opportunity between social classes, current policy is to concentrate resources upon the top third of the ability range and social classes.

(iii) Whereas past attempts have involved attempting to reorientate the system towards the attainment of more social goals (as in many comprehensive schools' personal and social education programmes for example), present policy is to redirect schools towards academic goals as of overwhelming importance and away from social goals.

(iv) Whereas past policies attempted to use the educational experience to distance pupils from their social class or origin by hopefully giving them a different social class of destination, present policies reduce the chances of class mobility by reorientating low ability pupils towards lower class vocational employment.

(v) Whereas past policies attempted to use the educational system to deliberately foster a questioning of the existing set of social relationships, present policy is to close off such questioning from the school curriculum in general, and for lower ability and working class pupils in particular.

Policy can be simply explained as aimed at maximizing the chances of class advantage for certain sections, together with the minimalization of the prospects of disadvantaged groups being able to resist that process by the acquisition of the really useful knowledge that would generate an understanding of the society around them. We will now proceed to look at how these goals are to be attained in the different areas of secondary education policy.

The Organization of Secondary Education

Policy since 1979 has been designed increasingly to differentiate between schools and between ability ranges within schools, leading to a return to forms of selection where class chances are distributed highly unevenly. The Assisted Places Scheme will — after the expansion to 35,000 places a year announced in May 1987 — take over 1 per cent of high ability, mostly more socially advantaged, children out of state comprehensive schools and give them the competitive edge (Halsey, *et al*, 1980) provided by the independent sector. Since all these pupils are likely to be in the top 10 per cent of the overall ability range, the actual effects of this creaming of state schools' 'O' level sets, sixth-forms and 'A' level subject sets (often already very small in subjects like languages) is likely to be dramatic, involving some schools losing perhaps up to one-tenth of their higher ability pupils. This creaming of the state comprehensives is likely to be exacerbated by the arrival of up to twenty new city technology colleges (CTCs) taking something like 1000 pupils from each city's existing comprehensive schools. Although publicly there have been statements that the colleges will take from the full ability range, it is difficult to believe that groups such as remedial children, special educational needs children and lower ability pupils will feature in the colleges in the proportions that they already exist in other schools. Given a likely oversubscription of middle and high ability pupils, no college is likely to take low ability children in over-large numbers. This creaming of higher ability pupils is also likely to be paralleled by the creaming of science, CDT and electronics teachers from the state comprehensive schools.

At the same time as the creaming is likely to affect the whole comprehensive sector — leading to poorer intakes and pupil outcomes for those pupils left behind and to greater chances for those sponsored out of the system — the comprehensive sector itself is already differentiating into 'good' schools (usually in middle class catchment areas) that are getting better intakes and 'poor' schools (usually with more disadvantaged catchment areas) that are performing relatively worse as their pupil ability range is altered.

This differentiation between schools is being aided by the following factors:

(i) It is clear that parental choice procedures are magnifying pre-existing academic and social differences between schools. In Welsh experience these choice procedures are mostly used by parents of higher social class to avoid their children attending schools in more disadvantaged catchment areas. This increases pupil differentiation in two ways: because pupils have *individual* effects upon their school's ability balance, and because pupils also have an additive *group* effect (Rutter *et al*, 1979; Willms, 1986).

(ii) Surviving grammar schools, or 'schools of proven worth' that have survived reorganization or tertiary schemes, are creaming an even higher proportion of the ability range in the 1980s because the substantial reduction in the size of the overall secondary age cohort is taking place against a background where these selective schools are maintaining constant pupil numbers. The tendency will be for comprehensive schools that are creamed in this way to resemble the academic intakes of former secondary modern schools, a tendency that will only increase as more and more LEAs move towards tertiary policies and thereby generate an even larger number of schools opting out.

(iii) Manpower Services Commission (MSC) schemes have already adversely affected the intellectual balance of the sixth forms in poorer catchment areas, with many former 'new sixth' candidates now opting into YTS schemes to put themselves in the employment 'shop window' for prospective employers.

(v) Increasing reliance upon parents as sources of school income, which can amount in some cases to approximately one-third of total capitation expenditure in more advantaged catchment areas, will magnify differences between schools in their effectiveness and in their results, given the relationship between resource levels and the effectiveness of schools as suggested by the Inspectorate.

(v) The movement into ordinary comprehensive schools of children with special educational needs and the growth in forms of intermediate treatment that necessitate children staying at their existing school rather than moving to a community home is likely to magnify differences between schools in their attainments, given that such children are highly likely to be school dependent in their learning (Reynolds, 1982). The 'advantaged' comprehensive and the 'disadvantaged' comprehensive will affect these pupils very differently and therefore the differences between schools will be magnified.

The net effect of all these changes is increasingly to magnify a selective division between schools, with the independent and the surviving selective schools and the most advantaged comprehensive schools in middle class areas increasingly having a more able pupil intake, a better balance of ability and therefore better results, with the remaining two-thirds of comprehensive schools increasingly creamed by the above policies both of higher ability and higher social class children.

In addition to maximizing differences *between* schools, differences *within* schools between pupils of different ability ranges are being magnified. By contrast to past liberal policies which sought to hand down through the ability range in a modified form the cognitive curriculum of the former grammar schools, the government aim is now to differentiate school experience for different groups. Whilst the new General Certificate of Secondary Education (GCSE) examination might not necessarily have been part of this differentiation process, the clear association in ministerial statements of the new exam's top three grades with 'O' levels and the next three grades with the former CSE examination (together with the use of the different CSE and 'O' level examination boards to draw up different portions of the new curriculum) have both created a clear differentiated vision in the minds of parents and of teachers. In Welsh secondary schools, pupils and teachers still habitually use the terminology of the ' 'O' level streams' and the 'CSE streams' in years 4 and 5. The increasing popularity of City and Guilds for lower streams, some LEAs development of non-examination Certificate of Education courses for lower ability children and the increasing use of vocationally-orientated link courses (usually with local technical colleges) that combine work experience with an acquisition of practical skills all suggest that the comprehensives' lower stream experience is increasingly to be only a passport to working class occupations for predominantly working class children.

Increasingly, then, there will be clear divisions between the top third of the ability range (targetted at the GCSE), the middle third (targetted at the Technical and Vocational Education Initiative (TVEI), some GCSE and some courses that are vocationally-orientated) and the bottom third (targetted at some TVEI, a little GCSE but mostly at work-related orientation and preparation courses). Such divisions will lead to children of different ability and social class receiving an education that will differentiate them and allocate them to occupational routes that will *reflect* their initial ability and social class or origin. Furthermore, the long accumulated 'excellent' knowledge in the bourgeois curriculum which may in parts resemble the really useful knowledge desired by many socialists (Reynolds and Sullivan, 1980) will increasingly be restricted to other than working class children. That this knowledge base is sufficient for social transformation to occur is unlikely, but it must be noted that the closure of this knowledge from most lower ability pupils' access is unlikely to advance the cause of social change and is likely to perpetuate the existing economic and social system.

It is important to conclude this section on the organization of secondary schooling by explaining in more detail why these policies are being pursued. There is much evidence (see Reynolds, 1988) that in the late 1970s and early 1980s the comprehensive sector (then educating over 90 per cent of all state secondary pupils) was developing a far more authentically 'comprehensive' philosophy and organisational style than formerly. Early comprehensive schools were in most accounts (for example, Reynolds, Sullivan and Murgatroyd, 1987) heavily grammar school orientated in that they concentrated their efforts upon the top third of the ability range and also concentrated very heavily upon academic success rather than on broader social development. Comprehensive schools — concerned with showing themselves to be no 'threat to the higher ability pupils and their middle class parents in their early controversial years — were simply *reactive* to outside societal pressures on them, not *purposive* in the sense of having a distinct comprehensive philosophy of their own.

This philosophy, which did begin to emerge by the early 1980s, was somewhat different to the 'grammar school for all' orientation of the early comprehensive schools. It stressed, at least in the schools we researched in

South Wales (see Reynolds, 1988), that the schools should concern themselves with the whole of their ability range including those lower ability pupils just above the remedial bands who had until then escaped special policy targetting. The new comprehensive philosophy also stressed that the social development of pupils was itself an important outcome of schooling which, although perhaps not quite as important as the cognitive or academic outcomes of school, had been seriously neglected in the schools' early years.

In these moves towards what can only be termed a more authentically comprehensive philosophy, the local comprehensives in our study seem to be performing in a very similar way to the comprehensive sector as a whole in the late 1970s and early 1980s. Moon (1984) outlines how the comprehensive schools surveyed in his volume were increasingly emphasizing social goals, were concerned to generate more participatory management styles, were attempting to relate to parents and were concerned to move away from what Hargreaves (1982) calls the 'cognitive intellectual domain' that typified the grammar school curriculum. Weeks' (1986) London comprehensives were also moving towards an emphasis upon social development, towards closer relationships with the surrounding community and towards a concern for the whole ability range. Extensive debate about aspects of the comprehensive school such as the need for a pastoral curriculum (Marland 1980), personal and social education (Her Majesty's Inspectorate, 1979), a community-based curriculum (Hargreaves, 1982), the need for participatory management structures (Murgatroyd and Reynolds, 1984; Weeks, 1986) and the integration of pastoral and academic structures (Best, Ribbins and Jarvis, 1983; Reid, 1986) all suggest that the comprehensive system nationally was either changing, or thinking about changing, in ways very similar to our Welsh comprehensives. From evidence in Weeks (1986) and in official publications such as *Aspects of Secondary Education* (HMI, 1979) it is clear that the schools were not simply seeking to reflect the initial predispositions of their pupils in their resource allocation in any direct *reproductive* fashion, but were — by their increasing concern with lower ability pupils and with pupils' social outcomes — seeking to be *transformative* of the wider society and its divisions.

It is interesting to speculate, then, that recent governmental policy towards comprehensive schools — involving returning them to concentration on academic outcomes and concentrating them on the needs of high ability pupils — may paradoxically have been because schools *were* beginning to succeed in generating authentic comprehensive education, not because they weren't. The schools' increasing concentration upon the bottom two-thirds of the ability range may have adversely affected the top third of the ability range and also the traditional sixth-formers — this is clearly shown by the virtually static proportion of the ability range getting 'A' levels compared with the rapidly rising proportion acquiring the lower level of 'O' and CSE qualifications (Rutter, 1980). The schools' increased concern with social goals, even more marked in other societies with the common schoool such as Sweden or the United States, threatened to open the curriculum and the schooling experience to forms of discourse and interaction much more suited to the expressive culture of lower social class pupils (Bernstein, 1959). The widening of the curriculum to include more relevant or 'new' knowledge may well have been a powerful spur to the learning of those of lower ability who had come to be labelled as culturally disadvantaged because of their non-possession of the 'cultural capital' (Bourdieu and Passeron, 1977) necessary to perform well in acquiring the old, traditional grammar school curriculum.

In conclusion, then, government policy is to concentrate attention upon the more able, differentiate them in schools, concentrate them in certain schools and give to them the conventional humanistic excellence of the old grammar school curriculum. The less able are to have a more narrow, vocationally-orientated education in schools deprived of large numbers of their middle class and more able pupils.

It should be clear that the selection of children into 'good' schools or 'poor' schools is to be based upon their social class or area of residence and not their ability. Past selection policies that involve examinations such as the 11+ often disadvantaged the dull middle class children, whereas comprehensive schools without any imposed balanced catchment areas favoured these pupils, because the 'good' schools are in the more advantaged catchment areas. This middle class advantage from comprehensivization probably explains why Solihull and the other LEAs trying to reintroduce selection by ability were opposed by large numbers of middle class parents whose children clearly benefited greatly from selection on the basis of catchment area rather than on the basis of ability. Recent policies allowing schools to opt out of LEA control and the removal of ceilings on the numbers of pupils at the 'good' schools will inevitably drain the remaining 'poorer' comprehensives of their surviving higher ability pupils, leaving a system that is heavily differentiated between even more advantaged middle class catchment area comprehensives and even more disadvantaged ones.

The middle class revolution in secondary school education is therefore becoming completed, with the restoration of schools which are academically orientated, concerned mostly with their more able children and which in addition systematically advantage any child living in a middle class catchment area. From selection by ability, we are moving full circle to the nineteenth century practice of selection by social class, except for the small scholarship ladder of brighter working class pupils who are 'sponsored' into the elite. The implications of these policies for the perpetuation of the existing class system are obvious.

The Curriculum

Policy in this area probably needs little elaboration. There has been a movement towards a nationally specified core curriculum for ages 11–16, to take up something like 90 per cent of pupils' school time. The specification of national criteria in the different subjects of the new GCSE and the related move towards more clearly specified curriculum goals are both part of this process of clearly demarcating the intended knowledge content of schooling. Testing at ages 7, 11 and 14 will enable parents and others both to check their children against others of a similar age but also check on the performance of their children's schools against the national guidelines as to what children should be capable of.

It is important not to overestimate the degree of central determination of the curriculum, since all the available evidence (for example, Morgan, 1980) suggests there cannot be easily be any such thing as a national core curriculum because of the enormous variability in the range of actual subjects available in different secondary schools. There is also a huge variability in the time allotted to the *same* subject in different schools — one study (Gorwood, 1983) reported a difference of almost two times in the number of timetabled hours for mathematics in thirty-six middle schools in only one borough. For French the ratio was 2.2 between the school with the least hours and the school with the most hours and for science the ratio between 'top' and 'bottom' schools was 3.2. Given this variability in subject availability and in the sheer 'quantity' of instruction, a National Curriculum will take a considerable period of time to generate any national entitlement to knowledge across schools. The variation between schools in their choice of examination boards, their use of optional courses and their choice of the precise curricular areas to be assessed (as say in the choice of English set texts) generates further variation in the curricular knowledge that children may be exposed to that is likely to last into the immediate future.

In spite of this evidence of widespread current curricular variation in terms of knowledge quantity and quality the attempt to move towards a national core curriculum is clearly an attempt to try to ensure an increased homogeneity of values in a society which has clearly become more ideologically heterogeneous and individualistic, partly as a result of increased economic differences but also as a result of the recognition of differences of gender and race.

The actual knowledge base of the curriculum itself is undergoing attempted change. At the most fundamental level of all there were the attempts of Sir Keith Joseph to reduce the proposed curricular coverage that stressed the impact of science upon society in various science syllabi and to make changes in the history national subject criteria that increased the attention given to what can loosely be called the supposed benefits of the British Empire for those ruled by it in the past. Attacks on various social scientific subjects (both verbal and financial) are part of the same strategy, as have been the virulent attacks on children's supposed left wing indoctrination by means of peace studies, or gay rights studies or multicultural education. The attempt to recreate a homogeneous, consensual, conservative value and belief system through use of the curriculum is paralleled by the attempts to improve the take up and the status of wealth producing subjects within the curriculum. The attempts to improve the image of industry, the emphasis upon better school/industry liaison, the TVEI itself, the bursaries for science and CDT teachers and the constant ministerial emphasis upon 'education for employment' is symptomatic of this trend, which involves an attempted biasing of the system towards the study of scientific and technological subjects for the more able together with the encouragement of more training in the acquistion of practical skills for lower ability pupils at secondary levels.

It is not difficult to see that the proposed specified secondary core curriculum, the more clearly specified curricular content, the testing to enable parents to hold schools accountable for their curriculum, the attempts to erode the position of the newer and more progressive subjects that have appeared in recent years and the attempts to generate more industrially relevant courses for some pupils are aimed at maximizing the chances of education being involved in wealth generation, but minimizing the chances of the growth of ideological positions that might influence pupils to question the unequal distribution of that wealth, both by closing some pupils off from 'dangerous knowledge' and also by ensuring that all pupils share a communality in their knowledge base that unites them.

Assessment in Secondary Education

It is clear from governmental policies that the examination system has been expected to determine the shape and nature of the school curriculum,rather than the nature of the curriculum determine the nature of the examination system. The desire to have effective, allocative selection mechanisms and perhaps the desire to select *per se* has outweighed the frequent and reasoned arguments that *only* removing the chains of 16+ examining would free the curriculum to be a learning rather than an assessment determined experience. Given that the stage of years 16–18 for the great majority of young people is still a semi-educational or training experience because so few actually get jobs outside the orbit of the Manpower Services Commission or the school sixth-forms, the continued presence of examinations at age 16 rather than age 18 can only be seen as the result of a desire to prevent the curriculum from being more learner-centred and directed. The examination and assessment system is clearly actually designed to restrain the curriculum from meeting learners' wider needs.

There are also grounds for believing that the new forms of assessment such as the GCSE and pupil records of achievement or 'profiles' may also have profound social consequences and may also, like other policies, act to increase the perpetuation of the existing system of social stratification. The new examinations represent a move to forms of continuous assessment where teachers will mark course work and allocate marks to pupils that they are already teaching. All the available evidence suggests that these subjective judgments are more class-biased than are closed examinations marked 'blind'. In the early 1950s when Hertfordshire LEA switched from the use of the 11+ examination to teacher judgments and allocations (the Thorne plan) as a means of allocation to grammar schools, there was a marked reduction in the proportion of working class pupils going through to selective education,

(Halsey and Gardner, 1953). It is interesting that this seminal article is rarely referenced within present-day sociology of education.

There are, of course, cultures where teacher-determined assessment is used extensively and within them there do not appear to be the same cultural or class biases as might be evident in Britain — America is an example where there are perhaps not the same cultural or class 'markers' that teachers can discriminate on the basis of, since the population is more homogeneous in its cultural markers of accents, clothes, and the like. In Britain, this situation does not exist — whether assessment by records of achievement and by increased teacher assessment is aimed at improving motivation or at increased surveillance seems of considerably less importance than the likelihood that these assessments may be class, gender and race biased by comparison with the present systems utilized.

It is worth pointing out in conclusion that the increased use of continuous assessment may also increase inequality of educational outcomes between social groups because some children will be directly able to add to their own ability and cultural capital that of their parents, as with using parents to help with continuous assessment exercises and with homework. To the past indirect effects of home background upon performance will now be added direct effects. Ironically, the potentially highly unequal effects of these new assessment procedures upon poorer children may well explain why it is that socialist and the labour movement have, until their recent supposedly progressive change of outlook, historically favoured closed examinations because of their likely minimization of the chances of the upper classes or middle classes obtaining benefits from school out of proportion to their ability.

Management

Emphasis in this area of policy has been on improving what is called the 'quality' of the education system by reforms in teacher education, by the proposed appraisal of the teaching force and the encouragement of more effective and efficient within-school management. The reforms on teacher education have been seen in most accounts as encouraging a more practical orientation to teacher training, particularly as shown by the emphasis upon the importance of school experience and of professional teaching skills rather than the parts of training that have a broader more 'educational' purpose. The past emphasis upon encouraging teachers to reflect on their practices, to question existing educational arrangements and to think about alternative educational features (as reflected for example in Woods and Pollard, 1987) is being rapidly replaced by a more utilitarian focus upon training as the acquistion only of the 'craft knowledge' of professional tips (see Rudduck's chapter in this volume). Given the local educational authorities' increased control over INSET budgets, this utilitarianism is likely to further pervade in-service education also.

Within secondary schools, emphasis has been put on the importance of a systematic teacher appraisal and currently a range of pilot schemes are underway that build on the well-known *Those having Torches* appraisal scheme commissioned from Suffolk LEA. Although there have been repeated assurances that teacher appraisal has formative implications and that it will be limited to personal career development rather than being linked directly to pay or to promotion (see the review of evidence in Reynolds, 1987b) the belief persists that the new responsibility allowances will be linked (if not overtly then covertly) with the new appraisal schemes. Looking at school management, the numerous initiatives on headteacher management training, the encouragement of school self-evaluation and the concern of the last Secretary of State for Education and Science for the introduction of more effective appointments procedures for headteachers (as in the 'Post' project of the Open University, 1982) are all well-known developments. In all of these initiatives, though, and in the pronouncements of the Inspectorate too, the emphasis has been put upon a 'top/down' managerial ethos of headteacher and staff relationships in spite of the mounting evidence of the ineffectiveness of such procedures in large institutions (Reynolds, Sullivan and Murgatroyd, 1987) and in spite of the movement amongst management theorists towards the third great management revolution involved in the new participatory or 'bottom/up' management styles that are widely argued to be more effective (Murgatroyd and Reynolds, 1984 and 1985). An increasingly hierarchical and ranked society is clearly not to be served by an educational system that devolves power to its teachers. The form of authority in the school is to parallel that in the wider society.

Power, Accountability and Control

Overall policy is to 'squeeze' the schools from the top down through the use of central government legislation and from the bottom at individual school level by using increased parental power to put pressure on their schools. This procedure is highly unlikely to generate any conflicts both because the government has given power to parents in only limited areas and also because the nature of parental power and of those parents who will utilize it is likely to generate effects upon schools that the government approves of. A centrally legislated core curriculum, government state patronage and support for schools wanting to 'opt-out' from LEA control *and* various parental choice and parental governor procedures are all therefore entirely compatible, since parental power as historically manifested will be used to tie back the schools to narrow instrumental goals, to teach conventional morality and to relate school experience more closely to later earning potential and to the world of work outside. Governmental avoidance of any policies that are concerned with the LEA level and their by passing of this level by funding the CTCs and any opted-out schools directly is clearly understandable given the LEA's generally Labour political persuasion, the latter's anger at government expenditure restrictions and the manifest evidence of past LEA ineffectiveness in delivering any school improvement (see Pearce, 1986 in the case of LEA advisers). The increased parental power and the school autonomy from the LEA that is intended will clearly restrict LEA impact in such areas as anti-racism and anti-sexism.

Whether these simultaneous top/down and bottom/up strategies will achieve the goals of improved educational standards is, however, highly doubtful given the complete absence of any helping initiatives for the schools caught in the middle of the policy sandwich. When the late Richard Crossman, by contrast, tried a very similar mix of central legislative pressure and direct local accountability in his reform of provision for the mentally handicapped in the late 1960s, he was insistent that this pressure should be accompanied by major initiatives in the areas of research and of developmental dissemination of good practice directly to the hospitals and professionals. The complete absence of such helping initiatives in secondary education, together with the alienation of the teaching profession because of governmental imposition of the 1987 pay award and the concurrent withdrawal of union negotiating rights, all suggests that whilst educational outcomes from schools may be redistributed between social groups in the ways outlined earlier in this chapter, it seems highly unlikely that the four-fifths of pupils who are going to be untroubled by school reorganization will be in institutions of any higher educational efficiency or effectiveness. To pressurize all schools without giving them guidance on how to cope with that pressure is simply a recipe for educational retardation.

Some Caveats

It would be wrong, though, to conclude this analysis of the nature of Conservative governmental policies in secondary education without making clear the inadvisability of any determinist form of analysis that sees government legislation as inevitably and quickly being reflected in changing form and changing content of secondary schools.

Firstly, the educational system in Britain has customarily possessed a considerable autonomy from direct central control that exceeds that of virtually all other industrialized societies (Reynolds, 1984). It has customarily exhibited multiple autonomies — of the school from the LEA, of the LEA from central government and of the school and LEA from the community. In such a system, variation in practice is large and the time that is necessary to actually change the basic organizational form of school, let alone change the *experience* of education consumed by pupils, is extremely lengthy. Although there is no doubt that this systemic autonomy has been reduced considerably, the within-system variation and school level freedom is still marked by comparison with other societies at the present time, although the freedom is clearly diminishing.

Secondly, it would be wrong to see too close a fit between the content and form of schooling and the wider needs of the economy. The curriculum, as proposed by the government and as outlined in the subject criteria, still leaves much of the knowledge base of the traditional liberal humanities that may be economically far from useful in the direct generation of wealth (Weiner, 1982). The industrial training lobby within the government would in some accounts (Ball, 1987) have wanted the breaking down of subject demarcations, the ending of any 'knowledge for its own sake' tradition and the encouragement of schools to develop the full range of pupils' social and academic skills to generate the 'rounded characters' that industry is said to need. The absence of initiatives on those lines (except for their marginal insertion in school practice through TVEI) strongly suggests that educational policy is not solely determined by economic needs and that history, past cultural styles such as 'the gentlemanly idea' of education and the wishes of members of the education system themselves all play a part in the determination of the nature of secondary school practice. In just the same way as it would be unwise to assume too great a determination of the education system by government policy formulations, it would be also unwise to assume too great a determination of educational policy by only the *economic* needs of the wider society.

Thirdly, it would also be wrong to underestimate the resistance to the policies that has emanated from within the educational system. LEA resistance has clearly been marked and the latters' contestation of government policies both ideologically and financially has been so marked that the government has overtly tried to reduce LEA power and to bypass LEAs by increasing the power of other educational sectors like parents. Resistance in the peripheral areas of Britain like Wales to the demands of the new vocationalism has also been marked and has its roots in the historical traditions that saw education as an escape for working class children from the need to be mere wealth producers for others. Schemes such as TVEI had initially a very low take up in LEAs in the periphery — seven out of eight Welsh LEAs, for example, refused to bid for TVEI money when it was first announced, not wanting to produce 'factory fodder' (in the words of one Welsh Director of Education). Also, teacher trades union opposition to appraisal schemes has halted the six LEA pilot projects. At school level, resources intended only for TVEI children have in the case of some schools been used to change the educational experience across the curriculum and ability range. There are schools who have refused to move in the direction of the new managerialism of government thinking and which have pioneered open, democratic and participatory decision making structures (see Reynolds, 1987a). There are also whole geographical areas like the Inner London Education Authority where the attempt is still made to develop children socially, to develop low ability children particularly and to maintain an emphasis upon progressive curriculum development. The precise strength of these resistances to government educational policy remain at the time of writing unclear but they obviously have the potential to reduce the possibility of the successful implementation of the governmental blueprint for education.

Fourthly, some of the present range of policies as they are implemented may have potentially transformative, not merely reproductive, effects. The equal opportunities for boys and girls to do what are usually gender stereotyped courses enshrined within TVEI, for example, may help to transform the practices of gender inequality perpetuated in schools. The experience of using new modular courses, again as in TVEI, may have effects upon the remainder of the curriculum. A staff group faced with the need for a more collective orientation to facilitate the development of new curriculum materials for the Certificate of Prevocational Education (CPVE), for example, may find the experience of working together so mutually satisfying that it generates a demand for a more collectivistic and less individualistic staff management structure. There may be a 'revolution of rising expectations' amongst lower ability pupils who — on finding that they are able to complete more practically orientated City and Guilds courses or some aspects of the Low Achieving Pupils Programme (LAPP) for example — then have the confidence and self-esteem to acquire more 'academic' subjects also. The transformation of the educational system, and therefore of the wider society, rather than the reproduction as intended of the existing set of class, race and gender relations, may be the unintended consequence of some of the contemporary policy initiatives as the potentially progressive aspects of some of the policies are worked on within the schools.

The Labour Party and Secondary Education

We have a set of Conservative policies, then, that aim to reproduce the existing set of economic and social relations, although there must remain doubts about the policies' chances of ultimate success. The system's increasing concern with academic and social development and with other than higher ability pupils is to be eradicated by a combination of central government legislative initiatives and local parental pressure upon individual schools. Class advantages are to be magnified and lower ability children denied access to high status knowledge. The school curriculum's more progressive orientations towards equal opportunities, multicultural education, peace studies and the like are also likely to be casualties of a new right wing educational populism. Schools themselves, in their own increasingly hierarchial managerial structure, are to reflect wider societal hierarchy. The school is to serve the needs of the economy, not aim to transform the wider economic and social structure.

The range of alternative policies that have been expressed from within the existing political system has been, it must be said, quite pitifully small. The Labour party has been particularly slow to recognize the increasing popular concern with education — even though recent years have seen 'education' running close to 'the economy' and 'the health service' in terms of issues of public concern. Only in Spring 1986 did Neil Kinnock and Giles Radice, then Labour education spokesman, attempt to *purposively* outline Labour's own so-called alternative educational policy rather than continue to simply *reactively* wait for the appearance of Conservative policies to oppose with boring repetition (see for example Kinnock, 1986, and Radice, 1986). Why has there been this past lack of concern with generating an educational policy?

Firstly, it seems likely that this absence of clear policies is in part a simple reflection of past historical neglect in the party, as evidenced by the fact that the Wilson government of 1964/70 is said to have discussed the reorganization of secondary education only a handful of times (see Reynolds, Sullivan and Murgatroyd 1987).

Secondly, the neglect of education as a policy area may well reflect the thinking of some members of the more left wing Tribunite or Campaign groups that educational reforms are merely ameliorative strategies that are inadequate substitutes for the root and branch reforms that are necessary in the class, income and opportunity structure. Educational policies, for these groups, are merely the focus of right wing Fabian and social democratic thinking which seeks the impossible of bringing about social change within an essentially unchanged capitalist economic system.

Thirdly, it is clear that the absence of educational alternatives reflects on the fact that a Labour government would itself have continued many Conservative initiatives had it won power. The moves to increase parental representation on governing bodies, the compulsory core National Curriculum, TVEI, pupil profiling and the emphasis upon educational training for industrial needs (which was itself the theme of Callaghan's 1976 Ruskin speech) are all policies that Labour have stated they would support. Avoiding educational discussion was therefore a way of keeping these policy communalities well hidden.

Fourthly, the absence of alternative educational thinking reflects upon the lack of any input of research and advice to the party from educational researchers or from the sociology of education that might have generated a more informed policy. Sociology of education has until quite recently eschewed directly policy relevant research, preferring to endlessly question educational policy goals rather than be concerned with developing more effective policy means. The result has been an absence of any informed thinkers who could have helped with the development of educational policies as did A. H. Halsey, Tyrell Burgess and Michael Young when Tony Crosland was Secretary of State for Education and Science in the 1960s. The blueprints of effective organizational means that were available to the party then were conspicuously absent in the 1980s.

Lastly, the absence of educational policy initiatives in the party reflects the absence of any strategic thinking in the party about general policy matters. The emphasis in the last few years has been upon how best to *present* policies and upon how to present personalities to the voters, not upon the *nature* of the policies themselves. Indeed, even after Labour's recent defeat, Neil Kinnock's first political utterance urged his party not to '. . . let up or slope off into self-indulgent seminars and painstaking internal analysis'. The party's problems, because of the absence of in-depth thinking about policy options in education, are compounded also by the absence of any coherent philosophical position that can act as an intellectual support to policy. Simple welfarism, labourism or 'do gooding' do not represent consistent world views in the same way as does Thatcherism, socialism or communism. In the absence of an underpinning world view of the nature of the society that the Labour party wishes for, the scope for coherent and integrated sets of policies is very limited — attitudes to the independent school sector depend, for example, upon a more general societal philosophy which balances individual exercise of freedom against its impact on the whole society, but where in the party has there been any philosophical discussion of this wider issue? Attitudes to the national core curriculum depend upon the extent to which individuals would be under a Labour government free to explore individually determined sets of knowledge or be constrained to have a knowledge base in common with others in the society — on this issue too philosophical discussion of the individual/society relationship has been conspicuously absent. Labour — quite simply — hasn't been thinking.

Labour Isn't Learning

The result of the absence of strategic thinking, of philosophical debate and of any input from academic researchers showed itself clearly in the educational policies upon which the Labour party fought the 1987 election, few of which carried the conviction of being able to deliver their promised societal and educational goals.

Overall, the party's emphasis was upon how equality of opportunity for members of society and higher educational standards overall were both attainable with the same sets of policies, yet these goals may well be mutually exclusive — a redistribution of effort to help lower achieving pupils may adversely affect overall standards because the resources given to them would have evoked a greater 'return' from the higher ability pupils they were formerly lavished upon. The pursuit of quality *with* equality carried little conviction as a theme, since it was never made clear *how* one could attain both goals at the same time.

Where direct policies were proposed to reduce class inequalities — as in the expansion of higher education and further education (Radice, 1986) — there was no apparent understanding of the last half century of educational experience which shows that opening up *access* to education is not the same as ensuring equality of *outcome* or *benefit* for different social groups. The Oxford Social Mobility study frequently used in public statements by Radice to apparently support his policy beliefs actually contradicts his views since it shows of course that expansion of educational opportunities over time does not necessarily reduce relative inequalities between social groups in their benefit at a point in time.

The policies that were to reduce overall educational inequality and raise educational standards were also highly unlikely to attain these goals. There was an emphasis in the public statements upon improving the quantity of resources available in schools, improving the fabric and maintenance of buildings and getting smaller class sizes, in spite of all the available evidence (summarized in Rutter, 1983, Reynolds, 1982) that these three factors are largely unimportant in affecting how pupils perform. Labour, it seems, was still more informed by the materialistic analyses of Marx than by those analyses which saw human beings as the products of both material and more independent cultural worlds.

The other drift of Labour policies was concerned with the 'quality' of educational organizations, rather than the mere quantity of resources available to them and involved among other things the prohibition of selection in all local education authorities, yet again the clear evidence is that the formal organization of schooling is less important than the informal world of school in determining educational outcomes. The selective process can work as much within comprehensives as it can between grammar schools and secondary moderns, and may be more damaging to development in the covertly selective comprehensive than in the overtly selective schools (Reynolds, Sullivan and Murgatroyd, 1987). Within apparently mixed ability classes, also, selective streaming may still take place (Ball, 1981). Also — as in the evidence on pastoral care systems — the establishment of *formal* mechanisms for pupil care and guidance are no guarantee that there is an *informal* or cultural ethos that is committed to those goals (Rutter *et al*, 1979). Simply, then, the party was historically grossly naive in thinking that in prohibiting selection between schools it was somehow necessarily establishing true comprehensive schools with a non-selective within-school ethos. Legislation to abolish selection may be necessary for comprehensive education to flourish but it is not sufficient. Ending the formal organization of selection does not end its informal manifestations and Labour showed no indications that it understood this.

It is clear, then, that the policies on education, as recently outlined by the Labour party, are highly unlikely to deliver their goals. Indeed, they seem strangely reminiscent of those policies originally outlined in the early 1960s which had subsequently such disappointing results. Now — just as then — the material determinants of learning were emphasized, together with the need for organization and structural reform, yet the ways in which the internal ethos and informal structure of schools like comprehensives may be the key determinants of pupil learning is not acknowledged in the policy formulations.

Most important of all, the policy leverage upon the system is to be the same mixture of increased central legislation and modest increases in parental power (as in the charter of parental rights) that was tried in the 1960s, yet there is no evidence that this leverage will now be able to change the nature of schools' internal quality any more than it was in the past. The LEAs who would be active 'improvers' or 'interveners' in changing schools simply do not feature in Labour policy as educational agents, presumably because of the supposed unpopularity of some of their efforts represented by the ILEA. The teaching profession itself is to be better paid, appraised formatively, better trained, involved more in school management and also involved in a National

Council of Education, but whether these limited 'helping' or 'enabling' initiatives to teachers and schools will be any more successful than their similar counterparts of the 1960s and 1970s must remain open to considerable doubt.

Concern with levels of spending and with the nature of parental/state power over schools are the hallmarks of an essentially sterile set of educational policies, since what comes out of schools is neither determined by their resources nor completely by their formal organization and since these policies would retain substantial autonomy at the level of the individual school. How to *directly* affect the people and policies in the 'black box' of the school is little discussed. The essential central or LEA delivered helping initiatives to improve secondary school practice that should be given to schools are never considered.

The Tory government has, of course, direct market based solutions to the problem of secondary school quality — the introduction of national curriculum benchmarks and national teacher appraisal — that are combined with a use of parental power and parental choice to use market forces to eradicate 'poor' schools. The variability in the quality of schools since comprehensivization probably greatly increased, since selection by ability probably generated more homogeneous social class groupings in different schools than does the current selection by catchment area into 'good' or 'poor' schools. Conservative education policy traded on the widespread public perception that many schools existed that 'weren't working' (to use their 1979 election slogan) and that there was large quality variability. It seems that their educational policies may well have been particularly popular amongst the skilled working class, since it was this group that was often finding its quite able children in comprehensives with disadvantaged catchment areas and since it was this group that may well have accurately perceived that their children might, under a more selective system, have been attending good quality selective grammar schools. Until Labour can generate non-market solutions to deal with the issue of school quality, it seems highly likely that the Conservatives' market based remedies will enable them to be identified as being more concerned with educational standards.

Rethinking Labour's Educational Policies

For Labour to generate effective and convincing educational policies, a number of problems have to be overcome. Effective comprehensive schooling, like effective multiracial or anti-sexist education, can probably only come about through a necessary statutory legislative commitment that specifies in legal terms what the internal organization, curriculum and processes in comprehensive schools should be, in much the same way as equal opportunities legislation or special educational needs legislation confers such rights and entitlements already. Such central state legislation, when combined with interventionist LEA policies as in the case of the ILEA's commitment to anti-racist policies, can generate transformed school practices and outcomes as shown by the recent ILEA evidence of those ethnic groups who now *overperform* relative to what would have been expected of them on arrival at school.

However, to move in this direction, the party needs not only to accept central government legislative interference (unpopular with teachers and their unions). It has to accept that effective comprehensive education, if enforced, may generate more disadvantaged middle class pupils, because of the shift of resources that will go to the more disadvantaged once they have a legal entitlement to them. The reaction against interventionist ILEA policies on multiculturalism from white parents is a reaction that would be magnified many times over if interventionist LEAs and legislative central government both acted upon the organization of secondary schools.

Legislation by itself, though, is unlikely to be enough to generate comprehensive internal school processes that reflect a concern for the social and academic development of all pupils. This will require both increased parental power and the availability of a large range of helping initiatives to enable schools to evaluate, improve and change their practices. On parental power, the party needs to overcome its dislike of it. This stems in part from Fabianism's historical concern with top/down policy making, rather than with policy seen as reflecting in a bottom-up fashion what parents might want. It also partly accurately reflects on the fears in the party that only a minority of more middle class parents may take the parental power and that they may subsequently use it to the advantage of their own children. Fabianism is an ideology of bureaucrats, not of democrats — it was once said of the Webbs that they believed that all that was necessary for human progress was sound intentions and a good filing system! Since all the available evidence points to the importance of school/parent links as determinants of school quality (see review in Rutter, 1983; Reynolds, 1982) and since parents would *have* to be involved in ensuring quality in the system to avoid even larger accretions of power to the interventionist LEA's and the legislative central government, the party needs to rethink its attitude towards parents. There is a substantial difference between giving parents direct power over schools (as have the Tories) and only giving parents the power to object if someone else *misuses* their power (as the Labour party has proposed).

Lastly, it is self-evident that the party needs to reorientate itself away from reflecting the needs of education *producers* towards the role of reflecting the needs of *consumers*. Much of the reluctance to directly intervene in the social life of schools is because of teacher union pressure to maintain teacher and school autonomy. The reluctance to deal with the issues of school or professional competence and quality (by the introduction of a General Teaching Council to ensure that the profession maintained its own standards for example) also testifies to an unwillingness to take on the entrenched vested interests of educational providers that are holding back educational standards.

In all these various areas it is vitally important for the Labour party to rethink the nature of its educational policies. The desired policy model outlined here is one of state legislation of entitlement to a comprehensive educational experience, with parental power being used to ensure school compliance. An interventionist LEA policy aimed at evaluating, improving and changing internal school policy, together with the direct provision of the helping initiatives of training and the like to the schools themselves are also likely to be necessary.

All the above is only inevitably a personal statement about what alternative policies on secondary schooling should be like, based on the evidence from the Welsh experience of secondary schools. Clearly there is room for many other contributions that will reflect both different personal ideologies and different sets of research evidence. The evidence is that the old link between research, policies and political policy making needs to be urgently remade to develop alternatives to the present Tory policies. In particular, educationalists and academics need to look at the following questions:

1 To what extent is it educational or perhaps non-educational policy areas that maximize educational benefits (as in the case of the impact of education maintenance allowances upon inequalities of opportunity)?
2 How much systemic autonomy is there at LEA and individual school level, since such autonomy is a prerequisite for successful educational social engineering?
3 At which levels of the educational system — LEA or school or LEA district — is there the greatest pay off from interventions and at which level is change most easy to obtain?
4 What precise interventions and improvement strategies generate the greatest practical changes in schools/LEA's? Top/down models? Consultative assistance? (Murgatroyd and Reynolds, 1984 and 1985; Reynolds, 1987a).
5 What should the goals of educational reform be? Improving overall education quality or reducing inequality of opportunity? The encouragement of individual self actualisation or of societal cohesion? The generation of wealth through education or the production of education for consumption?

All these are challenging policy areas where an input of ideas, knowledge and research data from the academic world of educational research might help the Labour party develop alternative educational policies. There is curently no sign of that input even beginning to occur. In its absence, it seems likely that liberal educational policies will lack all conviction and that radical right wing popularizers will be able to walk their educational streets in perfect safety for many years to come.

References

Ball, S. J. (1981) *Beachside Comprehensive*, Cambridge, Cambridge University Press.
Ball, S. J. (1987) 'Comprehensive schooling, effectiveness and control: An analysis of educational discourse', unpublished manuscript.
Bernstein, B. (1959) 'A public language: Some sociological determinants of linguistic form', *British Journal of Sociology*, 10, 4.

BEST, R., RIBBINS, P. and JARVIS, C. (1983) *Education and Care*, London, Heinemann.
BOURDIEU, P. and PASSERON, J. C. (1977) *Reproduction in Education, Sociology and Culture*, London, Sage.
DALE, R. (1987) 'Governments' education policy: A new direction?' in GREEN, T. and BALL, S. J. (Eds) *Inequality and Progress in Comprehensive Education*, London, Croom Helm.
GORWOOD, B. (1983) 'Curriculum continuity on transfer from middle to secondary school', *School Organization*, 2, 3, pp 229–38.
GREEN, T. and BALL, S. J. (Eds) (1988) *Inequality and Progress in Comprehensive Education*, London, Croom Helm.
HALSEY, A. H. *et al* (1980) *Origins and Destinations*, Oxford, Oxford University Press.
HALSEY, A. H. and GARDNER, L. (1953) 'Selection for secondary education and achievement in four grammar schools', *British Journal of Sociology*, March.
HARGREAVES, D. H. (1981) 'Schooling for delinquency' in BARTON, L. and WALKER, S. (Eds) *Schools, Teachers and Teaching*, Lewes, Falmer Press.
HARGREAVES, D. H. (1982) *The Challenge for the Comprehensive School*, London, Routledge & Kegan Paul.
HER MAJESTY'S INSPECTORATE (1979) *Aspects of Secondary Education*, London, HMSO.
KINNOCK, N. (1986) 'New deal for our schools', *The Observer*, 30 March, p 12.
MARLAND, M. (1980) *The Pastoral Curriculum*, London, Heinemann.
MOON, B. (Ed) (1984) *Comprehensive Schools: Challenge and Change*, Slough, NFER/Nelson.
MORGAN, C. (1980) 'The common core curriculum: Key issues for government', *Educational Research*, 22, 3, pp 182–7.
MORGAN, C., HALL, V. and MACKAY, H. (1987) *The Selection of Secondary School Headteachers*, Milton Keynes, Open University Press.
MURGATROYD, S. J. and REYNOLDS, D. (1984) 'Leadership and the teacher' in HARLING, P. (Ed) *New Directions in Educational Leadership*, Lewes, Falmer Press.
MURGATROYD, S. J. and REYNOLDS, D. (1985) 'The creative consultant', *School Organization*, 4, 3, pp 321–5.
PEARCE, J. (1986) *Standards and the LEA*, Slough, NFER/Nelson.
RADICE, G. (1986) 'Agenda for change', *Times Educational Supplement*, 9, May, p 4.
REID, K. (1986) *Disaffection from School*, London, Methuen.
REYNOLDS, D. (1982) 'Towards more effective schooling', special issue of the journal *School Organization*, 2, 3.
REYNOLDS, D. (1984) 'Relative autonomy reconstructed' in BARTON, L. and WALKER, S. (Eds) *Social Crisis and Educational Research*, London, Croom Helm.
REYNOLDS, D. (1987a) 'The consultant sociologist: A method for linking sociology of education and teachers' in WOODS, P. and POLLARD, A. (Eds) *Where the Action Is: A New Challenge for the Sociology of Education*, London, Croom Helm.
REYNOLDS, D. (1987b) 'Teacher appraisal and development', special issue of the journal *School Organization*, 7, 2.
REYNOLDS, D. (1988) 'Changing comprehensive schools', *Children and Society*, 2, 1.
REYNOLDS, D. and SULLIVAN, M. (1980) 'Towards a new socialist sociology of education' in BARTON, L. (Ed) *Schooling, Ideology and the Curriculum*, Lewes, Falmer Press.
REYNOLDS, D. and SULLIVAN, M. with MURGATROYD, S. (1987) *The Comprehensive Experiment: A Comparison of the Selective and Non-selective System of School Organization*, Lewes, Falmer Press.

RUTTER, M. (1980) *Changing Youth in a Changing Society*, Oxford, Nuffield Provincial Hospitals Trust.

RUTTER, M. (1983) 'School effects on pupil progress – findings and policy implications, *Child Development*, 54, 1, pp 1–29.

RUTTER, M. *et al* (1979) *Fifteen Thousand Hours*, London, Open Books.

SIMON, B. (1986) 'The battle of the blackboard', *Marxism Today*, June, pp 20–6.

WEEKS, A. (1986) *Comprehensive Schools: Past, Present and Future*, London, Methuen.

WEINER, M. J. (1982) *English Culture and the Decline of the Industrial Spirit*, Cambridge, Cambridge University Press.

WILBY, P. (1986) 'Teacher appraisal', *Journal of Education Policy*, 1, 1, pp 63–72.

WILLMS, D. (1986) 'Social class segregation and its relationship to pupils examination results in Scotland', *American Sociological Review*, 51.

WOODS, P. and POLLARD, A. (Eds) (1987) *Where the Action Is: A New Challenge for the Sociology of Education*, London, Croom Helm.

Chapter 11

Educational Policy and Educational Change: A Local Perspective

David H Hargreaves

When I left Oxford for the ILEA in 1984 my main motive was a simple one. During the late 1970s I developed a growing conviction that we were entering a period of considerable educational change, an era of action and not just words. The comprehensive schools were becoming established and it was clear, after the first flush of institutional reorganization, that internal factors, such as the curriculum and teaching methods, were coming under closer scrutiny. The comprehensive school had arrived: the issue was now about the success of this reform and the measures which would be needed to ensure effective schools that earned public confidence. Growing youth unemployment, and the consequent increase in the participation rate of the post–16 age group in schools, further education and various government schemes, raised important questions about 14–19 education, its purposes and content (curriculum, assessment and pedagogy) as well as its relationship both to 5–14 education and to various forms of higher and continuing education. My involvement with ILEA's *Improving Secondary Schools* suggested that teachers, politicians and the public were enthusiastic about a more coherent approach to education which promised to raise standards. It seemed to be quite natural to leave academic life to be part of the action.

Four years later I am struck by the fact that I underestimated the degree of change that would be introduced by central government, and I overestimated the degree of change that would spring from the teachers themselves. I could not have anticipated the more interventionist approach of Kenneth Baker and the set-back to school-based reform consequent upon the very long period of industrial action by teachers. In ILEA the recommendations of *Improving Secondary Schools* which could be more easily supported by the Authority related to curriculum and assessment (the scheme of units and unit credits in the fourth and fifth years) and such developments flourished. The recommendations which were most neglected were those which depended on the general goodwill of teachers, such as improving the partnership with parents and forging better links with primary schools. That they proved to be such a casualty of the pay dispute ironically seemed to strengthen the hands of central government to introduce fundamental reforms, since many parents felt a declining confidence in the profession and the government traded upon its (by no means entirely accurate) perception of parental dissatisfaction with comprehensive schools.

What has happened to my friends and former colleagues in the academic world during these four demanding years? Nowadays I have relatively little time to read their various published outpourings, but I enjoy the occasional opportunity, such as this, to exchange views and perceptions. Academic educationists are, it seems to me, in a defensive and reactive mood. Certainly they proved to be very defensive to the activities of the Council for the Accreditation of Teacher Education (CATE). The general attitude has been one of 'Leave us alone; we are doing a professional job; there is no need for a Secretary of State or his appointees or HMI to interfere.' In this respect, the academics have mirrored the school teachers, who have little wish to engage in constructive dialogue about reform with politicians, whether local or national. It is, of course, this very attitude of 'hands off education' which has confirmed politicians in their conviction that intervention is necessary and education cannot be left to teachers. Resistance to reform has reinforced the determination to impose reform. The educational community, it is felt, has simply become complacent, unresponsive to demands for change and hostile to the new accountability: and, I insist, this is common ground to politicians of the left as well as of the right.

No doubt the tension between educationists (teachers, academics, administrators/inspectors) and politicians has been exacerbated by the fact that the government is of the right whilst many academic educationists and the teachers' leaders lean heavily to the left. That much central education policy in the early Thatcher years was a direct heir of approaches developed under the Callaghan government was conveniently forgotten, though this fact remained more evident in some Labour controlled local education authorities. Many in the academic community have remained hostile to most central government policy initiatives and their writing is characterized by its negative tone — on YTS, TVEI, CPVE and so on. Indeed, it seems hard to find much differentiation in the writing despite the fact that some developments (for example, the Assisted Places Scheme, city technology colleges) seem much more damaging to maintained comprehensive schools than others. More important, it is hard to find in the vast amount of recent academic writing any positive alternatives to the developments that have taken or are taking place. Obviously academics should be critical of central government policy: this is part of the purpose of an academic community. But an academic community is also justified by its capacity to be creative, to generate fresh ideas, to pose new possibilities, to think the unthinkable. In recent times this branch of academe seems to have withered.

Academics attack central policies, plans and initiatives, almost indiscriminately: there can, it seems, be no good from that source. Because they have been much less energetic in generating new ideas, their cries of denunciation appear to defend the status quo. Without alternative visions, critique deteriorates to mere criticism. The consultation document on the National Curriculum provides a good example. Few would dissent from most of the objectives set out by the Secretary of State — the raising of standards, a broad and balanced curriculum for all pupils, a clearer statement of what pupils should be able to achieve, higher teacher expectations, removing the disadvantages of geographical mobility, and so on. Of course educationists may take the view that the Secretary of State has selected the wrong means of achieving these objectives, but then it is incumbent on them to set out alternative means of reaching the objectives. Controversies should be occasions for debating alternatives rather than for mere opposition.

In a period when central government (and not for the first time) takes bold educational initiatives, it is natural perhaps that the academic community should concentrate much of its attention on them. Central policies have widespread consequences, capture attention and generate substantial coverage in the media. Academic commentaries of various kinds upon such policies are thus of common interest to large parts of the academic community (though not, in the short term, to most of the rest of the educational community). It is perhaps inevitable that there should be much less interest in policy questions at the local level: studies of the many and very different local education authorities are likely to be less rewarding for academics, since such studies will seem relatively parochial and unexciting.

Yet it is frequently the LEA which mediates central government policies to educational institutions and teachers and such policies are affected in the process of transmission, in both political and administrative ways. Appraisal schemes will not, in the end, be simply a matter of teacher control; they will become a valued element in better staff development policies and programmes. I make this prediction on the basis of experience of how policies which may seem inimical to teachers can be turned to good effect by a sensible LEA. Secondly, central policy initiatives have multiple effects, some of which were not intended by their promoters or expected by their detractors. TVEI and CPVE are examples of this. TVEI schemes have, somewhat unexpectedly, been used to promote the arts and not just science and technology. CPVE can, as we have found in the ILEA, have beneficial effects in terms of methodology (for example, negotiated learning and assessment) on the teaching of fourth and fifth-year pupils. Both TVEI and CPVE have greatly advanced the cause of modular approaches to the curriculum of secondary education, especially in LEAs which happened to have more general policies to support such an approach. Such effects, intended or unintended, positive and negative, can be adequately described and analyzed only through local studies, and ones which include the LEA as well as the schools themselves.

Thirdly, some of the central initiatives — perhaps the policy on records of achievement provides a good example — spring from a kind of DES 'takeover' of what were originally local initiatives of a radical and innovative kind. The dynamics of this 'takeover' are extremely interesting, but there is a danger that too little of the local origins is adequately recorded, analyzed and explained. Fourthly, it is at the local level where the most notable achievements of the educational system are to be found. For example, there are many excellent comprehensive schools, but there are few academic studies of them. The ethnographic literature, which is now fairly extensive, abounds with studies of poor schools (and, *mea culpa*, I have contributed my share), but we still have to turn to an HMI document, *Ten Good Schools* (1977), to find an attractive celebration of effective schools. Fifthly, many important policies originate at the local level and are ignored or even opposed by central government. Equal opportunities policies provide a striking example. It is probably their local origins that have led to their neglect by some academics and the noticeable lack of black teacher educators partially explains the weaknesses of so much teacher education on anti-racist work, especially within subject specialisms.

Fortunately there have been a few among the academic community, and some are contributors to this book, who recognize the potential of local studies. But it is unhappily true that, if one judges from much academic writing, LEAs appear hardly to exist, or if they do they are no more than an inconsequential background factor. The picture presented by research is badly distorted.

The other side of the academic community is its teaching function, in initial teacher training and advanced courses of various kinds. The new so-called Grant-Related In-Service Training (GRIST) arrangements have been greeted with horror in many quarters of teacher education, not least because the conventional one-year courses for higher degrees seemed to come under instant threat. Indeed, some of my former colleagues have spoken as if they have some natural right to a quota of seconded students and seem to have given little thought to what an LEA (who provide funds of some £20,000 per annum for each seconded student) might gain from this arrangement. I predict, in fact, that one of the effects of GRIST will be to reform LEA policies for staff development and INSET in profoundly beneficial ways and, in the longer term, teacher education itself as well as the relationship between LEAs and institutions of higher education.

It is by no means uncommon to find teacher educators who see LEAs as little more than convenient suppliers of teaching practice places and seconded students. In such cases, not surprisingly, the very content of the initial training programme tends to contain serious defects from the point of view of the LEAs who provide the first appointment for most students. Indeed, I can say from experience that LEA induction courses for newly-appointed teachers are, in some cases, rectifying deficiencies in training rather than, as would be proper, building upon the foundations established during initial training. Perhaps I might cite some examples. Many new teachers arrive in their first appointment with little formal preparation for the teaching of mixed ability classes, unless they were fortunate enough to obtain some practical experience and support during teaching practice. Some have been offered few opportunities to think through the implications of achieving a match between work set and the abilities, aptitudes and previous achievements of each pupil. It seems relatively rare for new teachers to have been prepared for the setting of differentiated homework, with the result that able pupils are set little work or work that is insufficiently challenging because other pupils are using homework to 'finish off' classroom work. (It is all made worse by the fact that the very term 'differentiation' is, to many academics, an inherently nasty concept.) Too few have had opportunities to meet with parents and develop the skills of relating to them. Inevitably many such new teachers approach relationships with parents in a cautious, uneasy and defensive way, especially when parents are working class and/or black and lie outside the previous experience of the teacher. It seems more common to teach students about the importance of home background (with the danger of inculcating superficial pathological models of the home environment) than to provide some of the skills in relating to parents. Again, the whole pastoral area tends to be neglected, though many new teachers find themselves as a class tutor when they have never even heard of active tutorial work.

Cross-curricular work seems to find a small place in teacher education, which is often constructed around the subject specialism. This also has the effect of providing a poor preparation in whole curriculum understanding, an area in which so many schools have made immense progress in the last few years. And, perhaps most important of all, many new teachers are poorly prepared in understanding and being comfortable with new approaches to, and modes of, assessment of pupils, which constitute some of the most exciting (if still underdeveloped) advances in recent times.

Of course there are many exceptions to this: I do not want to overgeneralize or paint too gloomy a picture. I would, however, feel more confident if my colleagues (inspectors, headteachers and teachers) were more frequently consulted by teacher educators about our perceptions of what is needed for the most effective initial teacher training. Our views are not sought very often and this greatly weakens the transition between initial training and induction.

We all accept that there is a close relationship between teaching and research. Each influences the other in the best practice in higher education. My worry is that the neglect of the LEA in both research and teaching is mutually reinforcing. If more research were directed towards the LEA this would influence teaching. If teaching were more responsive to LEA perceptions, this would influence research. There is much good practice in these respects to be found, as I know from experience, and there are immense benefits for both sides. Much needs to be done to build on this good practice if the partnership between LEAs and teacher education is to reach its ideal of improving the quality and achievements of the teaching force.

Chapter 12

Reflections from an Observer

Maureen O'Connor

To an outside observer it begins to seem that the pace of educational change has reached break-neck speed. For the professionals it seems to have almost accelerated to a point wich saps vitality and morale, particularly when, as in so many areas of Britain, it has been combined with an enervating drain on resources right through from the nursery classroom to the university, and with a barrage of denigration from politicians which has clearly in the end, from sheer repetition rather than justification, been believed by significant sections of the public.

In 1986 I went to Bristol to listen to the British Educational Research Association (BERA) seminar perforce as a parent as well as a professional observer. And I know from personal experience that the tale the opinion polls tell is a contradictory one: a story of a generalized dissatisfaction with 'standards', 'discipline' and 'progressive methods' ironically allied to a quite specific satisfaction with the eudcation service as it is perceived at the level of individual families and their schools. In areas like the one where I live, the state education system is generally highly regarded by parents, whose main complaint is not of low standards but of chronic underfunding.

Even the much maligned Inner London Education Authority (ILEA) gains a high satisfaction rating from the people who actually use its services — rather than the mass of people who merely read about it in the newspapers. And neither the opportunity to break up the comprehensive system, where it has been offered since the Conservative government came to power, nor the latest proposals to break up the local education authority monopoly of school provision by allowing 'opt out', have met with parental approval either. If there is dissatisfaction it is certainly not with the present structure of schooling, whatever ministers may assert.

But change for parents with children in the State system can undoubtedly be a frightening, and quite possibly, a destablizing thing. These are MY children who are being taught new things in new ways for new exams with new objectives and methods of assessment. MY children whose schools are being reorganized and restructured, or even closed. MY children whose classrooms need redecorating, whose laboratory roofs leak, who have to share exam textbooks. And MY children only have one chance.

It takes a steady nerve and a lot of faith in teachers not to panic as the school system appears occasionally to spiral out of control through reorganization after reorganization of structure, curriculum, assessment and staffing. Small wonder some seek desperately for the certainties of their own schooldays in the private sector, if they can afford it, or in some surviving remnant of the grammar school tradition lurking in a comprehensive system which the ultra-conservative British have not, as a nation, taken to their hearts in twenty years. If we could only get back to that golden age, or indeed any golden age, then all would be well for our children, seems to be the theme of so much argument about education in the 1980s.

And what can one say as a journalist, even one who struggles to report honestly and comment without prejudice on the rapidly shifting kaleidoscope that the education service has become, and which was analyzed so dispassionately at Bristol? It would be naive to claim that the tatty, partial reporting of sections of the press does not impinge in two quite distinct ways: in the increasing level of suspicion which greets the most innocent enquiry — and who can blame headteachers for putting reporters at the school gate somewhere on a par with Old Nick himself these days? — and in an almost subliminal pressure to compete in the game of sharp headlines and simplistic exaggeration others get away with. Trying to tell the truth is harder, more complex and sometimes, in newspaper terms, just plain duller than doing it the other way.

In this depressing landscape, the need for impartial and unbiassed research has probably never been greater — nor under greater threat. There is no substitute for hard-won facts amongst the whirl of unsubstantiated assertion, difficult as they may be to quarry in a world of diminishing resources for, and increasing antagonism to, the social science research which could tell us precisely what does ail the education service and which of the panaceas currently being thrust upon it from all directions is actually effective.

What came out of the Bristol seminar clearly was an attempt from a number of research directions to unravel the various and often apparently contradictory thrusts of government policy since 1979. What is often hidden from view in the day-to-day hurly-burly of political and educational controversy becomes clearer under the impartial academic gaze. And that clarity is vital if initiatives which could damage what most of those at Bristol apparently believe in — equal opportunity for all young people to fulfil their potential in an educational system adequately resourced and without charges — are to be opposed effectively by the professionals on behalf an electorate which certainly appears to share that belief but has so far articulated it only feebly in face of strident and dishonest propaganda from those whose aim is an elitist system in which the weakest go to the wall.

So it is useful to have the themes of centralization, privatization and growing vocationalism teased out by academic research, even if it is increasingly difficult to obtain funding, get results published and even if one of the leading protagonists of this seminar has now, inevitably, brain-drained away to Canada. Because it is only if you can see the wood for the trees, the broad thrusts of policy which underly so many individual and distracting initiatives that a coherent set of alternatives can also be considered.

Simple things put in context can come as a shock. The contrast, for instance, between the unexceptionable definition of school education spelt out in the White Paper *Working Together: Education and Training*: 'children go to school so that they can develop their talents, become responsible citizens and be prepared for work'. And the DES's objectives set out on the back cover of the *Working Together* White Paper, produced jointly with the Department of Employment. In schools, all the DES can apparently aim at these days is the promotion of agreement on a broad and balanced curriculum, fostering the application of what is learnt to real problems and situations, 'stretching' pupils of all abilities, and the giving of more power and influence to parents and governing bodies. Not much there to enhance the human spirit, or develop the independent and inquiring mind.

But of course events have moved on rapidly since then, and 'promotion' and 'fostering' of even these limited aims has turned out to be too slow for the politicians and has been replaced by the compulsion inherent in the Education Reform Act.

And at the same time, the Department of Employment, through the agency of the Manpower Services Commission (MSC), with quite different objectives as Roger Dale and his colleagues involved in TVEI evaluation point out in their chapter, are becoming increasingly influential. Having in a sense bought their way into the schools by means of generous TVEI funding they are now moving into higher education in a similar way and with similar objectives: to promote 'training for enterprise' rather than education.

The themes raised at Bristol are all worthy of wide dissemination and consideration by a public apparently bemused by the pace of change. How far, for instance, can the comprehensive system, apparently still popular with parents on the ground however much they theoretically yearn for grammar schools in opinion polls, survive the pressures for differentiation in the school curriculum and the assessment system? Control of assessment has already been taken to the centre, through the National Criteria for the General Certificate of Secondary Education (GCSE), and Kenneth Baker's predecessor at the DES was quite clear that the GCSE would be a strictly differentiated examination. Add to that, blanket assessment at earlier ages and at 16 — if the young people can be persuaded to actually turn up to sit tests which will grade them delta minus minus — and one has to ask whether the schools can resist a return to streaming, even at the primary level? Are we on the edge of a return to the systematic branding of children as failures from the infant class onwards, in spite of all the evidence about self-fulfilling prophecies in the classroom?

And what of the clash, exacerbated by the proposed National Curriculum, between the new vocationalism of the Technical and Vocational Education Initiative (TVEI) and Business and Technician Education Council (BTEC) qualifications and the resurgence of a highly traditional subject-based curriculum, even if classics cannot be squeezed in? Is the apparent commitment to a common curriculum for all children up to 16 (except those in the private schools, of course) a sham? Or will that eventually be on offer to the 'most able' 60 per cent, leaving TVEI, or the Low Attaining Pupils Project (LAPP), or some other semi-vocational variant, for the 'bottom 40 per cent', in Sir Keith Joseph's inimitable phrase? That is not what the Manpower Services Commission (MSC) wanted when it introduced TVEI for, ostensibly, the whole range of ability, but the National Curriculum as at present proposed, leaves little scope for TVEI. Not that the MSC is apparently daunted. It is certainly showing no inclination to confine its attentions to those who do not fly very high pre- or post-16. It wants enterprise built into degree courses too. There is a potential clash of the Titans there.

And how can the comprehensive system, particularly at a time of falling rolls, resist the effects of privatization in its various guises: assisted places to boost the private sector at public expense; opting out, so that grant-maintained schools can join the city technology colleges in a third sector of schools which will almost inevitably introduce creeping selectivity; open enrolment, so that even within the weakened comprehensive sector there will be a pecking order of schools, with the weakest eventually going to the wall. Will the very structure of our schools soon enshrine the social hierarchy again as the competent, articulate, wealthy and white are offered means of securing educational advantage for their children at the expense of the poor, the inarticulate and the black? Or can the notion of equal opportunity survive? Separate but equal never struck me as a very convincing slogan all those years ago in Alabama: our own situation might not be too dissimilar in the brave new inner city world of CTCs and GMSs.

For someone who has watched with sympathy as the educational system has struggled to free itself from divisive selectivity — steadily though at times with painful slowness — it is a depressing picture. And one of the few gleams of optimism in the gloom is the certainty that the academic community, where it can find the resources and where it can make its voice heard, will eventually be able to add to the already convincing evidence that the future of Britain depends on raising the educational standards of all our children, not just of a selected, or self-selecting elite, and on extending access, particularly beyond the age of 16, rather than on erecting new barriers to exclude some children from the personal and social benefits of an education which may include some vocational elements but is liberal and liberating too.

As a journalist one is then left with the embarrassing question of whether academics can indeed make their voice heard. And the evidence is not encouraging. Serious journalism of the kind that can put across the sorts of message which were heard at Bristol is not yet an endangered species but it has suffered some setbacks recently, the death of *New Society* as we have known it only being the most recent. Trivialization and superficiality and political bias are not the prerogatives of the tabloid press, although they reach their apogee there. And in an atmosphere where the government is positively hostile to research results which tell them things they do not want to hear, the dislike of the message touches the messenger too, and the editorial response is too often to take the easy way out, and leave the uncomfortable truth unsaid. The market exerts its malign influence too: if it's difficult it must be dull, and if it's dull we daren't print or broadcast it, is an argument from the circulation departments and the ratings watchers which journalists often fail to counter effectively.

Short of taking the jumbo to Canada like Andy Hargreaves, what can be done? The only conclusion surely, for parents and observers like me, as well as for professionals, is that we have to try even harder. There are important messages to be got across, and in spite of what some politicians would have us believe, there is a sympathetic audience out there waiting to have its faith in a decent education service for all children reaffirmed. Like the NHS, the school system is a part of the welfare state which commands enormous loyalty from the people who are actually using it at any one time. Of course there is still massive room for improvement: far too many children leave school ill-educated, and too soon; far too many schools are underfunded in terms of what the economists call human capital which the nation cannot afford. And the problem is getting more urgent. We are falling further and further behind internationally.

The research shows all this, and illuminates which advances might put some of these things right, and which are unlikely to help. It is that, not the gut reactions of politicians, which will actually get us where we all want to be, raising standards, motivating young people, producing literate, numerate, creative, adaptable, aware citizens for a post-industrial democracy. We have no choice but to continue to try to put that across — do we?

List of Contributors

Stephen Ball	Faculty of Education, Kings College, Chelsea
David Burrell	Faculty of Education, University of Sussex
Richard Campbell	School of Education, University of Warwick
Roger Dale	Faculty of Education, Open University
Tony Edwards	Department of Education, University of Newcastle-upon-Tyne
John Fitz	Department of Education, Bristol Polytechnic
Andy Hargreaves	Department of Educational Administration, Ontario Institute for Studies in Education, Canada
John Harland	National Foundation for Educational Research, Slough
David Hargreaves	Department of Education, University of Cambridge
Roger Murphy	Assessment and Examinations Unit, University of Southampton
Maureen O'Connor	Freelance Journalist
David Reynolds	School of Education, University of Wales College of Cardiff
Hilary Radnor	School of Education, University of Exeter
Jean Rudduck	Division of Education, University of Sheffield
Brian Simon	Formerly School of Education, University of Leicester
Penelope Weston	National Foundation for Educational Research, Slough
Geoff Whitty	Department of Education, Bristol Polytechnic

Index